Stuka Attack!

Dedication

*To all who fell during the Junkers 87
Stuka attacks against the British Isles*

Stuka Attack!

The Dive-Bombing Assault on England During the Battle of Britain

Andy Saunders

Grub Street • London

Published by
Grub Street Publishing
4 Rainham Close
London
SW11 6SS

A CIP record for this title is available from the British Library

ISBN-13: 9781908117359

Design by Roy Platten, Eclipse, Hemel Hempstead
roy.eclipse@btopenworld.com

Printed and bound by Berforts Group, UK

Grub Street Publishing uses only FSC
(Forest Stewardship Council) paper for its books

Contents

Acknowledgements

AS EVER IN A WORK of this nature I have called upon the assistance of a good many friends and colleagues who have willingly and enthusiastically provided me with specific bits of detail, checked facts for me, provided illustrations or else have given advice on content and sources. I am greatly indebted to them all.

First and foremost I would like to single out my friend and colleague of over thirty years, Dr Alfred Price. It is no exaggeration to say that some of Alfred's early books helped inspire my interest in the subject and I have been privileged to know him. I also felt honoured to have been asked to help Alfred, many years ago, with aspects of some of his superb Battle of Britain studies. Now, in his recent retirement, he has helped me by generously providing his extensive archive material relating to the Junkers 87 along with a great deal of other Luftwaffe and Battle of Britain material. Thank you, Alfred.

Next, and very significantly in respect of this work, I must pay tribute to my friend of many years, Peter Cornwell. With his extensive knowledge and truly superb archive of personal research spanning several decades, Peter was generous in supplying a comprehensive listing of all Junkers 87 aircraft lost as a direct result of air operations against the British Isles in 1940. Such a list has never before been published and its inclusion in this volume adds greatly to the content and value of the book. Thank you, Peter.

In addition, a great many other friends have also helped. In no particular order of merit they are:

Steve Hall, Ian Hutton, Chris Goss, Philippa Hodgkiss, Robin Brooks, Tony Moor, Winston Ramsey, Norman Franks, Paul Baillie, Dennis Knight, Martin Mace, Ron Gammage, Larry Hickey, Richard Black, Hugh Trivett, Robert Forsyth, Simon Parry and Mark Postlethwaite.

Although he passed away in 2000, I really must make mention of my late friend and colleague, Peter Foote. He was the inveterate and tenacious researcher of all things to do with the Battle of Britain, especially aircraft losses, and he began his work in the immediate post-war period. Were it not for his dogged determination to root out the minutiae and the detail of Luftwaffe aircraft and crews who had been downed over the UK, I am certain that our knowledge would not be as rich as it is today. I have used a great deal of Peter's diligently assembled information in this book. He was a prodigious note taker, and a collector of photographs extraordinaire. Without his life-time of work there would certainly be gaps in our knowledge.

In addition to the above, I feel that I must single out the doyen of all information and writings related to the Junkers 87; Peter C. Smith. Thank you, Peter, for your valued comments during the early stages of preparing this book. I hardly feel worthy to be writing a book on Junkers 87 operations when Peter has written so many excellently researched and crafted books on the aircraft. All of them, of course, have been at the very top of my pile of Stuka reference works and it was comforting to know that I could be wholly reliant upon the accuracy and quality of information they contained. In research and writing terms they would be considered a 'secondary source', but to me they have hardly ever been that.

By now, I have become used to the excellent support, encouragement and guidance provided by John Davies and his team at Grub Street Publishing. It has been a joy working with you, and I must extend my thanks to Sarah Driver, Sophie Campbell and Natalie Parker who have responded instantly and helpfully to all of my queries along the way during the production process. I hope that working with me has not been too much of a trial. I am delighted to be able to continue producing books under the Grub Street banner.

Last, but by no means least, I must thank Zoe for her patience and forbearance whilst I locked myself away in my office writing this book. Also, of course, for the frequent cups of tea and plates of sandwiches she brought to sustain me – not to mention the odd glass of something a little stronger to cheer me up as I worked into the later hours! A big thank you must also go to my daughter Robyn for large chunks of data-input, not to mention her valued assistance when I tried to cope with sometimes baffling IT issues. Finally, my thanks to Lewis who also keyed in big chunks of text that I needed to take from contemporary letters and documents. It probably wasn't how he anticipated spending a major part of his time when home from university! How would I have coped without you all in this whole process of book writing? You have been invaluable.

Introduction

SOME MAY ARGUE, PERHAPS, THAT over-use of the word 'iconic' has rather devalued its significance in the English language. Too often we are told that some object or another, or some event or venue, is iconic – a description that is also quite frequently applied to famous weapons of World War Two. In some cases the word has been used in association with weapons that are perhaps rather more infamous than famous and such could probably be said of the much-feared Junkers 87 Stuka dive bomber, although if any one weapon of the period should be described as iconic, then surely this is it.

Strictly speaking the word 'Stuka' could be applied to any Luftwaffe aircraft employed in a dive-bombing capacity, including the Junkers 88 and some variants of the Messerschmitt 110. The name Stuka is, though, just a shortened version of the German word *Sturzkampfflugzeug*, or dive-bomber aircraft. However, despite the fact that it is a name that could be applied to other aircraft types it has become the exclusive moniker of the Junkers 87 – universally and exclusively known as the Stuka. As a weapon of World War Two there can be no doubting its fame and notoriety and it is readily and universally recognized with its angular lines and distinctive inverted and oddly cranked gull-wing configuration. Not surprisingly, its fixed undercarriage helped give rise to the notion that it was somehow predatory. It was certainly the case that in its death-dealing dives it looked remarkably like a bird of prey as it swooped down onto a helpless quarry. Certainly, it had swept through Europe from Poland to Norway and on into the Blitzkrieg across France and the Low Countries. Its reputation had been fearsome. Its success undoubted. For the most part it was very much at the spearhead of assault, taking out armour, bridges, troop concentrations and other pinpoint targets. Weaknesses and failings had, however, manifested themselves in the aircraft's early deployment, and these would ultimately be exploited by those engaged in the interception of Stuka raids. Nevertheless, the aircraft was used through to the war's end, in every theatre of operations, and to considerable effect. It is its specific use during the Battle of Britain, however, that is the focus of this book.

Once the Stuka-Geschwadern were established in France on the English Channel coast during the early summer of 1940 they faced not only the hazards of a two-way sea crossing but, for the first time, opposition from a well-organized air defence force and its integrated command and control structure. If the campaigns in the west had, until now, been a comparative walkover for the Stuka force then things would be very different over England and the Channel. Not by any means, though, did the defenders always have it all their own way. But, more often than not, the Stuka would be embroiled in the bitterest of fighting. Frequently, losses were high. On the other hand, however, successes were considerable if not somewhat mixed and it is frequently suggested that the Stuka force was eventually withdrawn from front-line service against England because of unacceptable attrition rates being suffered by mid-August 1940. But was this actually the case?

In this book I have examined in detail the history of most of the significant Junkers 87 Stuka operations against British targets between July 1940 and February 1941, looking at the specifics of those attacks by drawing on the experiences of participants, defenders and eye-witnesses. Losses and successes relating to those attacks are examined, and I have utilised contemporary official documentation from both sides in order to analyse the Stuka's overall role in that campaign.

Never before has a specific account of the Luftwaffe's Junkers 87 assault against the British Isles been comprehensively told in one volume. The story of the Stuka's dramatic deployment is an important and uniquely fascinating aspect of Battle of Britain history. This is that story.

Andy Saunders
East Sussex, May 2013

Right: The iconic and incomparable Junkers 87 Stuka. In this famous image a Stuka delivers its payload of one 250kg bomb and four 50kg bombs in the aircraft's typically very accurate and morale-withering dive attack.

Below: Reichsmarschall Hermann Göring visits his Luftwaffe in Poland shortly after the German victory over the country in September 1939. The Stuka force played a vital part and the Luftwaffe high command were no doubt confident that the resounding successes of the Junkers 87 would be replicated in the forthcoming campaigns against France, the Low Countries and Britain. Standing behind Göring to the right is Generalfeldmarschall Wolfram von Richthofen who would lead Fliegerkorps VIII during the Battle of Britain with a large complement of the Stuka force that was ultimately committed against British targets.

CHAPTER 1
First Encounters

"The outstanding success of the Polish campaign was the successful use of the Ju 87 dive bomber. With little or no opposition to hamper them the units equipped with this aircraft were able to exploit the accuracy of bomb-aiming inherent in the steep dive, as well as the demoralising effect on personnel exposed to dive-bombing attacks."

Air Ministry 1948: *The Rise and Fall of the German Air Force (1933 to 1945)*

I T WAS STILL DARK DURING the early hours of 1 September 1939 when Stuka pilot Fw Heinz Rocktäschel sat down for the briefing of 3./StG2 just prior to the opening shots of World War Two. Although he did not take part in the very first Stuka mission of the day (flown at 04.42 by I./StG1 against bridges over the Vistula river near Dirschau), Rocktäschel and his radio operator, Ofw Willi Witt, were amongst the very first Junkers 87 Stuka crews to fly an operational sortie when they took off with the rest of I Gruppe for their targets. For 1 and 2 Staffel this would be the airfield at Krakow, whilst Rocktäschel's 3rd Staffel were assigned other targets close the Polish/German border. It must have been with a degree of nervous excitement that the pair pulled on their flying overalls that morning. However, this was what they had trained for over many months. Now, they were flying off to make history in an aircraft type that would see service from the very first to the very last day of the war. Rocktäschel and his comrade, however, would not see the end of that war although the sortie flown on 1 September 1939 was the very first of seventy-six operational flights they would make together.

The next such mission was on 2 September when II Gruppe were assigned Piotrkow railway station. Here, a division of Polish infantry were de-training and forty Stukas from StG2 and StG76 wiped them out. And so, with an almost regular repetition the combat flights against Poland continued right up until the end of that brief campaign on 30 September. As the Air Ministry observed in 1948, the outstanding success of that campaign had been the Stuka and there can be little doubt that it also hastened the rapid achievement of total military superiority and victory in Poland. There was no reason to suppose that the pattern would not be repeated once Britain and her allies declared war on Germany on 3 September 1939, and Rocktäschel and Witt probably had little doubt they would soon be thrown against these new enemies.

The near invincibility of the Stuka and its awesome capabilities had been ably demonstrated, and the 'Stuka men' must have been buoyed up with confidence. That confidence, though, was described by RAF Intelligence Officer Fg Off S.John Peskett, who would later interview a captured Stuka pilot in France, as: "Sheer and unadulterated superior arrogance of a most unsavoury kind". At this stage of the war, however, there was certainly some good reason for the Stuka men to feel confident, and Peskett later went on to describe the Stuka's successes across France by quoting Milton:

"With ruin upon ruin, rout on rout,
Confusion worse confounded."

With the Polish campaign over, there remained very little for the Stuka crews to do apart from enter a period of intensive training in anticipation of an assault on the west that would surely come. On periods of home leave, though, the Stuka crews were treated as conquering heroes by a German public whose propaganda-stoked adulation knew almost no bounds. As one Stuka pilot said: "We were no less than Gods in their eyes."

For Heinz Rocktäschel and his faithful radio operator the assault on the west opened on 10 May 1940 with no less than *seven* sorties flown by them from their base at Gotzheim that day. It was a punishing schedule which had begun with a dive-bombing attack against Eben-Emael. Here, the crucial fort overlooking the Albert Canal was seized from Belgian forces by

Top: Hptm Helmut Mahlke, commander of III./StG1 during the battles of France and Britain.
Above: Preparing to load a 250kg bomb onto a Stuka during the Battle of France.

German airborne troops and the supporting attacks by Stukas against precise targets required absolute precision. Rocktäschel noted that his target was 'Fort Entrance' and a pilot from another Stuka unit operating against the fort pointed out: "The operation against such a pinpoint target in a very limited area, right next to previously landed gliders and paratroopers, did not only call for accuracy but our crews carried a heavy responsibility to our comrades on the ground and the success of the whole offensive." Certainly, the operation was a success and with Stuka support the fortress at Eben-Emael was taken in an operation that saw Rocktäschel and Witt flying three sorties against the fort that day; once with a 500kg bomb and twice with a 250kg bomb. Later that same day, and flying T6 + KL throughout, the pair attacked troops at Eben-Rimpst and Vellingen, a bridge at Bessingen and the airfield at St Trond where the destruction of twelve aircraft was noted.

Another Stuka pilot taking part on 10 May 1940 was Oblt Helmut Mahlke, then flying with 2./Trager Stuka Gruppe 186 (later re-designated III./StG1) as part of the opening salvo of the Blitzkrieg in an attack on Metz-Frescaty airfield. Mahlke takes up the story:

"We took off from our base at Hemweiler, near Trier, in complete darkness at 05.08hrs. I was flying Junkers 87 J9+KK, and we were led by our Gruppe commander, Major Walter Hagen. We had quite a lot of difficulty assembling in the dark with a full Gruppe of thirty aircraft, but for take-off and assembly we had our navigation lights on and took off singly because of the dark. Once we were formed up, it was lights out and we flew on to our target in the growing dawn light. We flew at 3,500m which was the highest we could fly without oxygen. On the way, it was radio silence; the leader waggling his wings meant 'close up' and an undulating flight meant 'open out'. We didn't have a fighter escort because the fighters had gone on ahead in *Frei Jagd* patrols to sweep the sky, and so we knew we shouldn't encounter any problems. We also knew that the French had no early warning system and so they couldn't tell we were coming. All of our Ju87s taking part in this attack had their sirens removed beforehand since we didn't want to advertise our arrival!

"We had some difficulty finding the target, but suddenly I spotted it. It was almost exactly at 90° on the port side. So, the leader ordered us into *Gefechtsreihe* formation – line astern. Suddenly, all thirty Stukas are strung out in a row as we did a three-quarters-of-a-circle turn. This would position us so as to let us attack from the east, and directly into the wind. As we lined up for our dives, the French flak opened up from below. But their shooting was very slow and it didn't bother us very much.

"The target assigned to my *Kette* (three-aircraft group) was the old airship hangar and during the manoeuvre I could see this clearly. When it was my turn, I followed the others into a bank which I then pushed into an 80° dive and then let go with a salvo of my five bombs at about 700 metres. I had one 250kg bomb and four 50kg bombs. I then swung over to one side and began my pull out. As I did so I looked round at the target and at first it seemed like nothing had happened. The huge hangar was still there. Our bombs had not gone off! Then, it seemed as if the whole place was expanding as though somebody was blowing up a toy balloon before the whole thing collapsed inwards in a cloud of smoke and debris. Our job done, we turned about and returned to an airfield at Ferschweiler. But we were not on the ground for very long! Over the next month we were worked to exhaustion, flying long hours and making several battle sorties each day if the weather was favourable for dive-bombing operations."

There followed for the Stuka force a hectic pace of activity over the coming month as German forces raced up through France and the Low Countries to the Channel coast and through the Netherlands to the North Sea. As the advance moved forward, so the Stuka units were leapfrogging northwards – sometimes operating from French airfields that had been over-run,

A 250kg bomb leaving the centre-line suspension cradle of a Junkers 87, typical of a dive-bombing attack against road, infantry and vehicle targets during the Battle of France.

and other times from suitably large pastures and fields. For Rocktäschel and Witt, still flying their trusty T6+KL, a move up to Beaulieu, via Libin, took place on 21 May but Heinz's diary entries illustrate the speed of events; Courtil-Normont against troops (three times) on 15 May, an attack on a railway station and armoured train at Soissons on the 18th, an attack on destroyers at Boulogne on the 23rd (three times) and then against ships at Dunkirk and Nieuport on 29 May. These are just a small selection of the missions being flown daily, and often up to four combat operations each day with Laon, Château-Thierry and Cherbourg East being some of the bases used.

Through France, of course, the Stuka force began to encounter often determined opposition from the hard-fighting French air force units and RAF Hurricane squadrons, but this was often sporadic and disorganised. In part, this may well have been due to the lack of any proper command and control structure for the defenders and with considerable reliance placed upon sightings of formations from either airborne patrols or from the ground. Then, of course, the problem existed of getting fighters off the ground and into position. And in doing so quickly enough. However, when fighters did engage with the Stuka force, the claims and the dive-bomber casualties started to mount and their aircrew began to realise that mixing it with high performance fighters was no picnic when flying the Junkers 87.

Quite likely the first RAF squadrons to engage in France with the Junkers 87 were the Hurricane-equipped 87 and 607 Squadrons on 11 May with both units making multiple claims against Stukas of StG2, the Geschwader losing eight aircraft with four damaged. Unfortunately, the detailed records of 87 Squadron were lost during the French campaign and, ironically, one of the squadron pilots, Plt Off John Cock noted, "I think they all went up in smoke during a Stuka

Above: 87 Squadron pilots race to their Hurricanes during a scramble staged for the cameraman in France during May 1940.

Right: Fg Off Derek Allen DFC, a Hurricane pilot with 85 Squadron.

attack!" Other squadrons, too, were having some success against the Ju87 in France and Fg Off Derek Allen DFC achieved 'ace' status (five destroyed) with a Stuka he shot down on 15 May over Ernage. His claim is likely to have been the machine of 9./StG2 which crashed near the village of Saart killing Uffz Urban and Ogefr Brandt, although no trace of Fritz Urban was ever found. Already, the vulnerability of the Stuka to RAF fighter aircraft was being painfully demonstrated with what had hitherto been its reputation of battlefield invincibility being severely dented. As Oblt Otto Schmidt of 3./StG77 remarked: "By the end of the first day of the campaign in the west, my Staffel had lost a third of its crews." It was a painful reminder to them that this wasn't Poland.

It is not the intention or purpose of this book to attempt anything like a comprehensive account of the part played by the Stuka in air campaigns before the 1940 assault against Britain. That has already been done successfully and more ably by others, although it is necessary in the context of this book to set the scene for an examination of the almost legendary part played later by the Junkers 87 in the Battle of Britain. Of course, apart from Poland and France, at least some passing mention must be made of the role of the Stuka in the campaign in Norway and in the air actions over Dunkirk. In Norway, I./StG1 with their longer range and drop-tank-equipped Ju87-R aircraft, had been employed to hasten the German victory and once again they proved their worth against specific targets and especially ships in the narrow fjords. On 30 April the sloop HMS *Bittern* had her stern all but blown off at Namsøs and with her steering gear gone she had to be sent to the bottom by a torpedo from HMS *Juno*. It was the first bitter lesson for the Royal Navy in terms of the vulnerability of its ships to dive-bombing attack, and the naval staff at the Admiralty must have been ruefully reflecting on the US Navy's 1920s exercises using dive bombers against warships when it was concluded "…there was no defence against it". Certainly, hitting a Stuka that was already in its bomb-delivering dive by either flak or fighter was difficult, but there was a defence against the Stuka if fighters could get through to them and on 27 May Flt Lt Caesar Hull made what was probably the first RAF 'kill' of a Junkers 87. Flying an obsolescent Gloster Gladiator biplane of 263 Squadron, Hull shot down a 1st Staffel Ju87 of StG1 putting the aircraft into the sea off Bodø from where its pilot, Fw Zube, and his radio operator were soon rescued. (As will be seen later, it was not the only time the RAF used outdated and outclassed biplanes in an attempt to counter the Junkers 87.)

The Stukas had caught the Gladiators on the ground, and Hull raced to get airborne and chase them but he didn't have it all his own way. He tells the story here in his own words:

"Got the Gladiator going and shot off without helmet or waiting to do anything up. Circled the 'drome, climbing, and pinned an 87 at the bottom of its dive. It made off slowly over the sea and just as I was turning away another 87 shot up past me and its shots went through my windscreen, knocking me out for a while. Came to, and was thanking my lucky stars when I heard a rat-tat behind me and felt my Gladiator hit. Went into a right-hand turn and dive, but could not get it out. Had given up all hope at 200ft when she centralised and I gave her a burst of engine to clear some large rocks. Further rat-tats behind me, so I gave up hope and decided to get her down. Held off, then crashed."

In the events running up to the Dunkirk evacuation, the battle for Calais was crucial and it was also another in which the Stuka played a major role. In fact, the citadel fell on 26 May, 1940, and its final collapse was certainly aided by several Stuka attacks. Rocktäschel and Witt took part in two such attacks that day. The RAF had no such weapon as the Stuka on its inventory, but they must have sincerely wished they had in order to use them against targets that may have hampered the German advance. It was with a degree of desperation, then, that on the very next day the RAF committed six Hawker Hectors of 613 Squadron from RAF Lympne to dive-bomb German artillery on the outskirts of Calais. The biplane aircraft were obsolete long before the outbreak of war, and the measure was as desperate as it was futile. Carrying only two 112lb bombs, the Hectors were outclassed and irrelevant. In any case, Calais had already fallen. But the Hector was the only answer the RAF had.

The part played by the Stuka in the events at Dunkirk is, of course, already widely written about. Again, it has been covered in other detailed histories but suffice to say that during the evacuation of British troops the Stukas accounted for numerous evacuation ships and an almost intolerable number of British and French naval vessels, amongst them the destroyers *Basilisk, Foudroyant, Grenade, Havant, Keith, L'Adroit* and *Mistral*. Not to mention the havoc and destruction caused amongst the assembling British and French forces around Dunkirk. An almost inestimable number of fatalities must have resulted amongst these armies from Stuka attacks.

Interestingly, Oblt Otto Schmidt of StG77 (who 'claimed' a 2,000 and 3,000-ton ship) observed of the Dunkirk operations:

"Over Dunkirk I was personally more worried about flak from the ships rather than the British fighters which caused us little trouble. Personally, I only saw one RAF fighter over Dunkirk and he did not attempt to attack my Staffel and our unit suffered no losses over Dunkirk."

For Otto Schmidt and others of the *Stukaverbande* it would be a different story over England. Thus far, Heinz Rocktäschel and Willi Witt of StG2 (the Immelmann Geschwader) had survived Poland, France and Dunkirk. But they were living on borrowed time.

Top: HMS *Bittern* crippled off Namsøs.

Above: Flt Lt Caesar Hull who was killed in action during the Battle of Britain whilst serving as a Hurricane pilot with 43 Squadron.

CHAPTER 2 Attack on Portland

DOWDING WOULD LATER DECREE THAT the Battle of Britain had not yet begun, but on 4 July 1940 the Luftwaffe struck what might be considered its first major blow towards securing air supremacy in the English Channel with a two-pronged Junkers 87 attack against a convoy off Portland (OA 178) and on the Portland naval base itself. It was to be the costliest blow suffered by British forces at the hands of the Stuka and was a classic demonstration, if one were ever needed, of the effectiveness of the Junkers dive bomber.

Whilst OA 178 was a convoy taking its passage through the English Channel, it was not a Channel convoy *per se*, at least, not of the type that almost weekly plied eastwards and westwards up and down the Channel – or 'Stuka Alley' as the mariners appropriately dubbed it. This, instead, was an 'Outbound Atlantic' convoy numbered 178 – hence OA. These convoys were escorted to the Western Approaches where the ships then dispersed for their onward voyages, although the OA convoys were re-routed immediately after this attack when they were sailed northwards. However, let us look here at the attacks on OA 178 and Portland naval base carried out by the Stuka force on 4 July 1940.

With long-range fighter cover provided by the Messerschmitt 110s of V./(Z)LG1 and Messerschmitt 109s of two staffeln of I./JG1 (re-designated as III./JG27 the following day), the Junkers 87 dive bombers of III./StG51 (also re-designated as II./StG1 two days later) struck Portland at shortly after 08.15, bombing the harbour, harbour installations and the ships within it. Twenty-six dive bombers took part in the raid, and one of the vessels hit was HMS *Foylebank*, an anti-aircraft ship converted from a pre-war freighter and stationed at Portland from 9 June 1940 to defend this important naval base against air attack. Mounted on the *Foylebank* were four twin four-inch high-angle guns, multiple two-pounder quick firing Pom-Pom guns and 0.5 inch-calibre machine guns. The Stukas dived on *Foylebank* before the gun crews on board properly had time to react to the 'Action Stations!' alert, and unlike many of the Stuka's later shipping targets in the English Channel she was, quite literally, a sitting duck – stationary, and within the harbour.

There was no question of this vessel being able to take avoiding action, or that the Stuka pilots needed to resolve sighting issues on a moving, twisting and turning target. In the onslaught, a good many bombs struck the *Foylebank* with direct hits; 250kg and 50kg missiles all rained down in salvos of four at a time – 104 in total being dropped. Other bombs fell very close to *Foylebank*, causing blast and splinter damage to the ship. One of them scored a direct hit and blew to matchwood the *Foylebank's* own tender that had been tied up alongside. On board the anti-aircraft ship herself it was sheer mayhem and carnage. One who was there described the ghastly scenes on deck as being like "…a cross between a butcher's shop and a scrap metal yard". In a

Top: The attacks on Convoy OA 178 and Portland naval base on 4 July 1940 were carried out by Stukas of II./StG1 and two aircraft of that unit are shown here.

Above: The anti-aircraft ship HMS *Foylebank*, sinking and ablaze, after being hit by Junkers 87 Stukas at Portland on 4 July 1940. The attack resulted in a huge loss of life to naval personnel.

few short minutes no less than 176 Royal Navy sailors had been killed and the *Foylebank* was sent to the bottom of the harbour. In the moments before she finally succumbed to the German attack, some of the gunners had got to their stations and had begun to ready themselves to fire back at the Stukas. Such was the surprise of the attack however, and so quickly was it all over, that only the ship's 'Y' four-inch gun was able to fire, managing to get off twenty-seven rounds from the port barrel and twenty-eight from the starboard. Meanwhile, Leading Seaman Jack Mantle was battling to get his set of Pom-Pom guns to bear.

In their diving attacks the Stuka pilot's usually adopted method was to dive as steeply as possible, and sometimes at up to 90°, towards the stern of the ship. At around 1,500ft the angle was decreased to 45° and the pilot's Revi gunsight was lined up on the target ship's stern as the pilot fired his twin forward 7.92mm MG 17 machine guns, mounted one in each wing. Gradually, the hail of bullets would move along the length of the ship and when the pilot saw them striking the water ahead of the ship's bow, the bombs were released. In this way, the machine-gun fire was an aid to sighting the bombs and had the additional effect of keeping down the heads of any would-be defenders who might be firing back. In addition, the altimeter was set to local altitude above mean sea level and when passing the set altitude for bomb release a loud warning horn sounded to tell the pilot to press the bomb release and pull out of his dive. As the Stuka pulled out and drew away from the target, so the rear gunner would take over the machine-gunning to maintain anti-aircraft fire suppression. So, when the Stukas dived on *Foylebank* they were raking her with high explosives and bullets almost

Leading Seaman Jack Mantle.

continuously for several minutes – and just at the moment that the gun crews were racing along exposed decks and gangways, and up ladders, to get to their stations. Some were lucky to escape, but many were cut down by machine-gun bullets or flying shrapnel – or literally caught in bomb blasts from direct hits.

Standing in his exposed gun position Jack Mantle was having difficulty with the change-over lever on top of the gun. Either through blast or gunfire it had become slightly bent, although he had managed to get away some rounds. Already, Mantle had been hit and badly wounded in the leg and was losing a great deal of blood but instead of seeking the medical attention that he so clearly desperately needed he stayed at his post. Just as he had won his battle with the damaged lever, a further wave of attacking Stukas came in over The Mole by Portland's South Ship Channel. As Jack Mantle opened fire, so too did the pilot of the diving Stuka and in his attacking-come-sighting burst of gunfire the hapless sailor fell across his gun, mortally wounded. He had been hit across the chest with machine-gun bullets. Lifted gently down from his bullet and shrapnel spattered station, and soaked in his own blood, Mantle was taken to Portland Hospital where the twenty-three-year-old seaman died later that same day. Of Mantle's action, the captain of HMS *Foylebank*, Captain H.P. Wilson, reported to the C-in-C Portsmouth who on receiving Wilson's report was moved to record that Mantle had "…..behaved too magnificently for words". It was magnificent behaviour that, ultimately, would lead to the posthumous award of a Victoria Cross for Leading Seaman Jack Mantle. His citation was fulsome in its praise:

"Between his bursts of fire he had time to reflect on the grievous injuries of which he was soon to die; but his great courage bore him up till the end of the fight when he fell by the gun he had so valiantly served."

Notwithstanding Jack's Mantle's courage, nothing that might be called a wholly effective defence was put up by HMS *Foylebank*, purely because the ship was not at battle-station readiness when the attack came and the attack was completely without warning. Although she was an anti-aircraft ship she had been sunk by air attack; the very type of attack against which she was designed to defend. Other defences that day were impotent, too.

During the attack on Portland the Messerschmitt 110s and 109s had circled protectively overhead to ward off the anticipated interfering RAF fighters. However, there was absolutely no response from RAF Fighter Command which had equally been taken by complete surprise – so much so that a solitary Fairey Battle of No 10 Bombing and Gunnery School from RAF Warmwell had not been recalled but instead found itself virtually caught up in the dive-bombing attack on Portland. It was also the only RAF aircraft anywhere in the vicinity. Piloting the aircraft (K9429) was Sgt A.W. Kearsey[1] who was steadily approaching the practice bombing range at nearby Chesil Beach when he noticed bombs falling off to his left at Portland with "…an angry swarm of bees above". He called to his two trainee aircrew in the rear cockpit to man the defensive Vickers 'K' gun before it dawned on him that they didn't have one. It had been taken out for airfield defence. Feeling somewhat vulnerable in such close proximity to a mass of Stukas, and with enemy fighters circling overhead, Kearsey beat a hasty and judicious retreat back to Warmwell. To quote Kearsey: "I was going downhill, balls-out, and as fast as I could!"

As smoke was still rising over Portland, a single Junkers 88 reconnaissance aircraft of 1.(F)/123 set out to check on the progress of OA 178 and reporting the shipping now south-west of Portland an immediate strike was ordered and carried out by twenty-four Junkers 87s of I./StG2 flying from Falaise, with an escort of a single staffel of I./JG1. Amongst the crews taking part in that attack were Rocktäschel and Witt of 3./StG2 (flying W.Nr 5129, T6 + KL) in what would be their first combat flight against what Rocktäschel described as "twelve ships". The pair would continue to fly as a crew in operations against British targets until they both died together during the attack on Tangmere on 16 August 1940.) The attack by StG2 was followed very shortly afterwards by another from the hastily re-armed and re-fuelled III./StG51 which sent out a further twenty-three Stukas.

The ships of the convoy were now sailing perilously close to the French coast. The Isle of Wight had looked a very long way away when they had passed by….whilst further on in the journey Cap La Hague, the Channel Islands and the whole coast of France had seemed alarmingly near. Of course, the passage of OA 178 had not escaped the attention of the 1.(F)/123 Junkers 88, and the Stuka strike was duly ordered although in reality the closeness or otherwise to the French coast of the OA 178 convoy was not a significant factor in the attack being ordered. When the Stukas pounced they hit the merchant vessels *Dallas City, Flimston, Deucalion* and *Antonio*. Of these, *Dallas City* was badly damaged and on fire. Eventually she would sink, but not before colliding with *Flimston* – the two vessels being locked together by the collision for an agonising fifteen minutes. On board the *Dallas City*, her gunner gave more than a good account of himself as he stood his ground, firing resolutely at the diving Stukas as they in turn machine-gunned him. Meanwhile, *Flimston* and *Antonio* had managed to limp, both of them badly damaged, into the bomb-shattered wreckage that had been Portland Harbour and where the *Foylebank* was still sinking.

---

1 Note: Sgt Arthur W. Kearsey transferred to RAF Fighter Command during August 1940 and flew Spitfires with 152 Squadron for the remainder of the Battle of Britain.

Again, there had been no interference with the attack on OA 178 from RAF Fighter Command, although two Stukas of 7./StG51 had been lost during the attacks on Portland to anti-aircraft fire; Lt Wilhelm Schwarze and Uff Julius Dörflinger were killed when their Junkers 87B-1 crashed into the English Channel south of Portland after its engine exploded and the crew of another 7 Staffel machine were rescued from the sea off the Cotentin Peninsula. In addition, one Messerschmitt 109 of I./JG1 had returned damaged and crashed on landing at Théville, its pilot unhurt. Out in the Channel the convoy was now in disarray and four of its ships had been lost. As night time approached there was another danger; E-Boats.

From their home port of Boulogne on the French coast, four motor torpedo boats of the 1.S-Flotille put to sea and headed for the already battered OA 178 where, just before midnight, the SS *Elmcrest* was struck on the port side by a torpedo. The attack had come out of the dark of the night, and with complete surprise. Listing, and clearly in a sinking state, the crew of *Elmcrest* were ordered to abandon ship. As they did so, the E-Boat came in to deliver a final blow and fired another torpedo into the starboard side. Unfortunately, this coincided with the moment that the lifeboat was pulling away from the stricken ship and the torpedo passed directly under the boat causing it to capsize and throwing all the survivors into the water. Sixteen men drowned. Moments later, another E-Boat put two more torpedoes into the merchant ship SS *British Corporal* and the crew abandoned what they believed to be a sinking vessel. Miraculously, she remained afloat and was later towed into harbour with two of her crew dead. The *Hartlepool* was also torpedoed and abandoned in what also seemed to be a sinking condition, although she too was salvaged and later beached at Weymouth. The nocturnal attackers had been S19, S20, S24 and S26, captained by Oblt.z.See Töniges, Lt.z.See von Mirbach, Oblt.z.See Detlefsen and Oblt.z.See Fimmen respectively. Also aboard the S24 was Kapt.Lt Birnbacher, the Flotilla commander.

Prime Minister Winston Churchill had been sufficiently alarmed by events in the English Channel on 4 July 1940 that he felt it necessary to issue an 'Action This Day' memo to the Admiralty:

"Could you let me know on one sheet of paper what arrangements you are making about the Channel convoys now that the Germans are all along the French coast? The attacks on the convoy yesterday, both from the air and by E-Boats, were very serious, and I should like to be assured this morning that the situation is in hand and that the Air is contributing effectively."

Of course, in respect of 'Air' involvement on 4 July 1940 there had not been any, effective or otherwise. The only RAF presence, and that only by accident, had been Arthur Kearsey's lumbering Fairey Battle. Whilst it was decided that the OA convoys should immediately be routed differently after the debacle and massacre of 4 July, it still remained the case that the CE and CW convoys needed to ply the English Channel. Clearly, it was imperative that so far as was reasonably practicable these Channel convoys should continue to run, but under protective cover of RAF fighter patrols or any other defensive measures against air attack that could be usefully employed.

Of the events on 4 July, Admiral Max Horton of the Royal Navy Northern Patrol was scathing, and called it "A disgraceful episode...." That said, it would have been difficult, if not impossible, to have provided standing fighter protection for the twelve ships of OA 178. Quite simply, she was too far out in the Channel for patrols to have been mounted effectively and once the attack was in progress, the attacking Stukas had it all their own way. Even if RAF fighters had been scrambled, the attackers would have been back at their home airfields before the defenders had arrived overhead the convoy. The failure to protect Portland was, however, just that.

The scourge of shipping in the English Channel was very often a double-act; Stukas and E-Boats. Here, an E-Boat of one of the Kriegsmarine Channel Flotillas shows off its threatening lines and it would be boats of 1-S-Flotille which would finish off the work of the Stukas against Convoy OA 178.

Whilst the earlier attacks on Channel shipping (not by Stukas) had illustrated the vulnerability of Channel traffic to bomber aircraft, the events of 4 July 1940 had been a clear demonstration of German military power in the English Channel and the virtual inability of the Royal Navy and Royal Air Force, thus far, to do very much about it. The Stukas and E-Boats had been demonstrated as a deadly force against the coasters and merchant ships running the Channel, and if lessons had been learned from 4 July it would yet still be the case that further convoys would come under the same sort of punishing attacks; Stukas by day, E-Boats by night.

These elements of attacks on Channel convoys became commonly recurring themes. It is also a theme that has a rich vein running through it; the utterly magnificent courage of Royal Navy gunners who were defending valiantly against air attack. Time and again their heroism shines out of the dark story that was the saga of these convoy attacks. It was a special kind of bravery, and one epitomised by that of Leading Seaman Jack Mantle VC. Courage during the Battle of Britain would not uniquely be the domain of RAF fighter pilots. Furthermore, the Stuka force had more than impressively flexed its collective muscle on 4 July and had forced the subsequent re-routing of OA convoys and a re-think on the protection of Channel convoys. It had also neutralised the key anti-aircraft defence at the Portland naval base, a key Royal Navy establishment. These had just been the first steps towards closing the English Channel, but there would yet be more Stuka actions during July that would have a further significant impact on shipping and Royal Navy activity along these shipping lanes. And these were shipping lanes that were absolutely vital for Britain's survival, both in the context of defensive operations as well as commercially.

CHAPTER 3

Fall of the Ironsides

T O A VERY LARGE EXTENT there was great reliance on the Messerschmitt 110 as the escort fighter that would shepherd the Junkers 87 on operations across the Channel and toward the coastal areas of Dorset, Hampshire and West Sussex. Really, there was no other choice. Quite simply, and as we shall see later, the endurance and range of the Messerschmitt 109 was not adequate for flying close protection missions to the lumbering Stukas at this, the widest point of the Channel. Thus, the losses to Messerschmitt 110s escorting Stukas back to Portland just one week after the attack on *Foylebank* and OA 178 must have been a shock to the Luftwaffe aircrew, still brim-full of confidence after the picnic that had been the attacks of 4 July. Those losses, on 11 July 1940, were significant for a number of reasons and are also inextricably linked to the Stuka story and its operations against Britain.

The Luftwaffe fighter force of 1940 could, broadly speaking, be divided into two distinct elements; the *Jager Verbande* (fighter arm) and *Zerstörer Verbande* (destroyer arm). Of these, the former comprised the Messerschmitt 109 single-engine and single-seat fighter and the latter the twin-engine, twin-seat Messerschmitt 110 *Zerstörer* (destroyer). Of the Me 110 it is fair to say that great store was placed in its prowess and virtual invincibility by the Luftwaffe chief, Hermann Göring. According to the Me 110 'ace' Wolfgang Falck it was Göring who stated in 1938 that an elite force was being set up to spearhead the Luftwaffe which would be a formidable offensive asset that Göring compared to Cromwell's Ironsides during the English Civil War. It was an analogy that would ultimately have a peculiar and eerie resonance – almost at the very first moment the Battle of Britain began.

Essentially, and indeed specifically, the Messerschmitt 110 had operational specifications which largely set out its role during the Battle of Britain:

- To penetrate deep into enemy territory in order to clear the skies of enemy opposition ahead of bomber formations
- Escorting and providing close defence for bomber formations
- The interception and destruction of enemy bomber formations
- Carrying out bombing and strike missions as well as ground-attack missions

Certainly, and with its concentrated package of firepower in the nose comprising two x 20mm cannon and four x 7.92mm machine guns, the *Zerstörer* seemed to live up to its name and it was indeed the case that any aircraft coming within its sights would be likely to receive a devastating fusillade of fire. The Me110's apparently overwhelming superiority, however, was to be short lived

The fighter escort for the Junkers 87 operations flown against targets from Selsey westwards very often comprised, at least in part, units of the Messerschmitt 110. Here one is seen in a head-on view and although it could pack a formidable punch from its two forward-firing 20mm cannon and four 7.92mm machine guns, it was not a success in such escort operations. Several would be lost in the close-cover operation flown in support of Stukas over Portland on 11 July.

when ultimately pitted against faster and more agile single-seat fighters. Nevertheless, in the prelude to war, it seemed to Göring that here was a wonder weapon to which the very cream of Luftwaffe fighter pilots would be assigned. It was, perhaps, a combination of that perceived elite status and a certain degree of family influence that saw Hermann Göring's nephew, Hans-Joachim Göring, posted to the *Zerstörer Verbande*. By the end of June 1940 he was serving as a pilot with 9./ZG76 on the Channel coast, holding the rank of Oberleutnant. Once or twice, Hans-Joachim had flown off on special leave to visit his

Among the losses sustained by the escorting Me 110 force over Portland was the aircraft of 9./ZG76 flown by Oblt H-J Göring (left) nephew of Reichsmarschall Hermann Göring. The Me 110 pilots had been ordered to ensure that no Stukas were lost that day. In the event, the Messerschmitt pilots succeeded in that goal albeit at significant cost to themselves.

famous uncle and had returned to ZG76 with fine cigars and cognac for the Geschwader aircrews, gifts from the Reichsmarschall himself. Once, on return to his unit, he had stressed to fellow pilots that Uncle Hermann had placed great trust in the Ironsides to protect the Stukas. Longer term, it proved to be a hopelessly misplaced trust. And yet, in the shorter term, Hans-Joachim and his fellow pilots would certainly give their all in protection of the Stuka force.

Hurricane UF-U of 601 Squadron stands at dispersal, ready for action.

In the wake of the 4 July 1940 debacle, the RAF and other defending forces were anxious not to be caught napping again. When another raid approached Portland exactly one week later it was fortuitous that fighters were up to meet them. That said, it was *almost* accidental that defending fighters had found the formations of German aircraft as they headed towards Portland. Quite likely, some of the Luftwaffe pilots flying in those formations had also been over Portland on 4 July. If so, they were in for a shock had they imagined that this would be yet another milk-run. And yet it so nearly might have been.

It had been around 11am that day when A Flight of 601 Squadron were ordered off from Tangmere to intercept what was supposed to be a lone reconnaissance aircraft returning to France. Tracked in over the coast at around 09.45, and up to Somerset and still further northwards, it had been decided to leave the enemy and deal with it on its return journey – thus the departure of 601 Squadron's A Flight Hurricanes later that morning. Instead, way south of Portland, the Hurricane pilots spotted a formation of about fifteen Ju87 Stukas at 15,000ft, escorted by thirty to forty Me 110s, advancing directly on Portland. It was certainly a very lucky encounter, because the RDF radar stations had either failed to detect the incoming aircraft or had plotted the formation as a single raider.

Hurriedly, other aircraft were scrambled including the remainder of 601 Squadron, six Hurricanes of 238 Squadron from Middle Wallop, and three from 501 Squadron at Middle Wallop, together with three Hurricanes from 87 Squadron and another nine from 213 Squadron – both of those squadrons Exeter based. All of these formations (with the exception of 213 Squadron) made contact with the enemy, although none arrived in time to prevent the repeat bombing of Portland harbour at 11.53. Fortunately, damage was relatively light and only one merchant vessel was slightly damaged. The raiders had been Stukas of III./StG2, with escorts comprised of the Messerschmitt 110s of III./ZG76 – including the machine piloted by Oblt Göring.

As the intercepting Hurricanes engaged the enemy force over the Dorset coast, it was Sqn Ldr John Dewar leading his three Hurricanes of 87 Squadron who was one of the first to get in amongst the 110s. Line astern, the three Hurricanes placed themselves between the sun and the enemy and swung in behind a defensive circle of the Messerschmitts. Dewar managed to put four bursts into one of them, whereupon the port engine exploded, the aircraft flicked onto its back and dived vertically to the sea. Having disposed of his first Messerschmitt, Dewar turned to review the progress of the battle and tried to get two other Me 110s off his tail. As he turned, he saw bombs exploding in the harbour and two other enemy aircraft diving towards the ground. Dewar takes up the story in his own personal combat report:

"One enemy aircraft was still pursuing me. The Hurricane turned easily onto his tail – he was vertically banked. He then dived for ground, going east. I followed, but withheld fire as I was getting short of rounds. Enemy aircraft pulled out at about 1,000ft and continued 'S' turns. I gave him a burst from 100yds and vapour came from both engines. I had to slam the throttle back to avoid overshooting. Vapour then ceased to come from the engines and he gathered way again. I was very close and saw no rear gun fire so I held my position and took careful non-deflection shots, using all ammunition. Enemy aircraft at once turned inland, going very slowly. Seeing me draw away he turned seawards again. I went to head him off and he, thinking that I had more rounds, turned for land again, sinking slowly. At 200ft another Hurricane coded UF-W came up and fired a short burst at him. He immediately turned and landed on Grange Heath. Both crew got out wearing yellow life jackets. The Army were nearby."

Dewar's adversary had, in fact, been Oblt Gerhard Kadow, the Staffelkapitän of 9./ZG76, and in 1980 he gave his first-hand account of the dramatic actions that day:

Oblt Gerhard Kadow (standing) was another of the 9./ZG76 pilots down over Portland on 11 July during the Stuka escort. Luckier than Göring, Kadow and his radio operator (Gefr Helmut Scholz) were both taken POW, when this photo was taken.

"I flew with my wireless operator/air gunner Gefr Helmut Scholz that day from our base at Laval. We had flown up to Dinard for re-fuelling and flew from Dinard to England at about 11 o'clock. I was the leader of the 9th Staffel and my unit, together with the two other Gruppen of the Geschwader, had orders to protect Ju87 Stukas flying against Portland. Just before we started my commander, Major Grabmann, told me that it was imperative no Stukas were lost and so we had to risk our own lives and sacrifice ourselves if necessary to ensure this. At the time, my unit only had seven aircraft combat ready and my order was to protect the right flank at 12,000ft, with one of the other Gruppen protecting the left flank at 18,000ft and the final Gruppe flying close escort to the Stukas. At the English coast we were confronted by enemy fighters and I counted about twenty specks in the distance but could not tell if they were Hurricanes or Spitfires. However, I knew that the two-engined Me 110 was no match for a single-engine fighter and the chance to win the battle was improbable.

"Our squadron of seven were outnumbered 3:1, but our order was to fight in order to ensure that the bombing was unhindered. I attacked the first fighter from in front, and my bullets and shells flew like water from a hose towards the oncoming fighter. The approach speed was very high and we both had to break away. In the next moment, two British fighters were behind me and opened fire hitting both engines which then stopped. The enemy saw his success and stopped further shooting, but just watched us from behind. I threw off my canopy roof in the hope that it would hit him, and told Helmut Scholz to do the same and to prepare to bale out but he reported that his cabin roof was jammed because of bullet strikes. So, I couldn't leave him and had no choice but to go down for a crash-landing which I now know was a place called Povington Heath, just outside Wareham.

"After we had stopped I found that I couldn't get out, because a bullet had hit my seat and caused a big hole in the aluminium. This had resulted in the 'fangs' of the metal effectively nailing me to the back-pad of my parachute and through my clothes to my flesh but I pulled forward and struggled free. I left the aircraft, and smashed in Sholz's canopy to free him and found he had been slightly hurt by splinters. The first thing was to destroy our aircraft, and so we opened the fuel tanks and with the muzzle flash of my pistol I tried to ignite the vapour but had no success. I used up to eight shots, and had it exploded I think we would have been dead.

"During this time I heard bullet strikes around us and went round the aircraft to see where they were coming from. In doing so, I got a blow in my flying boot and a bullet entered the rubber heel. The bullet turned and left the heel, causing a flesh wound as it did. After this, we both walked quickly away from the aircraft and looked around to find that we were surrounded by about twenty soldiers from whom an officer stepped forward, ordered 'Hands-up!' and took us as POWs. I told him that it was very unfair to shoot at fliers who had been shot down, but he replied that we had been trying to destroy the aircraft and he had tried to prevent this. 'You are lucky' he said 'that you didn't get a shot into your belly!'"

Kadow's 9th Staffel was faring badly, and in trying to keep the RAF fighters from getting past them to the Stukas they had taken the brunt of the attacks, although two of the survivors of his unit had been Oblt Urban Schlaffer and his back-seater Ogefr Franz Obser. Schlaffer, on Kadow's failure to return from the 11 July sortie, had been promoted to lead 9./ZG76 but only survived in that post for a little over a month until he was shot down at Clapham in West Sussex and taken

Kadow managed to put his Me 110 down in a respectable forced-landing and thus provided RAF intelligence officers with an intact example of the aircraft type.

Kadow's Me 110 was dismantled and taken to the Royal Aircraft Establishment, Farnborough, for evaluation where it was intended that the aircraft would be made airworthy. However, another captured Me 110 proved to be more suitable for this purpose and the aircraft from Povington Heath was used as a source of spares.

The final resting place of Oblt Göring's Me 110. A censor has obliterated the background.

prisoner along with Franz Obser, on 16 August. Later, whilst in the POW London 'cage' at Cockfosters, Obser had been secretly recorded discussing the disastrous mission of 11 July:

"During this attack Göring, nephew of the field marshal, was killed. In the distance we saw how two aircraft were trying to stand up to a whole swarm of Spitfires [sic]. One of them must have been Göring. There was no point in our going to help him alone. Graf zu Castell still tried to help him. But what's the use of that with just one aircraft? Sholz and Schröder are POWs, too."

Quite possibly this was the first indication British intelligence services had as to the fate of Herman Göring's nephew, and it was only when Kadow reached the POW camp where he met Lt Joachim Schröder (who had also been brought down in the same action) that he was able to piece together the fate of others from ZG76 that day. Coupled with information trickling back from Germany, and from those captured later like Schlaffer and Obser, Kadow was able to assemble in his mind the decimation of 9./ZG76 on 11 July 1940.

Whilst Kadow was battling with Hurricanes, and with the controls of his Messerschmitt 110, Göring's aircraft had been sent flaming vertically into the cliff top at The Verne, Portland, where it had exploded on impact and gouged out a deep crater in the Portland stone. The time was exactly twelve noon and the first Luftwaffe aircraft to crash on English soil during the Battle of Britain had fallen in defence of a Junkers 87 operation. Just a smoking and steaming crater marked the passing of aircraft and crew – and of the favourite nephew of the Luftwaffe chief. Of Göring and his gunner, Uffz Albert Zimmermann, there was simply no trace and both men are still listed as missing.

The 'Graf zu Castell' to whom Obser had referred was in fact Lt Friedrich-Wolfgang Graf von und zu Castell of the 7th Staffel ZG76 who had been seen bravely going to Göring's aid. He and his gunner, Gefr Heinz Reder, had been shot down into the English Channel and theirs was quite likely the Me 110 that Sqn Ldr Dewar had sent down vertically to the sea. Both men were killed and also posted missing. Scholz, to whom Obser referred, was of course Kadow's crew man and Schröder was the other 9./ZG76 pilot shot down that

Another of the casualties of 9./ZG76's desperate fight to protect the Stuka force was Lt Joachim Schröder.

day. He, like zu Castell, had gone into the sea but was fortunate to be able to ditch just off the breakwater where he was almost immediately rescued by RNLI Weymouth lifeboat, *William and Clara Ryland*, and brought ashore to captivity. His gunner, Gefr Franz Sorokoput, had evidently been critically wounded and did not survive the crash into the sea.

It had been a desperate day for the III Gruppe of ZG76, and an emotionally draining and exhausting one for its survivors. Already it was becoming obvious that the Messerschmitt 110 was not the invincible aircraft that Herman Göring had once believed. The loss of his nephew was proof enough of that. Furthermore, when he probed the circumstances, Göring must have been painfully aware of the price that would have to be paid for protecting the Stuka operations. On this operation, only one Stuka had been lost to British fighters. But this was more to do with the Me 110s getting in the way of the RAF pilots before they could get at the Stukas by their sheer weight of numbers, than it was to do with the Me 110 pilots dealing with the British defenders. Indeed, only one RAF Hurricane was slightly damaged in this encounter, its pilot unhurt. Major Grabmann had told Gerhard Kadow that it was absolutely imperative no Stukas were lost, and that they must protect them at all costs and by sacrificing their own lives if necessary. Although they couldn't prevent the loss of one Junkers 87 of 9./StG2 (shot down by Fg Off G.N.S Cleaver of 601 Squadron south-east of Portland) the Me 110 pilots of ZG76 had certainly fought desperately to keep the fighters away from the Stukas. Several of them had indeed paid with their lives, just as Grabmann had exhorted. Such would often be the cost of flying close escort missions for the Stuka against Hurricanes and Spitfires.

Quite apart from the irony that the first German fighter casualty on British soil was none other than a close relative of the Luftwaffe commander, the Messerschmitt had fallen not very far from Portland Castle. In the English Civil War the castle had predominantly remained in Royalist hands, the efforts of Cromwell's Ironsides consistently failing to take it. Over two wars, hundreds of years apart, Portland had seen the fall of the Ironsides.

Close the Channel!

CHAPTER 4

THE CONFIDENCE HELD BY THE Luftwaffe high command in the power of the Stuka force had been considerably buoyed-up by the successes of 4 July 1940, and although German intelligence could not have been in a position to know it, the OA convoys had been re-routed because of them. The obvious successes, though, were both visible and tangible; ships sunk and Portland hit hard. Though the high command were far from complacent and not unaware of the Stuka's vulnerability to determined fighter opposition, there was no reason to suppose anything other than that these early successes would just be repeated, over and over, until the job was done. And Stuka operations throughout July, for the most part at least, must have pretty much reinforced that view. To the Luftwaffe fighter pilots who had escorted the Portland operation, too, there had even been a degree of cockiness about the failure of RAF Fighter Command to show up. Writing home, Hptm Horst Liensberger, the commanding officer of the Messerschmitt 110 unit V./(Z)LG1, recorded:

Hptm. HORST LIENSBERGER,
Kommandeur einer Zerstörergruppe,
gefallen am 27. September 1940 über London.

Hptm Horst Liensberger, commander of the Me 110 equipped V./(Z)LG1, was another of those who flew Stuka escort sorties.

"Over the English harbour, and out at sea, the RAF fighters didn't come to meet us. We can only think that they could see our force was too strong for them, and they just stayed away. Our Stukas did their work, and we merely circled above and watched the whole performance. It was all too easy. They were even late and ineffective in getting their flak guns working! Now, Tommy knows what we can do. Our Stukas can get through unharmed and there is nothing they can do to stop us – especially when our fighter cover for the Stuka boys is so strong and invincible."

A massed group of Junkers 87 Stukas, typical of the formations deployed against British targets during the July and August of 1940.

This was not written for public consumption as a piece of jingoistic propaganda, instead it was penned in the form of a chatty postcard home from the front to Horst Liensberger's parents, and it surely represented the thinking in the minds of all of those involved in Stuka operations against Britain during the early part of July 1940. Ultimately of course, both the Stukas and their escorting fighters (especially the Messerschmitt 110s) would have a rather brutal reality check. However, it had been the Dornier 17s of Oberst Johannes Fink's KG2 that had first been allocated the task of closing the English Channel to British shipping and his bombers carried out a number of operations with varying degrees of success. Given the title of *Kanalkampfführer* (Channel battle leader) in July 1940, the Junkers 87 units that were newly established in the Pas de Calais and Caen areas were put at Fink's disposal on an *ad hoc* basis. His orders were specific; halt the coastal shipping, disrupt the assembly of ships for Atlantic convoys and drive the Royal Navy destroyer flotillas out of the Channel. All of this, of course, was the precursor for the anticipated invasion of the British Isles and for which control of the Channel, as much as air superiority, was essential.

Apart from the attacks already examined on 4 and 11 July at Portland and its adjacent sea areas, Fink's campaign against coastal shipping was pretty much begun further eastwards up the English Channel by his own Dornier 17s of KG2 on the evening of 7 July when forty-five aircraft of I and II Gruppen struck the convoy off Dover at around 21.30 hours. Despite this massive effort, and probably well over 200 bombs being delivered, little damage was done to the ships of the convoy and the withdrawing bombers were then harried by RAF fighters causing significant damage to two of them. It had hardly been an auspicious opening for Fink's leadership appointment and was ample demonstration that massed high level bombing against shipping was highly inefficient. This was not the role for which the Dornier 17 medium bomber was either designed or best suited, and it was clear that the accurate delivery of a small number of bombs rather than a weight of less accurate bombs was the way to go for such operations.

Despite the fact that the Stuka had already shown its worth in this respect, on 8 July it was still the Dorniers that were going for Channel shipping. Again, the attack was a failure – thwarted when Spitfires of 610 Squadron forced a Staffel of Dornier 17s to drop their bombs short of the target. It was the same story again the next day when more medium bombers were despatched to deal with a convoy in the Thames Estuary but were once more thwarted, this time by the interference of British fighters and the weather. However, further westwards that day the Stukas were again back to the English Channel as twenty-seven aircraft of I./StG77 dive-bombed a convoy during the late afternoon some fifteen miles south-west of Portland. Apart from damaging one vessel, the attack was not a success and, in fact, resulted in a severe blow to the Stuka force with the loss of StG77's Kommandeur, Hptm Friedrich-Karl Freiherr von Dalwigk zu Lichtenfels. One of the Stuka 'old guard', he had led by example in Poland, through France and on to the Channel battles and his loss was keenly felt with his death being marked posthumously by promotion to Major and the award of the Knight's Cross. He had fallen to the guns of a Spitfire of 609 Squadron flown by Flt Lt Michael Crook. It would be Crook's first combat victory, but not his last tangle with the Stukas.

On 10 July 1940, subsequently declared to be the first 'official' day of the Battle of Britain, Fink was still persisting with his assault against convoys in the Channel by using the Do 17, but once again, and despite considerable effort, no success was achieved against the ships in convoy and two aircraft of I./KG2 were lost and another seriously damaged with crew members killed and wounded. Whilst not substantially high, the attrition rate for the Do 17 was perhaps unacceptable when viewed against the dismal results achieved. In fact, there had been no positive results. The next day, of course, saw the attacks in Lyme Bay off the Dorset coast that have been examined in the previous chapter, and although only one vessel had been sunk (HMS *Warrior II*), the raiding force had escaped unscathed. Further eastwards, the Stuka units in the Pas de Calais were waiting to be unleashed against Channel convoys in the area of the Thames Estuary and Dover Strait and that chance finally came on 13 July.

Operating so close to the French coast there existed a much better opportunity to 'cover' the Stukas adequately in the narrow straits with escorting Me 109s operating from their bases around the Pas de Calais and on Saturday 13 July a single Staffel from II./StG1 was committed against a convoy off Dover. Escorting them were II./JG51 led by Major Josef Fozo:

"We started from Desvres airfield with the entire Gruppe and the mission to escort six Stukas that were to attack some vessels near Dover. In the middle of the Channel, we were warned to look out for many enemy aircraft and unfortunately some sixteen to twenty Hurricanes [56 Squadron: author] had managed to slide into firing position directly between the Stukas and our close escort Messerschmitts. We opened fire and at once three Hurricanes dropped out of formation – two dropping and one gliding down to the water smoking heavily. At that instant, I saw a Stuka diving in an attempt to reach the French coast. It was being chased by a single Hurricane. Behind the Hurricane was a Me 109, and behind that a second Hurricane. All were firing at the aircraft in front. I saw the deadly situation and rushed down. There were now five aircraft diving in a line towards the water. The Stuka was badly hit and it crashed on the sand near Wissant. The leading Messerschmitt, flown by Fw John, shot down the first Hurricane into the water with its right wing appearing above the waves like the dorsal fin of a shark just before it sank. My Hurricane dropped like a stone close to the one John had shot down."

Whilst the Stukas had delivered their bombs on the shipping (albeit without result) this operation highlights a number of factors common throughout the commitment of the Ju87 during the summer of 1940. First, and no matter how close or how good the escort, there would often be

A 56 Squadron Hurricane (R2689) gets airborne.

opportunity for the defending RAF fighters to break through to the Stukas. Secondly, when the RAF fighters did engage the Stukas overclaiming would be rife. In this instance, 56 Squadron claimed two confirmed as destroyed with five unconfirmed. In fact, the Stuka force had lost no aircraft and the speculative total of seven destroyed actually *exceeded* the total number of Ju 87s that had actually been involved in the attack.

The very next day saw another convoy (CW6) attacked by Junkers 87s in the Channel when IV.(St)/LG1 were engaged during the afternoon with an escort provided by the Me 109s of JG3 although two Ju87s were lost. Again, the results of the dive-bombing attack were disappointing although the 779-ton coaster *Island Queen* was lost. It was this attack that became famous for its live commentary by Charles Gardner which was broadcast on BBC radio. So famous was it, that no account of the Stuka war against Britain would be complete without including, verbatim, that commentary:

"Well now…the Germans are dive-bombing a convoy out at sea. There are one, two, three, four, five, six, seven German dive bombers, Junkers 87s. There's one going on its target now. A bomb! No!…there…he's missed the ship! He hasn't hit a single ship. There are about ten ships in the convoy but he hasn't hit a single one and you can hear our anti-aircraft guns going at them now. There are one, two, three, four, five, six….about ten German machines dive-bombing the British convoy, which is just out to sea in the Channel.

"I can't see anything. No! We thought he had got a German one at the top then, but the British fighters are coming up. Here they come! The Germans are coming in an absolutely steep dive, and you can see their bombs actually leave the machines and come into the water. You can hear our anti-aircraft guns going like anything. I am looking round now. I can hear machine-gun fire, but I can't see our Spitfires. They must be somewhere there. Oh! Here's a plane coming down. Somebody's hit a German and he's coming down with a long streak…coming down completely out of control…. a long streak of smoke and now a man's baled out by parachute. The pilot has baled out by parachute. It's a Junkers 87 and he's going slap into the sea…and there he goes now…*SMASH!* ….a terrific column of

This classic image from the Battle of Britain shows a Channel convoy under Stuka attack. Even near misses could sink or cripple ships when underwater shock waves ruptured hulls and bulkheads and it was certainly not the case that direct hits needed to be scored in order to ensure a sinking.

water and there was a Junkers 87. Only one man got out of it by parachute, so presumably there was only a crew of one in it.

"Now then…oh, there's a terrific mix up over the Channel! It's impossible to tell which are our machines and which are Germans. There's a fight going on, and you can hear the little rattles of machine-gun bullets (*loud explosion*). That was a bomb, as you may imagine. Here comes one Spitfire. There's a little burst. There's another bomb dropping – it has missed the convoy again. You know, they haven't hit the convoy in this. The sky is absolutely patterned with bursts of anti-aircraft fire and the sea is covered with smoke where the bombs have burst, but as far as I can see there is not one single ship hit and there is definitely one German machine down. And I am looking across the sea now. I can see the little white dot of the parachute as the German pilot is floating down towards the spot where his machine crashed with such a big fountain of water about two minutes ago.

"Well now, everything is peaceful again for the moment. The Germans, who came over in about twenty or twenty-five dive bombers delivered their attack on the convoy and I think they made off as quickly as they came. Oh yes…I can see one, two, three, four, five, six, seven, eight, nine…ten Germans hareing back towards France for all they can go….and here are our Spitfires coming after them. There's going to be a big fight, I think, out there, but it will be too far away for us to see. Of course there are a lot more Germans up there. Can you see, Cyril? Yes….there are one, two, three, four, five, six, seven on the top layer, one, two, three….there's two layers of German machines. They are all, I think, I could not swear to it, but they were all Junkers 87s. There are two more parachutists I think….no…. I think they are seagulls.

"You can hear the anti-aircraft burst still going. Well…that was a really hot little engagement while it lasted. No damage done except to the Germans who lost one machine and the German pilot, who is still on the end of his parachute, although appreciably nearer to the sea than he was. I can see no boat going out to pick him up, so he'll probably have a long swim ashore.

"Well…that was a very unsuccessful attack on the convoy I must say.

"Oh…there's another fight going on, away up, about twenty-five or even thirty thousand feet above our heads and I can't see a thing of it. The anti-aircraft guns have put up one, two, three, four, five, six bursts but I can't see the aeroplanes. There we go again…oh… what? Oh, we have just hit a Messerschmitt! Oh, that was beautiful! He's coming right down….you hear those crowds? He's finished! Oh, he's coming down like a rocket now. An absolutely steep dive. Let us move round so we can watch him a bit more….No, no, the pilot's not getting out of that one. He's being followed down. What? There are two more Messerschmitts up there? I think they are all right. No….that man's finished. He's going down from about 10,000ft , oh, 20,000 to 2,000ft and he's going straight down. He's not stopping! I think that's another German machine that's definitely been put paid to. I don't think we shall actually see him crash, because he's going into a bank of cloud. He's smoking now. I can see the smoke although we cannot count that as a definite victory because I did not see him crash. He's gone behind a hill. He looked certainly out of control.

"Now we are looking up to the anti-aircraft guns. There's another! There's another Messerschmitt. I don't know whether he's down or whether he's trying to get out of the anti-aircraft fire which is giving him a very hot time. There's a Spitfire! Oh, there's about four fighters up there, and I don't know what they are doing. One, two, three, four, five fighters… fighting right over our heads. Now there's one coming right down on the tail of what I think is a Messerschmitt and I think it's a Spitfire behind him. Oh, darn! He's turned away and I can't see. I can't see. Where's one crashing? Where? No…I think he's pulled out. You can't watch fights like these very coherently for long. You just see about four twirling machines, you just hear little bursts of machine-gunning and by the time you have picked up the machines they are gone.

"Hello? Look, there's a dogfight going on up there. There are four, five, six machines all whirling and turning around. Now…hark at those machine guns going. Hark! One, two, three, four, five, six; now there's something coming right down on the tail of another. Here they come. Yes, they are being chased home! And how they are being chased home. There are three Spitfires chasing three Messerschmitts now. Oh boy! Look at them going! Oh boy… that was really grand. There is a Spitfire behind the first two. He will get them. Oh, yes! Oh boy! I've never seen anything so good as this! The RAF fighters have really got these boys taped. Our machine is catching up the Messerschmitts. He's got the legs of it, you know.

"Now…right in the sights. Go on, George! You've got him. Bomb! Bomb! No, no…the distance is a bit deceptive from here. You can't tell, but I think something definitely is going to happen to that first Messerschmitt. Oh yes, just a moment…I think I wouldn't like to be him. Oh, I think he's got him. Yes? Machine guns are going like anything. No there's another fight going on…no…they've chased him right out to sea. I can't see but I would think the odds would be on that first Messerschmitt catching it. Oh look. Where? Where? I can't see them at all. Just on the left of those black shots. See it? Oh yes, oh yes…I see it. Yes, they've got him down too. Yes, the Spitfire has pulled away from him. Yes, I think that first Messerschmitt has been crashed on the coast of France all right."

After Gardner's report was broadcast there was quite widespread disquiet about the reporting of a life or death battle "…along the lines of a football match". However, his words captured the spirit of the moment and reflected very much how the public viewed the air battles going on above them at this time and who relished such jingoistic accounts of an apparent enemy rout. Unfortunately, however, one of the aircraft that Gardner so enthusiastically described as smashing in to the sea turned out to be a Hurricane of 615 Squadron flown by Plt Off Michael Mudie who died of his injuries the next day. Also, and despite Gardner's belief that not a single ship was hit, two were damaged and the coaster SS *Island Queen* was sunk.

By this stage, though, Fink might well have been wondering about the *real* effectiveness of the Stuka against the Channel shipping. Perhaps it was just a case of the Stuka pilots 'getting their eye-in' more than anything else, and although it was to be nearly a week before the Stukas re-appeared over the Channel they did so with rather more devastating results on 20 July. This time, it was again II./StG1 who were thrown into action against Convoy CW7 at around 18.07 when one of the escorting destroyers, HMS *Brazen*, was singled out for special attention. Eventually, a bomb burst underneath the destroyer broke her back and she finally sank at around 20.00 that day although, remarkably, with the loss of only one life. It was, though, a significant loss for the Channel-based destroyer flotilla and although the Stukas had also managed to sink the 960-ton collier SS *Pulborough*, and damage the SS *Westown,*the *Brazen* was a very important prize. It was the beginning of the end for Dover-based destroyers, and worse was to come just five days later.

On Thursday 25 July Stukas of II./StG1 and IV.(St)/LG1 attacked Convoy CW8, in three waves, in the Dover Strait during attacks between 14.55 and 16.20. The Admiralty commodore's report added a little of the detail:

"14.55 Convoy attacked by about forty 'planes. Three ships were sunk and another four damaged. SS *Gronland* (the Convoy Commodore's ship) damaged and taken in tow. Hoisted Commodore Pennant on board SS *Arctic Pioneer*, position off 'A' Buoy.

"16.20 Convoy attacked by at least twenty 'planes. Two ships were sunk. Two destroyers were observed on starboard quarter. Firing heard and smoke screen observed."

As ever, such official reports as these belie the true nature of the action, and in these two attacks five merchant ships had been sunk out of the twenty-ship convoy by Stukas: *Corhaven, Polgrange, Leo, Henry Moon* and *Portslade*. Things had suddenly got really bad for the coastal convoys, and were getting worse for the Dover destroyers. Steaming out of Dover to pick up the convoy, and making smoke screens as they did so, HMS *Boreas* and HMS *Brilliant* were both picked off by the Junkers 87s and badly damaged although it is also known that the specialist precision-bombing unit, the Me 109 and Me 110-equipped Erp.Gr210, were involved in the attack on *Boreas* with eight of their Me 110s attacking the destroyer from ahead but failing to score any hits. Disabled, both vessels had to be towed into Dover. Fifteen men had been killed on *Boreas* and twenty-nine injured, but miraculously there were no casualties on *Brilliant*. The Stuka boys had finally got their 'eye-in'!

Further down the Channel, off Swanage, another attack had been carried out toward Portland during the late morning by Stukas of III./StG1, although the raid was repulsed by RAF fighters. During this operation a Dornier 17 operated by the staff flight of StG1 (Stab./StG1) was intercepted and shot down at East Fleet, Dorset, when on a photo-recce mission but, unusually, it had been flying with the Stukas on this mission. The aircraft was shared destroyed by four Spitfire pilots of 152 Squadron.

On 27 July, off Swanage, there was further Stuka activity when a convoy was targetted by I./StG1 during the early morning, although that had been preceded by an 'armed reconnaisance'

The scattered wreckage of the Dornier 17M of Stab./StG1 shot down at East Fleet Farm, Fleet, Dorset.

by I./StG77 during which a Stuka of 2./StG77 was shot down south-east of The Shambles lighthouse by Plt Off C.T. Davis of 238 Squadron with its two crew missing. It was at Dover, though, that the main and most significant precision-bombing activity of the day took place. Unusually, it was carried out by the Me 109s of Erp.Gr210 which effectively set the seal on the Royal Navy's inevitable decision to withdraw its destroyers from Dover.

At 14.30 that day the Me 109s of the unit's 3rd Staffel streaked in at high speed and low level from landward and attacked Dover Harbour, targeting the Royal Navy ships berthed there. HMS *Walpole* had several near misses and was put out of action just the day after joining the Dover Command. The attack, in bad weather that would have precluded Stuka activity, was over before the defenders knew what was happening and there was worse to come. Another attack by the same unit at 18.00 found the destroyer, HMS *Codrington* moored alongside the depot ship HMS *Sandhurst* and the repeat attack saw both ships hit. The flotilla leader, HMS *Codrington*, was crippled in the attack and with her back broken she sank at her moorings alongside the damaged *Sandhurst*. Although not Junkers 87 Stuka victims *per se*, the losses were a further demonstration of the vulnerability of these important Royal Navy vessels to dive-bomber attack. Two days later, on Monday 29 July, the Stukas came back to Dover. This time, eleven Spitfires of 41 Squadron were scrambled from Manston to strike at the incoming raid's right flank whilst 501 Squadron's Hurricanes, ordered up from Hawkinge, took the left. One of 501 Squadron's pilots was Flt Lt George Stoney who later made a BBC radio broadcast about that interception:

"On Monday we were up bright and early and waited by our Hurricanes enjoying the fine sunny morning and wondering whether we would be sent up before breakfast or not. Suddenly, we received the alarm. Enemy bombers were over the Channel. We raced to our aircraft and just as the engines were starting up so the air raid siren was sounded. I a

An unusual shot of 238 Squadron Hurricanes at dispersal; the aircraft regularly flown by Plt Off C.T. Davis (P3462) may be seen in the background.

HMS *Sandhurst* burning at Dover on 29 July 1940 after a Stuka attack, alongside the already wrecked HMS *Codrington*.

The Hurricane pilots of the Hawkinge-based 501 Squadron were heavily engaged against the raid on Dover shipping of 29 July. Here they relax at dispersal. Standing (L to R): Fg Off S. Witorzenc, Flt Lt G.E.B. Stoney and Sgt F. Kozlowski. Seated (L to R): Fg Off R.C. Dafforn, Sgt P.C.P. Farnes, P/O K.N.T. Lee, Flt Lt J.A. Gibson and Sgt H.C. Adams.

wondered as we took off how I was going to behave when I saw the enemy. I was excited, of course. It was a strange sensation to find myself going out on my first action against the enemy. Would I be frightened? Would I want to bolt? I genuinely wondered.

"When we were at about 8,000ft we made a turn and saw the German aircraft. There were about thirty or forty Junkers 87s in threes about to dive down and bomb four ships in Dover Harbour. As we raced in to intercept them I watched the first lot about to begin their dives. They dropped their bombs at 2,000ft and I saw them explode in the water. There were ten bombs at one time, and the water all around the ships heaved up into huge fountains. As we raced along at 300mph I could see the bombers waiting their turn to go into the attack. Not all of them got a chance. Somewhere above us were the escorting Messerschmitts, but they were already being looked after by a squadron of Spitfires so we had the bombers pretty well to ourselves.

"It was only a matter of seconds before we were diving down to our targets. First, I saw a Junkers 87 being chased by six Hurricanes. I felt like cheering when the bomber went down in flames. Immediately afterwards another Junkers flew right across my bows. I hared after him for all I was worth. I got him in my gun sight and let him have it. I was overtaking him fast, and when I stopped firing he was covering my entire windscreen and only fifty yards away. I stopped firing because he blew up. Then, below me, I saw three Junkers 87s tearing off for home. They were only about fifty feet from the surface of the water going away from our shore as fast as they could. I dived down and attacked them in turn, chasing them about a dozen miles out to sea. I gave the first one a good burst, and I know that I hit him. Then I was attacked from behind and had to break off.

41

"We were in the air for exactly thirty-six minutes, although I suppose the fight lasted no more than five minutes and when we got back we had breakfast. When I first saw the Germans I felt a kind of fascination, and I was surprised that I was able to see so much of the battle. After I had dealt with my first Junkers 87 I was able to notice other members of the squadron shooting down other German bombers. There is no doubt that it shook them up an awful lot. As I said, some of them didn't even get a chance to drop their bombs.

"One thing that stuck out in my mind was a sailing boat with a big red sail simply passing down the coast. Aircraft were blazing away at each other in the sky above, occasionally one would crash into the sea and disappear, but this little boat with its red sail took no notice at all. It was a cheerful sight. Our squadron, by the way, came out of the combat untouched except for one bullet hole through the wing of one of our aircraft[2]. One bullet hole for four bombers destroyed and six damaged.

"I have been a pilot for English and Irish airlines and have got in over 5,000 hours flying time, but I don't think I have ever had a more enjoyable few minutes in the air."

The attacking Stukas on this occasion had been the massed formations (forty-eight Ju87s in total) of IV.(St)/LG1 and II./StG1 and despite suffering some losses they did manage to sink the armed yacht HMS *Gulzar* whilst further bombs hit the already crippled *Sandhurst* setting her well ablaze and finally sank the SS *Gronland* which was in Dover Harbour after being damaged in the attacks of 25 July. On the debit side, the Stuka force had lost two Ju87s destroyed with four crew killed and three damaged and one man badly wounded – all of these losses from II./StG1. Although attributed to and claimed by RAF fighter action, the Stukas that day had also faced another weapon at Dover; the unrotated projectile (or UP). This was effectively a rocket that trailed a curtain of wires, and its use had resulted in claims by the RN operators that they had entangled two of the dive bombers in the wire curtain and brought them down. This seems most unlikely, and the UP operators probably saw aircraft being brought down by RAF fighters and believed they had been responsible. Whether or not the three aircraft that returned damaged were hit by UP wires it is impossible to say. Either way, the UP weapon was not developed or widely deployed after its initial 'trial' at Dover.

Events on board the already damaged HMS *Sandhurst* during that attack were set out in a secret report filed by her captain:

"On Monday 29 July 1940 at about 07.20 a 'Red' warning was given and shipkeepers and a small party working on *Codrington* took cover in Tunnel 'G'. The remainder of the ship's company had not arrived and took cover ashore. Guns were not manned when an attack was made at 07.25. Full details of the attack made by many bombers supported by fighters cannot be given, but one incendiary bomb started a fire in the sick berth and one high explosive bomb wrecked the Church Flat and demolished five cabins, library space and Captain (D)'s office, church fittings and books being destroyed. About six large high explosive bombs as well as incendiary bombs fell on the jetty alongside the starboard quarter and also created damage on *Sandhurst's* upper deck and to boats, derricks and rigging. A machine-gun attack was also carried out from the air on *Sandhurst* during both raids. A further bomb hit HMS *Gulzar* setting her on fire. As she burnt down the oil fuel floating on the surface of the submarine basin set on fire and enveloped the after part of *Sandhurst's* side causing it to

2 This was the Hurricane flown by Plt Off J.W. Bland of 501 Squadron.

Bombs fall among a group of moored merchant vessels in Dover Harbour during the 29 July attack by IV.(St)/LG1 and II./StG1 Stukas.

> become red hot and starting further fires on board. Oil stored in drums on shore was also ignited and ran down the jetty side and helped ignite the oil on the surface."

The report went on to praise the work of Dover AFS in getting the fierce fires under control and asked that the Chief Constable of Dover be informed of the good work they carried out. Ultimately, four Dover men were awarded the George Medal for their work in dealing with the aftermath of the Stuka attack on HMS *Sandhurst*. They were, from the AFS: Deputy Fire Chief Sgt C.W.A. Brown, Executive Officer E. Harmer and Section Officer A. Campbell whilst another George Medal went to Harbour Tug Master Captain F.J. Hopgood and six Mentions in Despatches went to officers and men of the *Sandhurst*. The list of those recognised for courage and devotion to duty in the face of attack by Stuka would be ever-growing throughout the summer of 1940.

Whether the Stuka attack on Dover had been worth the effort is open to some doubt, especially given that the total 'bag' was two lame-duck vessels destroyed and a small naval vessel of limited significance sunk. What it had done, however, was to reinforce the decision already taken; the port was not longer tenable for the Dover Command's 1st Destroyer Flotilla.

Further down the Channel that day the vulnerability of Royal Navy ships to Stuka attacks was boldly underlined when, at 19.25, twenty-three Stukas of III./StG2 bombed the destroyer HMS *Delight* thirteen miles south-west of Portland. Leaving the ship crippled and clearly doomed, the Stukas returned to France un-challenged by any RAF defenders. Set ablaze by direct hits and shattered by near misses, the *Delight* somehow managed to limp back to Portland where she finally sank later that day having sustained the loss of nineteen men. Today, she still lies on the sea bed. Her central hull is inverted, her bow twisted and broken off and her stern ripped apart to expose her propeller shafts and steering gear down to the keel. More than seventy years on the wreck is a symbolic reminder of the success of the Junkers 87 Stuka in Luftwaffe efforts to close the Channel and of the considerable loss of life sustained during that campaign.

CHAPTER 5 Convoy Peewit

THE CONTINUING ATTACKS BY STUKA against Channel shipping in 1940 had led the Admiralty to consider what further methods of defence could be employed against the dive bomber in light of the clear and demonstrable inability of RAF Fighter Command to protect coastal convoys at all times. One of the answers seemed obvious; barrage balloons. The concept of protecting convoys at sea by towed balloon was hastily conceived that summer through the provision of several RN vessels, each towing a single balloon, and with the balloons being operated by RAF crews on the small ships that would be positioned around each convoy. The curtain of steel cables, it was reasoned, would protect the ships below from dive-bombing attack. That, at least, was the plan.

It was a plan first put into operation on 7 August 1940 with the sailing of Convoy CW9[3] from Southend, that convoy being protected by six vessels from the newly formed Barrage Balloon Flotilla. One of those little ships was HMS *Borealis*, a converted Antwerp tug under the command of Lt Arthur Hague. It was Hague's first command, and also the first real outing of the seaborne barrage balloon defences. Unfortunately, things would not go well. Passing through the Dover Strait the convoy was spotted by German observers at Wissant against the

HMS *Borealis* was a converted Ostend tug that had been modified to tow a single barrage balloon. The object was to surround convoys with a balloon barrage in order to prevent or hamper attacks by aircraft, and especially from dive bombing.

3 To the Admiralty, this was Convoy CW9 (Convoy Westbound No. 9) but was assigned the codename Peewit by the RAF. A full and extended account of all the events of 7/8 August can be found in the author's book *Convoy Peewit*, also published by Grub Street.

setting sun behind Dungeness, their attention being attracted to the bobbing balloons around the smoke streaks from the convoy's twenty-four merchant ships and eleven naval escorts. The trap was about to be sprung.

Shortly after two o'clock in the morning of 8 August, four E-Boats of the 1.S-Flotille (1st E-Boat Flotilla) ambushed the convoy in pitch darkness off Beachy Head, managing to get right amongst the plodding colliers and coastal tramps to begin a rampage of destruction. Loosing off their torpedoes at what were literally

The strung-out Convoy CW9 Peewit heads westwards down the English Channel and is photographed here from HMS *Borealis* before the attacks.

sitting ducks, the E-Boats were able to sink three of the merchant ships in rapid succession and cause pandemonium amongst the previously ordered convoy columns of CW9. With their torpedo loads fired, the E-Boats continued to roar amongst the scattering ships firing their 20mm cannon almost at will into wheelhouses, bridges and deck structures at near point-blank range and continuing to deliver mayhem until first light. By this time, the shell-riddled survivors had no cohesion as a convoy and were strung out, disorganised, severely shaken and way behind schedule. Still chugging along amongst the motley procession, unharmed, was HMS *Borealis*. It had been a hard and bloody night for all of the ships in convoy, but things were to get much harder and far bloodier.

At 04.30 hours in the morning, and shortly after the vicious E-Boat attack on CW9 had ended some seventy-five or so miles further east, six merchant vessels laying at anchor in the eastern approaches of The Solent at St Helen's Road set out to join the battered convoy. They were to rendezvous at 07.00 with convoy CW9 off St Catherine's Point and continue their passage westwards to Falmouth under convoy protection. The column of ships, led by the SS *Balmaha*, arrived for the rendezvous at 07.18, but of the convoy there was no trace to be seen. At first, there was concern that CW9 had somehow been missed. However, there was not time for it to have passed out of view over the horizon and yet there was simply nothing in sight. Looking back eastwards and down the English Channel they could see no ships there, either.

Unfortunately, CW9 had already been behind schedule when the E-Boats had fallen on it and that attack had caused further delay to the convoy's already hindered progress. It was not until about 06.20 that the straggling remnants of the convoy were just passing Selsey Bill, a position getting on for some fifteen miles distant of the crocodile of six ships, led by *Balmaha*, as they had sailed down into Sandown Bay, past Shanklin and enroute to the planned rendezvous point. When the order to sail was given there had been no inkling that CW9 was behind schedule, nor any knowledge of the night-time attack off Beachy Head. Consequently, the six merchant vessels were sent off to the 'protection' of a convoy that wasn't there.

Meanwhile, and by sheer bad luck, a snooping Dornier 17 had spotted the straggling CW9 off Selsey Bill at precisely 06.20. Unfortunately, six Hurricanes of 601 Squadron from Tangmere, led by Flt Lt Archibald Hope, had already left and were landing back at Tangmere by 06.25 just as the Do 17 was arriving on the scene. Unhindered and uninterrupted in its work, the Dornier was soon headed back with information on the convoy's course, speed and composition. Back on the ground in France that information was flashed to operational planning staff and with the position and course of the convoy now known, and its timings accurately predicted, an attack by the Stukas of Flieger Korps VIII was set in train. The likelihood that all of the ships would have been annihilated by the E-Boats overnight was not high. There were surely likely to be at least some left for the Stukas to finish off, and the report from the Dornier 17 confirmed so.

Consequently, by 08.00, fifty-seven Ju87s of StG1 had been re-fuelled, bombed-up and were ready to go; their crews duly briefed and already preparing to board their aircraft for final preparations and checks. Ten of I./StG1 Stukas carried a single 500kg bomb whilst the other nineteen were loaded with single 250kg and four 50kg bombs each. As for the III./StG1 aeroplanes, nine of them carried a single 500kg bomb under the fuselage, with another nineteen carrying a single 250kg bomb and four of the wing-mounted 50kgs each. At 08.25 and 08.30 hours respectively, the Stukas of StG1 became airborne; the I Gruppe from Picauville led by Major Paul-Werner Hozzel and III Gruppe, led by Hauptmann Helmut Mahlke, from Théville. Over the Cherbourg peninsula the forty-seven heavily-laden dive bombers set course in the direction of the Isle of Wight covered by large formations of Messerschmitt 109s of I and III Gruppe JG27.

On board the Dutch vessel SS *Ajax*, Captain Jan Lits was following in the *Balmaha's* line when, at around 09.00, he was startled by the shout of his first officer from the bridge: "Fifty enemy aircraft attacking!!" Although there were fifty-seven in total it was a pretty good count in the heat of the moment, but what happened next for the crew of the *Ajax* was all over in little more than five minutes; five minutes which saw the appearance of the Stukas, being bombed and getting in the lifeboat before seeing their ship slide beneath the waves. Lits takes up the story:

"I immediately ran to the bridge but could not actually see the planes which attacked us owing to the bridge protection, but I understand that three enemy aircraft approached on our port beam. They flew athwartships and dropped a salvo of three [sic] bombs. I saw the first bomb fall on the foredeck in the fo'castle, the other two fell almost instantly on No.2 hatch, also forward. As the 'planes flew off they gave us a burst of machine-gun fire, but did not return for a second attack.

"The ship shuddered violently and listed 25 degrees to port. I think the whole of the port side forward was blown out. There were four men in the fo'castle, which had collapsed; two of the men went down through No.2 hold and managed to get out that way, but the other two were trapped and lost. There was no fire, but all the steam pipes broke, thus enveloping the ship in clouds of steam.

"Our naval gunner was at the gun on the bridge when the aircraft appeared and he let go at the enemy immediately they attacked. He continued to fire after we were hit, in fact he continued to do so until the very last moment, and I consider he was very good indeed. He told me afterwards that he thought he had hit one of the 'planes as they flew over, but I cannot vouch for this.

"We lowered the port boat after we had been hit; the chief engineer, chief officer, a steward and a trimmer jumped overboard, the rest of the men got into the boat. I called out to the gunner, who even now was still manning his gun, and he jumped overboard as I stepped into the boat. The crew, including myself, numbered nineteen and we had on board one naval gunner. Of the crew, four men were killed and four injured. The confidential books went down with the ship."

When she sank with her cargo of wheat, *Ajax* was approximately 9.5 miles south-west of St Catherine's Point and it wouldn't be long before Stukas sent other vessels to join her on the bottom of the English Channel.

The attack on the six vessels in *Balmaha's* formation came without surprise to RAF Fighter Command since a formation of some thirty enemy aircraft had been detected off Cherbourg by the Ventnor CH radar station at around 08.40. Fifteen minutes later a formation of equal strength was located between the mouth of the Seine and Selsey Bill. Already, Fighter Command had a standing patrol over Convoy Peewit in the form of six Hurricanes of 601 Squadron led by Flt Lt Archibald Hope. Unfortunately, the Hurricane pilots had again returned to Tangmere before there was any sniff of action, landing back at 08.50 and just at the moment the Stukas were bearing down on the ships. It was the same story, too, with twelve 609 Squadron Spitfires ordered off from Warmwell at 09.00 and arriving just too late to engage the enemy. Also too late were three Spitfires of 234 Squadron's Yellow Section, airborne from St Eval since 07.55. Vectored onto Peewit, the three arrived after the enemy had left and by now the Spitfires were low on fuel. Having flown at full throttle to reach the convoy, and having over-extended their operational endurance, the three Spitfires failed to make it back to base and had to undertake hasty landings enroute to home. However, Hurricanes from 145 Squadron, up from Westhampnett, had just taken 601's place and Squadron Leader J.R.A. Peel led his Hurricanes off at 08.30 and was just in time to intercept the Stukas off St Catherine's Point – although not before the German aircraft had already bombed the ships. Peel takes up the story:

"I was leader of A Flight of 145 Squadron ordered to patrol convoy off St Catherine's Point. Received warning of enemy aircraft approaching from SW and climbed into sun at 16,000ft. Saw large formation of Ju87 approaching from SW in vic formation with Me 109s stepped up to rear at 12,000ft. Approached unobserved from sea and went into attack on rear Ju87s with Yellow Section before enemy fighters could intercept. Gave one Ju87 a five-second burst at 250 yards but did not observe results as I broke to engage two Me 109s. These fought by half rolling, diving and zooming in climbing turns. Got on tail of one Me 109 and gave him two five-second bursts at 100 yards. Smoke came from starboard wing and he dived to south at sea level. Followed second Me 109 up in a zoom and caught him with a deflection shot at the stall. Enemy aircraft immediately dived to sea level and made off at fifty feet. Gave chase for three minutes but unable to close up enough for effective shooting. Turned back towards engagement and found about twenty Ju87s flying southwards at about 1,000ft in a vic on my beam. Attacked one straggler and shot him down into the sea. Me 109 then carried out a beam attack but didn't give enough deflection. Attacked another Ju87 some distance behind with a beam attack but my guns stopped after a two-second burst. Enemy aircraft dropped to sea level and flew off in a right-hand turn very unsteadily and appeared badly damaged."

As for the dive bombers, two Junkers 87s of 9./StG1 had failed to return and their crews were lost; another 9 Staffel machine and one from the 8 Staffel got back to France damaged after the engagement with 145 Squadron. Some of the Me 109s flying as escort were also almost certainly shot down or damaged by the same squadron, but surviving records do not make specifics of these Messerschmitt losses particularly clear.

The formation of Stukas that 145 Squadron engaged had, in fact, chanced upon the isolated group of six ships off St Catherine's Point although the Germans had quite expected to find and attack a much larger formation of ships that comprised Convoy CW9. The ships of CW9, of course, were still some miles astern and eastwards down the Channel. Unwittingly, the *Balmaha* and the five other ships in her group had become decoys for CW9 and would pay a terrible price. Although CW9 had made some good headway it was still some

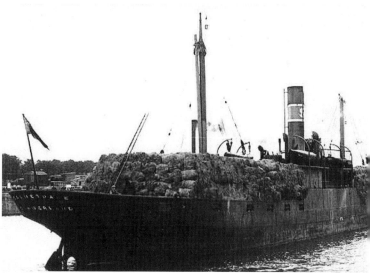

Captain William Harvey's SS *Coquetdale* took multiple hits from the Stuka attack on 8 August and finally sank fifteen miles south-west of The Needles.

miles astern of these six vessels and when spotted through gaps in the 6/10 cloud cover by the Stukas they were presumably taken to be the CW9 convoy. On board the commodore ship of CW9, the *Empire Crusader*, some miles astern of the *Balmaha*'s group, the explosions of the attack were heard and falling sea-spray could be observed in the far distance, though the precise nature of the action could not be assessed.

On board the SS *Coquetdale* Captain William Harvey recorded events that day in his account to the Shipping Casualties Section:

"We were fifteen miles to the SW of St Catherine's Point and travelling at about eight knots, visibility was good, and the sea fine with a WNW wind. I had just given instructions to the engine room and as I glanced up I caught sight of a number of planes very high up on my starboard bow approaching from the WNW. I had three naval gunners on board, one of whom at that moment was at the wheel. I took over the wheel so that he could go and man one of the Lewis guns. The 'planes swooped down on us, almost vertically, and all three gunners opened fire immediately but I do not think they registered hits. The bombs, some of which made a whistling noise, were numerous and started dropping all around us, and many of them struck the ship.

"Not knowing what damage had been caused we stopped the ship. There was a few seconds lull in the bombing and we saw the *Ajax* sinking very quickly. I started up the engines again and put her hard to starboard, issuing instructions to lower two port lifeboats to within two or three feet of the water, but before we could get her round there was another attack and the planes circled all around us. I tried to communicate with the engine room to stop engines, but we could not get in touch as it turned out the engine room was full of water. So I gave instructions to shut off steam.

"Bombs were still dropping and some of the splashes of water rose to a height of fifty or sixty feet. The water was very black. Some of the bombs hit us right amidships about 170 feet from the bow and the whole port side was blown out. Three of the bombs dropped aft onto the gun and blew it to smithereens. The gunner was badly injured.

"When the planes pulled out of their dive they machine-gunned us all along the decks. Unfortunately, during the second part of the attack the gunner on the port side had used up all his ammunition, and the Lewis gun on the top deck had jammed. All three gunners behaved exceptionally well throughout the entire attack.

"I signalled to the *Balmaha* to come alongside and take off my crew but as she was in a sinking condition herself she did not think it advisable."

Quite how many bombs actually hit *Coquetdale* it is impossible to judge, but she suffered multiple hits and finally sank fifteen miles south-west of The Needles. That anyone on board actually survived is something of a miracle, but incredibly only two were injured. As for the *Balmaha*, her fortunes were slightly more favourable than those of the *Coquetdale* although after the attack the early indications were that she was also sinking. *Balmaha's* captain, J.M. Forsyth, tells his story:

"At 09.15 hours, and fifteen miles west of St Catherine's Point, I observed a number of 'planes approaching from the starboard quarter. There were at least eight, and I think they were Junkers 87 bombers. I had just left the bridge and was standing on the lower bridge deck when, five minutes after I first sighted them, the first machine dived steeply, flew diagonally across the ship, and dropped a salvo of five bombs which fell very close to our port bow. As he pulled out of the dive he let go with his machine gun, wounding the gunner who was at the Lewis gun on the bridge. This man, Seaman H. Antrobus, who was one of the naval gunners, had a bullet right through his leg but refused to leave his post at the gun. This salvo caused the whole ship to lift out of the water, perforated the plates, and the water from the explosion splashed right up over the bridge to a height of about forty feet. This water was much discoloured, black and smoky, and with a strong smell of cordite.

"The enemy aircraft were flying in single line; some dived over us one after the other to a height of about 200 feet, while others attacked the *Coquetdale*. I ran up to the bridge, and as I did so a second salvo of five bombs fell almost in the same position as the first, very close to our port bow. The effect of each salvo was to lift the ship out of the water. Every wooden bulkhead was blown out, the wooden structure was blown off the bridge, the fo'castle had perforated steel plates from the machine-gunning, doors were blown off, beams fell off the hatches and No.2 tank started to leak. A number of bombs fell aft, but I do not know how many were dropped as I was not watching.

"I stopped the ship after the first salvo fell as I thought we had been hit, but finding this was not so I re-started the engines, swung the ship round and went full speed ahead again. She was not making any water as far as I could see.

"The attack lasted between five or ten minutes, during which time we had opened fire with the two guns aft and with one of the guns on the bridge. These all worked very well, and the gunners got off three or four drums each. One of the gunners reckoned he put a burst into the first plane, but without any apparent damage. I did not see this, but I watched some of the tracers and they appeared to be going just ahead of the planes. There was no protection at all round the guns but everyone behaved very well, especially Antrobus, who refused to leave his post although wounded.

"After about ten minutes our fighters came out to engage the enemy who very soon flew away.

"I turned my ship round then picked up the crew of the *Surte*, having to use the derrick

Stukas of I./StG2 in flight during the summer of 1940.

to get the boat on board. Another ship, the *Scheldt*, had had her engines damaged so I put a rope across and was able to tow her into St Helen's Road where we anchored at about 13.00.

"The sides of the ship were riddled with holes, some small round ones, and other fairly large jagged ones which I think were made by shrapnel. There were also a number of dents in the plating, but from the sound of it the enemy were only using machine guns."

The dramatic accounts of the Stuka attack illustrate the appalling carnage and damage that the onslaught had unleashed. The recurrent accounts of machine-gunning after the dive-bombing was simply the manifestation of the adopted tactic for rear gunners in the Junkers 87s to 'hose down' the target area with their single 7.92mm calibre MG15 machine guns in order to suppress anti-aircraft fire. In other words, it had an intended purpose rather than being some kind of terror tactic as is often suggested. The hit on the seaman Antrobus, as he valiantly manned the anti-aircraft Lewis gun, was exactly what the German gunner had intended.

Perhaps the sheer horror of the Stuka attacks are summed up by a comment made by Captain W.H. Dawson of the *John M*. His ship had endured the E-Boat onslaught overnight and then the dive-bomber attacks later on in the day. In his official report he stated: "The Mate and one of the Able Bodied Seamen have since cracked-up completely, and I do not think they will ever go to sea again."

As the battered *Balmaha* struggled back eastwards with the crippled *Scheldt* in tow, the two vessels now passed Convoy CW9 steaming westwards, doubtless wondering what on earth had gone wrong. However, if the six little ships in *Balmaha's* original grouping had been unwitting decoys for the main part of CW9, it wasn't going to throw the Luftwaffe off the scent for very long. Quite possibly, the escorting Messerschmitt 109 pilots in the attack, or maybe the Stuka crews themselves, had spotted the main assembly of ships way off to the east with the devastating assault on the six merchantmen in full swing. Either way, post operation de-briefing established that the ships attacked had nothing at all to do with the seventeen vessels spotted during the early morning by the Dornier 17. For one thing, the convoy was eleven ships light. Not only that, but they were not in the right position given the convoy's previously plotted location and speed. Back on the ground in France, feverish activity was again underway to prepare yet more Stukas for another attack on the convoy.

This time, it was the assembled might of the Junkers 87 Stukas of I and III./StG2 which were called into action to finish the job and, again, a similar number of Ju87s were assigned to the operation; forty-nine of them being loaded up with no less than 245 high-explosive bombs. At 11.45 the aircraft slowly climbed out of their airfields for a rendezvous with their escort; the massed Messerschmitt 109s of I and III Gruppen of JG27 and the Messerschmitt 110s of V./LG1. At Ventnor chain home radar station on the Isle of Wight, almost overlooking the scene of the earlier action, operators had picked up a trace of this large enemy formation, at least one hundred strong, and about twenty miles north of Cherbourg headed on a course that would take it directly to CW9.

With only the six aircraft of 609 Squadron over the convoy itself, and a force of one hundred plus advancing, the controller ordered six aircraft of 601 Squadron up from RAF Tangmere at 11.55. Already airborne were the Hurricanes of 145 Squadron, although they were headed eastwards to intercept a threatening raid in the area of Brighton, but when the new threat against Peewit became apparent 145 Squadron were turned around and back towards the convoy. Quite likely, the plot being chased by 145 Squadron had been a diversionary raid to draw RAF fighters away from the main force. Unfortunately, valuable time was lost for 145 Squadron in what had turned out to be a futile pursuit and it delayed their arrival over CW9 where they were needed most. Meanwhile, more Hurricanes were scrambled; 257 Squadron from Tangmere, 238 Squadron from

Among the escorts for the Stuka formations during the attacks on 8 August were the Messerschmitt 110s of V.(Z)/LG1. Here, the unit commander Hptm Horst Liensberger prepares to take off for another operation.

Middle Wallop and 213 from far away Exeter. All three extra squadrons were airborne between 12.09 and 12.15 and were vectored toward CW9.

Having survived the ordeal of the E-Boat attacks, Lt Hague and his crew on board HMS *Borealis* were, at that moment, sailing at the head of the port column and watching Lt Cdr Owles' balloon vessel, HMS *Astral*, off to their starboard. On board the *Astral*, Flt Lt Puckle had ordered down his balloon to engage in seaborne inflation trials when, at 12.19 exactly, Hague spotted enemy aircraft diving down on them. Almost at once, the Me 109s

The bomb-shattered view down the deck of HMS *Borealis* on 8 August 1940. Lt Arthur Hague (seated left) takes in the dismal scene.

of 9/JG27 shot up the balloon that was being towed at 3,500ft (just below a bank of cloud at 4,000ft) by *Borealis*. The balloon immediately erupted into flames and descended, burning, into the sea. As its charred remnants fell hissing into the water, the Ju87s of Stuka Geschwader 2 followed it down in their attack, diving through the broken cloud directly above the convoy. At 12.20 precisely one of the bombs scored a direct hit on *Borealis*.

The 50kg bomb struck the foremast, bringing it down over the starboard side of the bridge before the missile was deflected through the deck which it pierced about half way between the bridge and stem, before finally exploding below. Here, the blast blew a hole in the starboard bow just on the water line causing an immediate in-rush of water which flooded the forward compartment. The explosion from the bomb had caused havoc on the bridge, which it almost entirely wrecked, and had totally destroyed the gun positions on top of the wheelhouse. Of the chart table, charts and convoy orders there was no trace to be found and the principal steering position had been demolished along with the improvised concrete blocks that had been piled up as protection around the wheelhouse itself. On the bridge, all electrical switching gear was destroyed and every window had been broken. The thick glass of portholes in the hull had been holed by bullets and shrapnel. Behind the wheelhouse, the gravity diesel feed had ruptured and fuel oil was spewing out onto the deck which was liberally strewn with assorted debris; wood, glass, metal splinters, bits of smouldering balloon fabric and wrecked equipment. Incredibly, there were only six casualties and only three of these were serious.

Still intact on the after deck were the big hydrogen cylinders for re-charging the balloon. There was not a mark or scratch on them, despite all else being liberally peppered with holes. In a moment, however, Arthur Hague's tidy little ship had been reduced to a wreck, and he at once noticed that the ensign mast had been carried away by the falling balloon cable and, rather incongruously, he went off to the flag locker with the attack still in progress to find another White Ensign. Finding what he wanted, Hague managed to scramble over the mass of debris in order to lash the replacement to the after rigging. After all, naval tradition had to be upheld come what may. As she fell out of line, *Borealis* was at least still afloat. Just.

Overhead, the relentless Stukas dived one after the other onto the two columns of merchant ships. Apart from the *Borealis*, the Norwegian vessel SS *Tres*, with her cargo of 1,096 tons of coal, was hit by bombs in this attack with four bombs falling amidships at 12.25. All of them were 50kg weapons. She was lucky, since the single 250kg bomb that would have been in that same salvo with the other four bombs had missed the ship by feet. Had it struck, *Tres* would have been literally torn apart. As it was, the bombs had set her on fire and she was immediately in serious difficulty. Captain Vermund Kvilhaug, seconds after the four bombs had exploded, ran down from the bridge to the chart room to save the ship's papers but, on his way, he was struck by something that knocked him out. For a while, he was unconscious but managed to pull himself together enough to head again for the chart room. When he got there, he found it a mass of flames and made his way instead to the boat deck where all hands were present except for the cook. By this time, Captain Kvilhaug was in intense pain from burns to his face and hands, although he had no idea how he had been burned or what by.

The cook, Bjarne Arnsten, had been in the galley preparing lunch for the fifteen crew and three gunners on board the *Tres* and had finally managed to struggle up to the deck of the blazing vessel. When he got there, Arnsten found that his crew mates had given him up for dead and had already cast away from *Tres* in the lifeboat. Seeing the cook appear on the smoke-shrouded deck, they returned to rescue him. Painfully, the injured Arnsten managed to lower himself down on the ship's derrick although unfortunately he lost his grip and fell into the sea. Willing hands hauled the injured man into the lifeboat where he was gently covered with jackets, sweaters and tarpaulin as the crew awaited rescue.

The *Tres*, a fortunate escapee from the night-time E-Boat attacks, had not been so fortunate now – although surprisingly the crew were picked up and taken ashore to Portsmouth later that day, but not before the men in the lifeboat had come under machine-gun fire. Ashore at Portsmouth, the captain was admitted to Haslar Royal Naval Hospital with perforated ear drums, severe burns and shock. Bjarne Arnsten died of his injuries in the same hospital five days later.

With so many aircraft diving to attack the ships in convoy it was not just the *Borealis* and *Tres* who were having a hard time. Things were getting difficult for Captain W.H. Dawson and his men aboard the *John M*, too:

"At 12.15 when in a position ten miles south of The Needles we were attacked by enemy aircraft.

"There were about fifty bombers of the Junkers 87 type flying at a height of 2,000ft. They dived out of the clouds at an angle of forty-five degrees, to a height of about 400ft, when they released their bombs. Two of the bombers concentrated on our ship, diving over our stern to about 400ft when they released their bombs, then turned to port or starboard, but mostly to port, climbed out of the dive, circled and again dived over our stern. They did not machine-gun us at all, but I could see bullets spattering on the water ahead of us, and when the crew of the *Tres* took to their lifeboat the bullets spattered all around them.

"About fifty bombs fell very near us, within a few feet, in eight salvos with each salvo containing from four to seven bombs [Author's note: In fact, if there were eight 'salvos' falling near the ship she must have been targeted by eight individual Ju87s rather than the two which Dawson mistakenly thought had repeatedly concentrated on them. With five bombs per Stuka, we can conclude that forty bombs fell immediately around the *John M* in total. Given the stressful conditions under which Captain Dawson made his observations it is understandable that his accuracy might have been somewhat compromised!]

"The effect of each salvo was to lift the ship completely out of the water. The first salvo fell on the starboard bow. Two of these exploded on impact and two rebounded from the water, almost struck the ship, then fell back and exploded. The next salvo fell right ahead. The third salvo fell on our starboard quarter, two bombs exploded immediately, but the other two had a few seconds delay, then exploded and threw out about ten incendiary bombs to a height of about nine feet which then fell into the water. The fourth salvo fell right aft, the fifth salvo alongside the port quarter and the sixth almost amidships on the port side. The water thrown up by the explosions was a brownish colour."

Armourers load a 250kg bomb underneath a StG77 Stuka as the aircrew look on. These weapons were devastating against surface ships, even if only near-misses were scored.

Dawson's observations about the bombs, and their behaviour, are interesting. First, he talks of bombs exploding some seconds after impact with the water and this was something observed, too, by others on CW9 who noted the delayed-action of the detonation. The answer to this is provided by Hptm Waldemar Plewig, a Stuka pilot and Gruppen Kommandeur of II./StG77 who participated in other attacks on CW9 later that day:

"It did not matter about scoring direct hits on the ships themselves because all our bombs were fitted with delayed fuses so that they didn't actually explode on hitting the sea but after penetrating the water. This caused a strong pressure wave which could badly damage a ship's hull."

On board the *John M*, Dawson and his crew knew all about the pressure waves described by Plewig, and as it would turn out those blasts had buckled the plates of the hull sufficiently for her to take on water. Without doubt, the consequences of forty near misses had been dramatic to say the very least:

"The vessel had stopped and everything breakable on board was smashed. The only thing left intact was the main engine. The auxiliary pipes, pumps and even the fresh water service pump were all useless. The only drink we had was the brackish water out of the lifeboats."

With the situation on board so dire it was fortunate that none of the 'incendiary bombs' ejected from the explosions had landed on the ship. Quite apart from the threat this would pose to the cargo of 650 tons of coal, anything else flammable on the vessel might have ignited, too. From

Dawson's description, it would appear that at least some of the bombs used in that attack were *Phosphorbrandbomben* – literally phosphor fire bombs. These weapons contained glass ampoules of phosphorous that were flung out on detonation, the bomb casing either being of 50kg or 250kg size. Had any of these cascading burning projectiles hit the ship and caused a fire there would have been precious little that Dawson's men could have done to extinguish it, given the virtual incapacity of all the main on-board pumps. For the duration of the attack, though, some of his men were manning the guns rather than the pumps:

"The gunners had taken their stations during the attack and they did remarkably well. However, all three Lewis guns jammed. The cause of stoppage being the same in every case and when one bullet was in the chamber the one in the barrel had failed to eject. There may have been a misfire, but there was no mark on the cartridge. Our own gun worked very well."

Munitions-Lexikon Nr.: 62 100 - 100 - 8	Brand C 50 A PHOSPHORBRANDBOMBE

Verwendung: Deutschland, 2. Weltkrieg
Zünder: AZ (25) D mit kz. Zündldg. C/98
Gesamtgewicht: ca. 41 kg
Füllung: 12 kg Flüssigkeitsbrandmasse mit Phosphorzusatz in Ampullen

A German schematic diagram for the Brand C 50 A 50kg phosphorous incendiary bomb which seems to have been carried by some of the attacking Stukas on 8 August 1940. The glass ampoules were ejected on impact and burnt when the projectiles smashed open on contact with any solid surface.

Once more, Royal Navy gunners were working with extraordinary courage and efficiency in difficult and trying circumstances. The reference by Dawson to "our own gun" relates to the *John M*'s own designated defensive weapon, another single Lewis, as opposed to the three RN weapons on board. Apart from the four Lewis guns, however, the *John M* was one of the Merchant Navy ships equipped with the singularly ineffective Holman Projector, a weapon designed to launch air-bust bomblets into the path of attacking aircraft. Again, Dawson tells the story:

"The first salvo of bombs threw a column of water right over the ship and down into the engine room. At the same time I heard an inrush of water and thought the ship had split open. I found afterwards that this sound was in fact the air bottles of the Holman Projector. The blast had disconnected the pipes. The second salvo threw all the bombs out of the stowage tray and onto the deck at the side of the projector. The seaman-gunner, Thomas, threw all the bombs over the side. He was a very brave man."

It is impossible to conclude anything other than that the Royal Navy gunners were very much the heroes of the day. They certainly fought overwhelming and impossible odds with woefully inadequate weaponry and the courage of Dawson and his crewmen cannot be doubted:

"At the third salvo I noticed that the ship seemed to be listing and labouring somewhat, probably owing to the shock of explosions taking a certain amount of weigh off her. She seemed to me to be making water. All the after hatches were lifted out of their beams, and at that time I was under the impression she had broken her back. Each time the water splashed up I thought we would be swamped, and as she appeared to be settling I ordered away the starboard lifeboat – not knowing, of course, that she had been damaged. Immediately we put her in the water she sank, as the whole of one side had been blown away, probably during the night-time E-Boat attack. There was so much gear in the boat that we could not see the damage until she was lowered.

"About this time the chief engineer reported that she was making water in the engine room. I asked him if he thought they could stick it out down below and he said they would try. I told him to keep her going full, and then let me know how things were going. We have a gadget fitted whereby we can shut off the fuel. I pulled on this and it just came away. Then I noticed that its flywheel was just throwing up water.

"We had by this time received about eight salvos near us, then our fighters came into action and the attack was over as far as we were concerned."

Exhausted, but physically unharmed, the crew finally got ashore later that evening and thankfully left their battered *John M* riding at anchor in Weymouth Bay. Later that evening, however, it was decided unsafe to leave her off Weymouth and she was towed into the Royal Navy Dockyard at Portland, a harbour fast becoming a graveyard for Stuka victims.

Despite all that the convoy and its associated shipping had endured, CW9 continued to sail on westwards with the commodore ship *Empire Crusader* still in control of her charges, although she too would be hit by the Stukas of StG2. Her chief engineer, J.E. Cowper, was able to tell his tale of high drama after surviving the overnight E-Boat attacks:

"At 12.15 we were ordered to action stations again. I was having lunch in the saloon at the time with the 2nd mate and a naval rating when there was a terrific explosion forward as a bomb struck the fore deck. Both the men immediately left the saloon and went towards the bridge. I made for the engine room. Just as I got to the engine room there was another violent explosion, approximately two or three feet from the ship on the port side which lifted the ship into the air. A huge column of black water was thrown up about sixty feet and completely deluged the ship. The engine room skylights were broken and the steam pipes burst. The whistle control was shot away and this added to the general pandemonium. Bombs were falling astern of us in all directions.

"I got hold of the 2nd Engineer and asked him if he was all right and then he went aft to see about lowering the raft and I went forward to see the damage. The main mast had gone, the para-vanes had gone, all the hatches had been stripped off and there was a crater in the coal which was now on fire. The front of the bridge had been completely blown in. I went alongside the starboard lifeboat which was hanging by the falls and where I found the 2nd mate who had had his hand shot off and he had a very bad wound.

"I looked over the side and realised that the engines were still going full speed ahead, although I thought they had been put out of action. I stopped them by the engine control on the deck. I then went to see what I could do for the 2nd mate and noticed an attempt being made to get out a boat, although the 2nd engineer and 3rd mate succeeded in getting a raft out.

"I then got a naval rating to assist me in getting the wounded 2nd mate across the skylights to the boat. While he was assisting me he was hit by a machine-gun bullet, and although wounded he did not complain until we had got the 2nd mate onto a raft. Until the naval rating was hit I did not even realise that we were being machine-gunned – I could not hear anything because the noise from the aircraft and the bombs falling round us was so terrific.

"By this time a boat had been partly lowered and the commodore went down the rope into it and we managed to get the 2nd mate into the boat. The commodore said that the captain had last been seen on the bridge and had said that he was going to the chart room. I went to the chart room but could not see anybody there. The whole front of the chart room had caved in and there were papers, books and drawers all lying in a heap. As I came out of the chart room I found two naval ratings. One of them was dead, and the other was so seriously injured that I knew I could do nothing for him. [Author's note: Only one naval rating is shown as having been lost on *Empire Crusader* and that was Ordinary Signalman Peter J. Turner and so it is likely that the second body Cowper saw was, in fact, the master for whom he had actually been vainly searching.]

"In the meantime, the fire was travelling to the front of the ship. The bridge had also caught fire and the ship seemed to be going down by the head. There were about eight or nine of us who were not injured and we managed to get away in the boat together with the injured.

"We rowed to the escort trawler which was coming towards us. The wounded were taken on board the trawler and first aid was immediately administered to them. The 2nd mate died as a result of his wounds.

"We proceeded on board the escort trawler and on the way 'Action Stations' were sounded again, but there were no further attacks. We were landed in Portsmouth, where there were ambulances waiting, at about four o'clock in the afternoon.

"I should like to recommend the naval rating [Able Seaman William Robson; Author] who was afterwards wounded. If it had not been for him we should never have been able to get the 2nd mate into the boat."

After abandoning ship, *Empire Crusader* was left to sink fourteen miles south-east of The Needles. From land, and as far away as Portland, the funeral pyre from this and other stricken vessels could be seen coiling upwards 2,000ft into the summer sky.

Racing back westwards from their unsuccessful attempt to intercept the raid off Brighton, the twelve Hurricanes of 145 Squadron were straining every last ounce of power to get quickly back to Convoy Peewit and the towering pillars of smoke they could see growing in the west. Below, broken cloud left dappled dark patterns flecking across the blue-green sea whilst the summer sun blazed above them at its zenith. The apparently tranquil sea and azure blue sky belied the deadly intent of the Hurricanes and of the fierce battle that was about to be joined. That battle would be a whirling maelstrom of Stukas and fighters, including the Hurricanes of 257 and 601 Squadrons and the Spitfires of 609 Squadron. In total, well over 160 aircraft milling around in a furious aerial battle in quite a small space of sky; little wonder that claims and counter-claims were confused and confusing. That said, there seem to have been two distinct seats of combat; one involving the Stukas and escorting Me 109s directly above the ships and the other involving circling escort fighters a few miles distant.

The dive bombers exploited the conditions of broken cloud above the convoy to dive through into attack, the cloud at least partly hiding where they were coming from to the ship's gunners below and partly shielding them from the view of attacking RAF fighters above. Meanwhile, the main formations of escort fighters circled in two areas of fairly cloudless sky to the south and to the east of the convoy. It was a clever tactic that resulted in both these groups of German fighters standing between the attacking Stukas and the RAF aircraft that were approaching from the west and from the direction of Tangmere and Westhampnett. It was only the Spitfires of B Flight of 609 Squadron, approaching the convoy from the north after flying down from Middle Wallop and then across the Isle of Wight, which actually engaged the dive bombers. As 609 Squadron approached the convoy, led by Sqn Ldr H.S. Darley, they witnessed the Messerschmitt 109s of JG27 diving to shoot down the remaining barrage balloons – at least one of them falling to the guns of Oblt Max Dobislav of 9./JG27. One of the attacking Spitfire pilots of 609 Squadron was Flt Lt J.H.G. 'Butch' McArthur, leader of Green Section:

"I only had my number 3 with me and took off behind Blue Section and stayed behind them until over the convoy. I then heard the controller tell Blue Leader [Sqn Ldr H.S. Darley; Author] to come down below clouds. In trying to follow him down I lost Blue Section. At the same time my number 3 became separated from me. Below the clouds I saw a balloon in flames and many aircraft of all types in a general scrimmage. Owing to my inexperience I could not pick out a suitable target with any certainty so I climbed into the sun and headed out to sea. On reaching 6,000ft, where there was just about 4/10 cloud, and after having cruised about for around five minutes I saw one Me 110 down to sea level."

McArthur had flown off and away southwards from the attacking Stukas and had headed out towards the circling and waiting fighters, although by now the Stukas that had been the first into attack were already headed home:

"I dived down and on the way down I found that the Me 110 was following a squadron of Ju87s in vic formation heading for home. I dived on the outside Ju87 from about 3,000ft and fired a seven-second burst. I saw him turn over on his back and go into the sea. The formation then split up and I regained 4,000ft very quickly. The height of the Ju87s was about one hundred feet. I then dived and gave another long burst of ten seconds on another Ju87 which started to emit black smoke and dived into the sea. I then found the Me 110. I climbed up a bit and was coming in at him from the port side and slightly above him. I turned quickly away from him and after a turn or two found myself quickly on his tail. I then found that I had no more ammunition so pulled the over-ride tit and hurried home."

Apart from McArthur's claims, Darley claimed a Messeschmitt 110 as having being shot into the sea and he also took 'pot shots' at a number of Ju87s with the squadron operations record book noting: "Though a good day for 609 Squadron this was a bad day for the Navy. The convoy advertised its presence by flying silver barrage balloons and made it difficult to bring prompt aid by sailing fifteen miles out to sea."

Apart from 145 and 609 Squadrons, 601 Squadron and 257 both threw their Hurricanes into the fray, with six Hurricanes of 601 Squadron leaving Tangmere at 11.55 and the twelve Hurricanes of 257 Squadron (flying from RAF Tangmere as their forward operating base and away from their home station of RAF Northolt) getting off at 12.10. With the attack literally closing on the ships of CW9 Peewit, and despite the short flying distance from Tangmere, there was precious little time to get the fighters into position. Quite likely the controller had been wrong-footed after he had sent 145 Squadron haring off towards the feint attack to the east. Now it was a case of getting 145 Squadron back as quickly as possible and plugging the potential hole in defences with 601 and 257 Squadrons – although he still had 43 Squadron's Hurricanes in reserve and on the ground at Tangmere.

Meanwhile, 601 Squadron were ordered to orbit Tangmere at 20,000ft instead of making directly for Peewit, notwithstanding the clear indications that were already coming in from the radar station at Ventnor showing a big German force bearing down on the convoy and just minutes away. Possibly, and until the Germans' intentions were clear, the controller had preferred to keep 601 Squadron covering the airfield, and at least until 257 Squadron were up. Either way, 145, 257 and 601 Squadrons were some minutes from the convoy and 609 Squadron were still some minutes away to the north. Also racing up the Channel from Exeter were six Hurricanes of 213 Squadron, but their departure at 12.15 did not put them over the convoy until long after the Luftwaffe had left for home. From the north, too, came yet more Hurricanes – this time twelve aircraft of 238 Squadron operating out of Middle Wallop which had become airborne at 12.09, hot on the heels of the recently departed 609 Squadron. The convoy, already badly mauled, was dangerously exposed. And yet, given the advance warning, it would have been possible to have had all three Hurricane squadrons from Tangmere and Westhampnett up and over it long before the Stukas had got there. With the advantage of height (the squadrons would have had sufficient time to climb to altitude) and the mid-day sun at their backs, the impact those three squadrons might have had on the attackers can only be guessed at.

It was not until 12.30 that the Hurricanes of 601 Squadron finally had contact with the enemy; the Me 109s of JG27. Led again by Flt Lt Archibald Hope, the six fighters tore into the enemy some ten miles south of St Catherine's Point. In a hectic combat, Plt Off J.K.U.B. McGrath accounted for two Me 109s claimed as destroyed. Breaking away from his section on sighting the enemy, McGrath did a stall turn onto the tail of a Me 109 that was, in turn, on the tail of a Hurricane and did a head-on attack. Stall turning again as the enemy aircraft passed dangerously close underneath him, he caught sight of the Messerschmitt as it rolled onto its back and spun down into the sea. Now though a Messerschmitt was on McGrath's tail.

Diving at full throttle he then zoomed up vertically and fell off the top of a loop, flattened out and did another stall turn only to find that despite his aerobatics the Messerschmitt was still firmly on his tail. Truly, this was dog fighting. Sweat poured from under his flying helmet and trickled down his face as he twisted and turned and, after some minutes, he finally got onto his opponent's tail. A two-second burst did the trick. The Messerschmitt wobbled and dived into the sea with McGrath following him down. Later he noted: "Presumably the pilot was killed immediately". For no loss, 601 Squadron had claimed three Me 109s destroyed but, crucially, had failed to get at the dive bombers.

Flt Lt Noel Hall led the twelve Hurricanes of 257 Squadron into the engagement with fighters south of the Isle of Wight, and here, in the frantic combat, Plt Off A.C. Cochrane and Plt Off K.C. Gundry each claimed a Me 109 destroyed, with Gundry also claiming another as damaged. Sgt R.V. Forward, meanwhile, claimed a 'Dornier 17' as damaged, but since no Dornier 17s were involved in the action he must have mistaken the twin tails of a Me 110 for those of a Do 17. On

Flt Lt D.E. Turner of 238 Squadron was shot down in the battles over Convoy CW9 Peewit. No trace of him was ever found.

the debit side, things were not good. Flt Lt Hall, Fg Off D'Arcy Irvine and Sgt K.B. Smith had failed to return and nothing had been heard or seen of them by the rest of the squadron. Meanwhile, Sgt R.H.B. Fraser in Hurricane P3775 had experienced some difficulty that had resulted in him beating a retreat to RNAS Lee-on-the-Solent, and from where he did not return to Tangmere until 18.40 that evening. Despondently, Plt Off Gundry went off again from Tangmere in Hurricane P3708 at 13.50 to search the sea area where the combat had taken place to look for Hall, D'Arcy Irvine and Smith. Despite a search of one hour and fifteen minutes he found only the depressing detritus of war drifting about on the tide.

According to the 238 Squadron operations record book:

"When our aircraft arrived the enemy aircraft were dive-bombing the convoy. Flt Lt D.E. Turner and Fg Off D.C. McCaw have been missing since this engagement although at least one of them is believed to have baled out and landed by parachute. Fg Off McCaw came to the RAF through the University of Cambridge and had been with an Army Co-Op squadron before coming to 238 Squadron, of which he was an original pilot. Of Celtic colouring, blue eyes and black hair, which was already tinged with grey, and his slightly dreamy dignified personality he is greatly missed. He was clearly material from which the best type of Officer is made.

"Flt Lt Turner's keenness, energy and good humour made him very popular with everyone and his strong reliable character made him an excellent second-in-command. He has been greatly missed."

When the head count had finally been completed for all the returning RAF squadrons, and a reasonable time had passed to allow for any stragglers to get back, it was clearly apparent that the two pilots of 238 Squadron were not coming back to RAF Middle Wallop. Unsettled by their disappearance, the commanding officer, Squadron Leader Harold Fenton (who had not participated in the action) decided to go off in Hurricane P2497 at 13.20 to carry out a search where the combats had taken place. Like Plt Off Gundry of 257 Squadron who was searching the same area at the same time, Fenton would find no trace of his pilots. Arriving over a sea littered with debris, floating coke, oil slicks and burning ships drifting listlessly on the distant horizon, his anxious search for the unfortunate Turner and McCaw was suddenly interrupted by the appearance on the scene of a Heinkel He 59 seaplane, low over the water, itself searching for downed Luftwaffe airmen.

Approaching the seaplane and going in to attack, Fenton was surprised by a brief burst of fire from the He 59 and before he could even think of any retaliation it quickly became apparent that a single unlucky round had severed an oil feed pipe in his engine. Acting quickly, and as oil pressure began to drop and temperatures ran higher, he started to climb. If he could gain some altitude it may allow him to glide back to land or, if need be, to bale out. However, as he reached 3,000ft his engine promptly seized and the propeller jerked alarmingly to a halt. One way or another, this was journey's end; it was just a question of whether he now baled out or rode his Hurricane down and ditched in the sea. The first option did not seem very attractive. After all, at least one of the two pilots he had just been searching for had been seen to bale out and was now missing. If Fenton jumped he might end up being posted missing as well. Alternatively, he might be fished out of the sea by prowling He 59s. Captivity wasn't attractive, either. By good fortune, and as his altitude began to fall away, Fenton spotted a distant naval trawler of some sorts about five miles south of St Catherine's Point and decided that it would be best to attempt a landing as near to it as possible.

To make his water landing safer, Fenton undid his parachute and the Sutton seat harness. When the impact came he would need to get out, and mightily quick! As it was, the radiator scoop of the Hurricane dug into the sea resulting in the nose going under and the tail shooting high into the air. The result was that the unsecured Fenton was catapulted forward on impact with the sea, with his torso striking the instrument panel, control column, and gun sight causing injuries to his face and chest. As he was thrown upwards and outwards he hit his head hard on the canopy frame causing severe cuts and abrasions. Additionally, he had badly injured his leg on something lower down in the cockpit.

Fenton had put down approximately one mile from HM Trawler *Bassett* whose captain, Lt Nigel Herriot, at once altered course and proceeded under full speed to the stricken pilot's assistance although it took Herriot a full half-hour to reach him. Arriving on the scene, *Basset* found Fenton struggling in the water and if it were not for the courageous and prompt actions of Second Engineman J. Alexander the outcome may have been rather different. The crew of *Basset* were not easily able to get the injured squadron leader aboard, and so Alexander unhesitatingly jumped into the water with a line and secured the rope around the battered and dazed pilot so that he could be hauled up onto *Basset's* deck in another instance that day of selfless valour from a Royal Navy sailor.

On board the *Basset*, Fenton was given first aid treatment and taken below to warm up and dry out in the boiler room. What happened next is best described by the writer of 238 Squadron's operations record book:

"Later, the trawler picked up a German officer of Flt Lt rank whose total luggage, a special Very pistol with cartridges, and a large packet of twelve contraceptives, gave the crew an amusing interlude. The pistol and its cartridges are used to draw attention if a pilot comes down in the sea. Whilst Sqn Ldr Fenton and the Bosche were drying out they had toast and tea but were much interrupted by bombs which were falling with insistent regularity. After a time they got used to it and they were in a somnolent state when the boat hove to. On enquiry they discovered that port had not yet been reached, but that they had hove-to in mid Channel to pick up a Dutch skipper from a raft. Closer examination showed that he was dead as a result of accidental strangulation by a line which had caught around his neck. He was left, and the trawler headed for port where it arrived at around 1am, putting ashore Sqn Ldr Fenton and the Bosche who were both transferred to the Haslar Hospital."

The German airman who became Fenton's reluctant travelling companion on board HMS *Basset* was, in fact, Stuka pilot Oblt Martin Müller the Adjutant of Stab I./StG3 who had been shot down off the Isle of Wight during the attack by 145 Squadron's Hurricanes. His radio operator, Uffz Josef Krampfl, had been killed and his body later washed ashore on the French coast. Meanwhile, and whilst the rescue of Fenton and Müller was going on, preparations were already underway in France for yet another attack on the battered remnants of Convoy CW9 by Stukas. This time, it would be the turn of various elements of Stuka Geschwaders 3 and 77. It had, in fact, been their bombs that had so rudely interrupted the tea and toast of the two drying-out pilots.

After the mid-day attack that had damaged Hague's little ship, HMS *Borealis* had bravely limped on with the intention of at least reaching port. No longer effective for her intended purpose, and now barely afloat, her master was determined to save her if he possibly could. Unfortunately, the Luftwaffe had other ideas. Hague takes up the story from the point when he had stopped the engine and fallen out of line after *Borealis* was first struck:

"With my chief engineman I inspected the collision bulkhead which was holding well and then put the ship into hand steering from aft – the bridge steering gear being no longer effective. The chief engineman, J. Taylor, with great difficulty had caulked the fuel supply tank sufficiently to keep the main engine supplied and it was found that the ship would still work.

"At this time HMS *Astral* came to my assistance and ordered HMS *Elan II* to take me in tow and for me to send all hands not required to work the ship to *Astral*. I had already transferred my three serious casualties to HMS *Greenfly* and I retained my two officers and seven ratings.

"HMS *Elan II* took me in tow with three hawsers stern first because of the pressure on the collision bulkhead. It was found impossible to steer *Borealis* however, so *Elan II* cast off and came alongside with her bow to my stern and was secured. Owing to the rising westerly wind and sea this method was also found to be impracticable and likely to cause too much damage to *Elan II*. In the meantime, HMS *Renee* had arrived to stand by and an attempt was made to tow *Borealis* stern first by *Elan II* while *Renee* made fast forwards and steered her. This method proved highly satisfactory and the three vessels proceeded towards Portsmouth."

However, the adventures of *Borealis* and her crew at the hands of the Stukas were not over yet.

CHAPTER 6

Peewit in Their Sights!

THE FINAL STUKA RAID OF 8 August 1940 was first picked up by radar as an estimated eighteen-plus force of aircraft detected at 15.34 hours off Le Havre and was headed, once again, directly towards CW9. However, the slightly deteriorating weather in the English Channel during the mid to late afternoon period had earlier caused a question mark to hang over further Stuka operations that day. Indeed, at around 14.25 Major Paul-Werner Hozzel had again led his I./StG1 off towards the convoy for another attack, this time with twenty-two aircraft. However, he aborted the mission when it was found that cloud cover in the target area was too low to press home an attack.

Although the day had remained dry and with moderately good visibility, broken cloud had gathered to the extent that by 15.00 the Germans were reporting 9/10 cloud cover and with a cloud base down to somewhere between 3,000 to 4,500ft. Hardly optimum conditions in which to conduct dive-bombing operations against a convoy. In fact, the broken cloud during the first attack of the day had most likely already caused some difficulty in properly identifying the correct target.

That the continuation of the late afternoon operations (which were to be flown by no less than three Stuka Gruppen) had been in some doubt was certainly borne out by Hptm Waldemar Plewig, the Gruppen Kommandeur of II./StG77. Frustrated by the refusal of the *Oberbefehlhaber der Luftwaffe* to give the green light for the late afternoon attack because of weather conditions encountered during Hozzel's aborted mission, Plewig took up the Gruppe's Dornier 17P to have a look for himself over the target area. As an experienced Junkers 87 combat pilot, Plewig was able to make an objective assessment and satisfied himself that even if these were not optimum operating conditions, they were currently quite within operational limits. Moreover he could see the convoy and felt that the targets were

Hptm Waldemar Plewig.

Oblt Klaus Ostmann of III./StG1 in the cockpit of his Stuka. The naval influence in the unit's emblem is because this Gruppe was originally designated I.(St)/186 and had been destined to operate from an aircraft carrier although that plan never materialised.

clearly recognisable. Returning, he made his report. By early afternoon the attack was given the green light.

For many of the waiting crews of III./StG1 this may have been the second operation of the day. Tiredness and nervous exhaustion was an ever-present and aggravating factor for combat fliers. Uncertainty just made matters worse. Waiting with the twenty-two Junkers 87s of III.StG1 for the word to go before Plewig's confirmatory reconnaissance were twenty-eight others from I./StG3, and another thirty-two from both the Stab and the II Gruppe of StG77 – eighty-two aeroplanes and 164 aircrew in total. And another 328 high-explosive bombs destined for CW9. When the word to go finally came, the aircraft of I./StG3 departed from Barly between 15.30 and 15.45 with Major Walter Sigel leading the formation to rendezvous with their escort, the Messerschmitt 110s of II./ZG2. The aeroplanes of StG1 and StG77 departed a little later at between 16.08 and 16.20. Plewig of II./StG77 tells the story:

"Besides the Gruppen commanded by Sigel, and another commanded by Hozzel [sic: Hozzel had in fact led the aborted raid earlier in the afternoon and did not participate in this action; Author] my Gruppe was to assemble over Cherbourg and carry out a large-scale attack. My Gruppe started as ordered, but noticed that one of the other Gruppen was not ready for take-off. Climbing up steadily, we proceeded to the gathering point. As we approached the coast, I realised that the third Gruppe was already hanging over the Channel above us, and long before the stated time. Our own fighters must have split up as only a few 109s and 110s were to be seen. The majority of the fighter escort must have already flown to the target area with the Gruppe of early starters. Only this could explain why my Gruppe, when later approaching the convoy, flew right into the arms of the RAF fighters which had been lured up by the first Gruppe; our escort then split up, the first Gruppe returning with the escort whilst my far weaker fighter escort had to fight against overwhelming odds."

Thus, the carefully planned massed-group attack with its fighter umbrella had lost its cohesion long before any ships were sighted. The groups of dive bombers, with their fighter escorts, were now strung out over many miles across the English Channel. Almost a full hour had separated the departure of the first and the last Junkers 87s from their French bases. Additionally, the escorting Messerschmitt 109s had a limited operational endurance, especially over the sixty miles or so that separated the Cherbourg Peninsula from the Isle of Wight area. Given that distance of travel, the Messerschmitt 109s' available time to 'loiter' over the target area and protect the dive bombers was severely restricted and there was certainly no margin that would allow them to hang around waiting for straggling groups of their charges to catch up. As it was, and even if things were going entirely according to plan, their low-fuel warning lights would already be winking during their return flights. Although the Messerschmitt 110s had a greater range and endurance their effectiveness against the more agile RAF fighters did not best suit them to this kind of operation. These escort problems were ones that would dog all Stuka operations in this area by Fliegerkorps VIII aircraft.

If it was the weather, the disorganised start of this particular Stuka operation or the appearance on the scene of considerable numbers of defending RAF fighters it is difficult to say, but the fact is that the Stuka attacks that day had seen diminishing returns for effort expended. In addition, by the time the bombers were over the target area during the late afternoon, convoy CW9 had begun to disperse. This, the last attack, was by far the least successful and it also saw the greatest number of Luftwaffe casualties. In view of the massed formations of Stukas once again ranged against them, the actual ships of Convoy CW9 and its various survivors and stragglers would this time get off more than lightly. Again, it would be other ships which took the brunt.

As the Stukas approached the Isle of Wight it seems that at least some of the Gruppen, if not all of them, were initially attracted by the columns of smoke from the burning ships of the earlier attack, and especially the blazing hulk of *Empire Crusader*. By now, the rest of the convoy was sailing on and was well past the Isle of Wight and getting towards Weymouth Bay. Some of the vessels had already split away and were going in to Yarmouth Roads at the western end of The Solent. Other ships, though, were in the vicinity of the burning and sinking hulks from the previous attack, and were trying to give assistance. HMS *Basset* was already on station, as were other sundry smaller craft including the RAF launches HSL 116 and 121. Present too were a number of other vessels sent out to assist, and these included HMT *Cape Palliser*, HMS *Wilna* and HMS *Rion*. Adding to this varied collection of shipping, HMS *Borealis* was still just afloat and limping along in the general vicinity with the *Elan II* and *Renee* still in close attendance. It was this disparate group of shipping that the Stukas had chosen to attack, and, in so doing, they finished off *Borealis*.

Again, we return to Arthur Hague's report:

"At about 17.00 [sic. This was, in fact, nearer to 16.15 to 16.30; Author] however a further enemy dive-bomber attack was made, and with the ship being unmanageable and it being impossible to make any effective defence, I abandoned her with my remaining hands in the only boat that was left and lay off until the bombers had been driven away by our fighters. We then pulled back to the ship with the intention of securing her again as bomb splinters had severed the tow ropes. Unfortunately, we found her listing heavily to port apparently having suffered a further direct hit or near miss which had started [sic] her bulkhead. There

Lt Arthur Hague RN who commanded HMS *Borealis*.

was the sound of escaping gas which suggested that the hydrogen bottles on her after deck had been hit. I therefore considered it unwise to board the vessel again and we were picked up by the *Renee*."

As they stood on the deck of *Renee* the crew of *Borealis* watched as her list to port steadily worsened. Finally, the end came at about 17.20 as she slid beneath the waves, bow first, fifteen miles south-east of The Needles.

Of the *Borealis* crew, Arthur Hague and two of his men would be recognised for their meritorious service that day and were Mentioned in Despatches. In addition to Hague, Second Hand Cyril White and Engineman Joseph Dell Taylor (both of the Royal Naval Patrol Service) were rewarded with MIDs.

Five minutes before *Borealis* had finally gone to her watery grave, the crew of the Bembridge lifeboat, *Jesse Lumb*, were called out at 17.15 to go to the aid of an aircraft down "ten miles SSW from Bembridge Point". Quite which aircraft this might have been it is impossible to say. There were certainly plenty to choose from and *Jesse Lumb* made way to the position given. Here, an RAF Blackburn Roc aeroplane circled over the lifeboat, went off, returned and repeated the operation to show the direction she should take. There was no sign of any aeroplane in the water, but *Jesse Lumb* found instead the RAF's HSL 116, disabled and flying a distress signal. During the last of the Stuka attacks she had been raked with machine-gun fire, her relatively flimsy construction offering little or no protection to the men on board. Sadly, one had been killed and another badly wounded although she was unable to make her way ashore for aid as a rope amongst the floating debris and wreckage of Peewit had fouled her propeller.

Consequently, the lifeboat towed HSL 116 to port putting the wounded man, Sgt Wilfred Vosper, ashore for admission to Haslar Hospital. They also took ashore the body of the seventeen-year-old wireless telegraphist, AC1 Raymond Wheeler. A local boy from Southampton, Wheeler's praises were later sung in the *Southampton Daily Echo* of 12 August 1940. The newspaper described how Raymond, suffering terribly from seasickness, had remained at his post in the small wireless cabin of HSL 116 sending messages as the launch sped to the aid of a downed German airman. So ill did Wheeler become that another crew member had to sit beside him to support the wireless operator as he tapped away at his signalling key. As they made towards the reported position of the enemy flier the RAF craft was machine-gunned, killing the young signaller instantly while he sat at his post.

Despite the dive-bombing attacks on the eclectic grouping of ships that the Luftwaffe had again mistaken for CW9, and the alarming and deadly experiences still being lived through by those on board the various vessels, the Stukas and their escorts were far from having it their own way. Plewig again takes up the story:

"Despite our predicament with the fighter escort, there was no turning back and I ordered the three Staffeln of II Gruppe to attack. I, along with the reinforced Stabs Kette, waited until the end. As we could see more and more enemy fighters appearing above us, I decided not to climb up to the usual altitude and started the attack instead from about 12,000ft. After the three Staffeln had attacked their targets, I chose mine and went into a dive and released my bombs from about 1,800ft. The Spitfires and Hurricanes dived with us but we were able to observe some near misses on the ships.

"Now, I attempted to throw off my adversaries by irregular flying at sea level – we always flew that way as it gave fighters less of a chance to hit us. However, during the descent, I was repeatedly shot at. My gunner, Fw Schauer, fired back until he was hit. I think he was hit in the neck and the thigh, because I noticed a jet of blood. In the meantime, I was hit in the right arm and right calf and had to fly with my left hand. At the same time, the oxygen supply was hit and a box of ammunition was struck by tracer bullets. When the 'plane started to show signs of burning on the right side, I decided to bale out. My gunner did not reply over the intercom, and I could see him hanging lifelessly in his harness. As he did not react to my orders to throw off the canopy, and I had levelled off above the water and the 'plane was well alight, I decided to jump at the last moment. I had failed in my efforts to throw out the gunner – he was certainly dead and I just hoped that his body might be washed up somewhere. So, I said goodbye to my companion and friend, Kurt Schauer."

At 16.15, and at the same time that *Borealis* had been on the receiving end of her further unwelcome attention, HMS *Wilna* was also coming under Stuka attack. In fact, it is clear that *Wilna*, along with HMS *Rion*, (both anti-submarine yachts) and the anti-submarine trawlers HMS *Cape Palliser, Kingston Chrysoberyl, Kingston Olivine* and *Stella Capella* – in company with the *Borealis, Elan II* and *Astral* – were the group of ships that the attacking Stukas had found and targeted. The ships of CW9, meanwhile, steamed safely off to the west and far out of harm's way, as six little Royal Navy ships that had sailed out to help them became the second group of unwitting decoys for the Stukas. From HMS *Wilna*, Commander A.D.W. Sumpter reported of events that day to the commander-in-chief, Portsmouth:

"At 16.15 on 8 August 1940 *Wilna* was in approx position 160° St Catherine's Point, steering 045° at 14 knots. At this moment a large number of aircraft, estimated at 60-80, were observed southward at a great height, perhaps 15,000ft. In a diesel ship at full speed it is impossible to hear aircraft at a distance. The alarm was at once sounded and I stepped into the chart house for my telescope. Before I could use it, however, I saw three dive bombers attacking from vertically overhead, and at too great an elevation for my Lewis gun to bear. No R/T signal was made as the first salvo put the wireless out of action. Before the enemy released their bombs I ordered 'Lie Down' and did so immediately before each attack. Six attacks were made in ten or twelve minutes, each being made by three Ju87s and each machine dropping a cluster of five bombs. These burst on the surface of the water. Some of these machines, but not all, fired on *Wilna* with machine guns.

"All of the salvos of bombs were very close, I should describe them all as 'inners' but fortunately there were no 'bulls'.

"The groups of three all dived vertically from a great height and appeared to flatten out at about five hundred feet; fire was opened on each group after they had flattened out with the Lewis gun, *Wilna's* sole anti-aircraft armament, and it is possible that a couple were hit. One round of four-inch shrapnel was also fired.

"It was not possible to take avoiding action beyond going at full speed as the electric steering gear was deranged by the first salvo and the hand gear was rather difficult to engage. The course therefore remained at approximately 045°.

"After about ten minutes Hurricanes were seen to be engaging the enemy and the bombing ceased. Three of my men were killed, one of them inside a half-inch thick steel shelter on the bridge that was penetrated by splinters. The other two were on the port side, aft, below the promenade deck. I cannot say whether these two were lying down or not. Eleven were wounded in varying degrees. Fortunately, just before being ordered to sea I had landed liberty men at Seaview, so that the 1st Lieut, chief engineer and seven of the ship's company were out of the ship, leaving a total of thirty on board. A greater number on board would have made no difference, except that there would have been more casualties. It was also a comfort, on our return to St Helen's, to have some fresh and unshaken hands to secure ropes etc.

"It is hard to speak highly enough of the conduct of my ship's company; nearly all of them fishermen or yachting hands. Though we were quite helpless to ward off these alarming attacks, and this ship being by no means constructed to withstand such treatment, there was not the slightest sign of any 'wind up' and some might have thought they had been used to that kind of thing all their lives. None of the wounded made any complaint and all were most patient. Leading Seaman Stuttle, though wounded early in the attack, was very smart each time in jumping up and firing the Lewis gun after the bombers had straightened out. Lieuts Behennah and Dimmick, RNVR, and the boatswain, Little, all of them wounded slightly, were indefatigable in doing all in their power for the badly wounded men on our way back, with no thought for themselves. A fire in the wood store, forward, caused me some anxiety as it was at no great distance from the depth charge for the demolition of ASDIC if necessary. No pump would work and the fire extinguishers had all been deranged by shock and the smoke was too thick for men to remain below for more than a minute or so. However, the pistol of the depth charge was finally removed and our fire was extinguished by hoses from an examination vessel at St Helen's.

"Damage to the ship cannot at present be stated, she is riddled with splinter holes above the water line but appears to have suffered no structural defects.

A.D.W. Sumpter (commander)"

As she limped back to St Helen's Road, the *Wilna* passed the floating wreckage from earlier attacks, including an empty lifeboat with its sides bullet-holed and splintered and the complete wheelhouse of a Dutch vessel with its ship's bell still hanging inside. The muffled sound of it ringing whilst it floated past was like some ghostly tolling for ships and lives already lost that day.

In all, *Wilna* had evidently been singled out by virtually one fifth of the entire attacking force of Stukas. The ship had not, in any way, been part of CW9 and her significance (as that of the others with her) as a naval vessel hardly warranted such comprehensive attention from the dive bombers. It was attention that had cost the lives of Quartermaster Edgar Brown, Able Seaman Alfred Fullick and Carpenter Samuel Keat. In addition, a further eleven wounded men were admitted to Haslar Hospital which was now rapidly filling up with casualties from the actions that day; RAF and German aircrew, an RAF marine craft man, merchant seamen of various nationalities and an increasing number of British sailors. Again, in this action, we have shining examples of Royal Navy seamen being exemplary and courageous in the execution of their duties. Again, we have wounded men staying at their stations to fight, or assisting others perhaps more badly wounded than they. In respect of *Wilna*, however, we also have formal recognition of that gallantry and the devotion to duty of the Lewis anti-aircraft gunner, Leading Seaman George Alexander Stuttle, P/JX 129588, who received a Mention in Despatches for his bravery in sticking at his post and defending the ship despite his grievous wounds. The story on board *Rion, Kingston Chrysoberyl, Kingston Olivine, Stella Capella* and *Cape Palliser* was pretty much the same.

The captain of HMT *Cape Palliser*, Lieutenant Dennis C. Hayes, also compiled a comprehensive report in which he described how "three formations" of Stukas dived on the little group of ships, with the attack on *Cape Palliser* coming from the third formation. Quite likely this had been the group of Stukas led by Waldemar Plewig. However, and like all of the vessels in this group, *Cape Palliser* was not well equipped to defend herself against air attack with a single four-inch gun and two Lewis guns. Once again, we have the gunners of the latter giving good accounts of themselves – although this time with fatal results for both:

> "Lieutenant McEwan was in charge of the Lewis guns and continued to keep them firing until two of the Lewis gunners were killed and one badly wounded. We were only able to get off one round of four-inch when all of the gun's crew, except one, were badly wounded. Everyone stuck to their guns magnificently and continued to fight until they were killed or wounded."

In all, around fifteen salvos were aimed at *Cape Palliser*. Of these fifteen or so attacks some of the bombs fell within fifteen yards of the ship but the majority dropped between twenty-five to thirty yards away. Hayes also talks of some bombs being dropped "….as far as half a mile away once British fighter aircraft had appeared on the scene", thereby implying that the attackers had ditched their bombs and fled. Although this is entirely possible it might also have been because so many aircraft were attempting to dive on so few targets. With the sky so crowded, and Stukas almost literally queuing up to attack, it may have become clear to some of the dive-bomber pilots that the limited target opportunities presented by the little group of ships, and the increasing menace of defending RAF fighters, meant that the only real option was to dump their bombs and head for home. After all, trying to avoid Spitfires or Hurricanes with the weight of a full bomb load was not the best option for survival! At the end of the attack the *Cape Palliser* was badly damaged, the onslaught leaving Seaman Isaac C. Bowles and Engineman Fred Pile killed. Of the seven crew members left wounded, Seaman (Cook) Jeffery W. Hinton died in Haslar Hospital the next day. The officer in charge of *Cape Palliser*'s Lewis gun crews, Temporary Lieutenant Ronald McEwan, was Mentioned in Despatches for his gallant action.

On the *Rion*, the crew found they were entirely defenceless when the sole Lewis gun jammed before even a single round could be fired. Drawing back the cocking handle the gunner discovered that the full withdrawal could not be made and that he was gazing impotently up at a Stuka which drew closer and got bigger by the second. Losing his battle with the recalcitrant cocking lever, the seaman flung himself to the deck as five bombs crashed into the sea around him while the departing Junkers raked the ship from stem to stern with machine-gun fire. Two ratings were injured by gunfire, but during that first attack the captain, Commander J.K.B. Birch, was also seriously wounded as he stood on his bridge. Unfortunately he succumbed to his injuries in Haslar Hospital on 14 August 1940. Birch, aged 59, was no stranger to war at sea and had served on board HMS *Duke of Edinburgh* at the Battle of Jutland in 1916.

The *Rion*, meanwhile, was a mess. All her windows were gone, the anti-submarine recorder and wireless were wrecked, the dinghy was lost and both launches were badly shot-up and holed. Bullets had punctured the funnel, split open a water tank and severed air lines. More seriously, bomb shrapnel had split open the casing of a depth charge and damaged one of the others. The consequences had the explosive fillings detonated would have been disastrous; the small ship would have simply been blown to smithereens. There could have been no survivors from such a blast. It was just one of many lucky escapes that day.

Whilst the absence of any form of armour plating for the gunners on *Cape Palliser* and other RN ships was cause for concern, the perceived existence of under-belly armour plating to Spitfires was also a worry to one particular gunner of I./StG3 after this particular attack. In the ULTRA intercepts for 19 August is to be found the following: "On 8 August, in a battle with Spitfires five kilometres south of the Isle of Wight, he noticed his machine-gun bursts glancing off the underneath of the Spitfire's cockpit. It was to be presumed that the Spitfires had recently been armoured in that part."

Of course, the unknown Luftwaffe airmen's perception was a little like his shooting and rather wide of the mark. No such armour had been or ever was fitted, and what he had observed must have been either just a fluke or a trick of the light. On the other hand, one gunner from Stab II./StG77 on that operation (Uffz Karl Witton) had claimed a 'confirmed' Hurricane destroyed over the English Channel.

The late afternoon attack by the Stukas that had been directed against the ships of Convoy CW9 had been an abject failure. Not a single ship of the convoy had been hit, nor had the attackers come anywhere near them. Further, the collection of Royal Navy vessels and the RAF launch that were attacked were relatively insignificant. Whilst all were damaged, and fatalities and casualties had been sustained, none were sunk with the exception of the already crippled *Borealis*. The vessels targeted were hardly ships of the line, and really not important within the Royal Navy's Home Fleet. When set against the losses sustained by the attacking force, and even taking into account the losses to the RAF's defending fighters, the effort was certainly disproportionate for the results obtained.

Well over a hundred Stukas (in three raids) and scores of escort fighters had been pitched into that last battle of the day. The cost to the Luftwaffe in aircraft and crews during that attack was very heavy with twenty-three of their airmen killed. With hindsight, the decision by Paul-Werner Hozzel to abort his earlier attack and the subsequent refusal of high command initially to sanction any others had been the right calls. By late afternoon the Hurricane pilots of 43 Squadron must have been frustrated by the lack of any call to action. Since early that morning they had seen their colleagues on 145 and 601 Squadron come and go to do battle with the Luftwaffe. Worse, an 'imported' Hurricane unit from RAF Northolt, 257 Squadron, had had *its* share of the action, too! The famous Fighting Cock's squadron was hoping to live up to its motto *Gloria Finis*… glory in the end. And in the end, that day, they would surely have their glory.

When an incoming raid was again plotted off Le Havre at 15.34 it was clear that, once more, the Luftwaffe's intentions were directed towards CW9 Peewit. Since the various RAF fighter squadrons had departed home after the lunch-time engagement the convoy had been unprotected by air cover and the fighter controllers sought immediately to rectify that by sending off at 15.40 the Hurricanes of 43 Squadron from Tangmere and Spitfires of 152 Squadron from Warmwell with orders for 43 to proceed at once to Convoy Peewit with 152 headed for St Alban's Head and Weymouth Bay. As the threat grew more immediate, so the controller bolstered his forces over Peewit by sending off 145 Squadron for its third operational sortie that day at 16.00, and with 238 Squadron again being called on at 16.20. The former squadron was sent to its by now familiar battleground off the Isle of Wight, with 238 Squadron following 152 Squadron down into Weymouth Bay. Doubtless the controller didn't want to get caught again being so tardy in getting his defences in place over the convoy, and on this occasion he was a little more timely. This time, the Stukas were actually caught over the ships – even though they were not actually the ships of CW9 Peewit.

In Waldemar Plewig's account of the dive onto his target he speaks of the RAF fighters "diving with him", and that is indeed what the Hurricanes of 43 and 145 Squadron succeeded in doing. Not quite early enough on the scene to prevent at least the majority of Stukas diving to attack, the massed Hurricanes certainly managed to wreak some havoc as they got in amongst the enemy

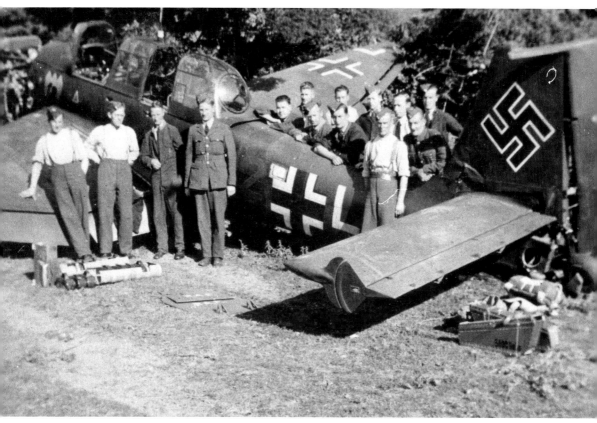

The Junkers 87 of 4./StG77 shot down on 8 August 1940 at St Lawrence, Isle of Wight, by Plt Off Parrott of 145 Squadron. The pilot, Uffz Pittroff, was captured although his radio operator, Uffz Schubert, was killed. This was the first intact Junkers 87 to fall into RAF hands on British soil.

aircraft. Plt Off Peter Parrott was also in action, and managed to get a positively confirmed victory over one of the Junkers 87s:

"The best strategy was to hit them as they pulled out. I got one from the beam as it recovered from dropping its bombs. I followed it as it flew on towards the Isle of Wight after pulling out of its attack. We were very close to the sea, about a hundred feet or so, and its only evasive action apart from flying low was to make a series of gentle turns each way."

Parrott managed to get in a short burst which severed the aircraft's fuel lines and killed its rear gunner, Uffz Schubert. With the damage sustained by his aeroplane there was no chance that Uffz Pitroff would be able to make the return flight across sixty miles of English Channel and he had no choice but to put down on land. Wobbling on past the St Lawrence Hospital, the Stuka pitched down in a field by Orchard Bay, bounced across a small depression and careered into the next field where it finally rolled to a halt in a hedge. Of all the enemy aircraft shot down in operations against CW9 Peewit that day this was the only one to fall on land, and on its final approach local lad Alan Twigg decided he would lend Plt Off Parrott a helping hand. Grabbing his Daisy air rifle he took a pot shot at the Stuka as it went overhead, only to be admonished for his apparently extreme foolhardiness: "What if you'd hit one of its bombs?" shouted one of his elders and betters "…you'd have blown us all to kingdom come!"

Gradually, the targets became fewer for 145 Squadron as the fighting spread out like the ripples on a pond and then dissipated as the enemy aircraft finally withdrew southwards and the defending RAF fighters returned home out of ammunition.

Whilst we have read of Waldemar Plewig's experiences that day there also exists a contemporary account given in a German radio broadcast by one of the participating Stuka crewmen who flew in this attack with II./StG77. Clearly, it was made with propaganda in mind but it provides an interesting insight from a German perspective:

A close-up of the emblem of the 4th Staffel of StG77 which was emblazoned on each side of the fuselage of the aircraft brought down on the Isle of Wight. It depicts a black cockerel on a yellow shield with a red top.

"At the briefing we were told that our target is a British convoy trying to force the Channel route. We were given a codename for our attack; 'Puma'. We had no proper location and so we had to fly our mission most accurately by compass. Our wing leader had to give each squadron commander short and accurate instructions from what he knew, then everyone got dressed. The most important piece of clothing is the life jacket. Then, shortly before 16.00 [sic] the whole group is ready, the first formation to take off being our commander's formation. A small signal lamp flashes and like a flock of large birds the squadrons rose up one after another into the sky. We all circle our base and collect information, then head off towards the Channel battleground. After only a few minutes we are at the coast. Below us, as far as the eye can see, is the Channel. Once it was the busiest shipping lane in the world. Now it is the largest ship's graveyard.

"Water – nothing but water below us. We cannot see the coast or the enemy ships. Our thoughts are with our engines, those reliable humming helpers in our operation. Our eyes go from instrument to instrument checking; water cooling, tachometer, pressure gauge – all of them are regularly checked. If our engine gives up there is only one thing for us and that is 'The Ditch'. The Channel is large and wide, and on the other side is the enemy island.

"There, carefully, one would like to whisper that there is a light strip emerging from the blue-green water. At first you can hardly make it out. The English south coast, and the white cliffs of the steep shore. A few hundred metres above us fly some squadrons of fighters – Me 109s and the long-range destroyer Me 110s as protection for us. Half-right in front of us at about 3,000 to 4,000 metres the first air battle has already begun. You can hardly tell friend from enemy. We can only see small silver specks circling. Now we must be especially alert. The coast is getting nearer, to the left, below us, the Isle of Wight and we already see ten or twelve ships. They, as they in turn spot us, try somehow to avoid our attacks by zig-zagging turns. We fly steadily eastwards towards them. Suddenly we hear through our R/T 'Number four aircraft has crash-landed!' One of our 4th Staffel machines has had to go down into the water. His engine must have failed. We hope everything goes well for them as we press on.

"'Puma one – to all Pumas – Puma attack!' We are above the convoy. It all seems to be small ships, coasters. Our 1 Staffel has already started to attack. Now the formations pull apart. Each one of them chooses a ship that has not yet been hit by one of the other squadrons. Our Staffelkapitän's formation starts its attack dives near to the coast. But what is this? I cannot believe my eyes. There is a third formation which attacks with us in a dive from the left. At the same instant I hear 'Puma – alert. Enemy fighters diving from above!' When we are diving and banking vertically the English fighters have virtually no chance to shoot our Stukas so they always tried to intercept us earlier or catch us later on when we have pulled out of our dives. On account of them being so much faster than us we always form up for mutual protection.

"That's for later. Right now I select my formation's target which is the most southerly ship of the convoy. Before I commence my dive I make sure by asking my radio operator if everything is clear behind us. I receive the reply 'All clear!' Then we dive down. My bombs land close alongside the ship, my left-hand *Kettenhund* aircraft also scores a near miss by a very near margin, but the third aircraft of the formation hits the ship square amidships with his bombs. Within seconds a huge flame shoots up from the ship and a large cloud of smoke bellows out of her insides. As we fly away, we can see her listing badly and on fire.

"Now the English defenders are right on top of us! Spitfires and Hurricanes. From a distance you cannot distinguish these from our own Me 109s. Above the Isle of Wight it makes for a terrible battle. About sixty aircraft of all makes, German and English, all fighting for their very lives. Some of the English draw back towards the coast of England, on the left of me a Me 109 drops into the sea. The pilot is able to get out and slowly he guides his parachute towards the water. Another aircraft, the make I cannot see clearly, circles in flames like a bonfire above us. Then it explodes and falls in many small pieces. You can only recognise the engine compartment as it falls.

"When we all collect towards the south, the English take us on. Only weaving helps you if you want to escape the eight machine guns of the English fighters. Our radio operators shoot whenever they can get their guns to bear. Again and again the English attack from astern. Again and again I feel the bullets striking my aircraft but I don't think the engine has been hit. The motor is quiet and smooth. The closer we get to the centre of the English Channel the fewer English aircraft attack us. Our squadrons find each other bit by bit and we form up. To the left of us flies our 4th Staffel. One of the planes has a smoke trail behind it. The pilot gives the message: 'Aircraft damaged, going into the water!' At that moment a Spitfire [sic] comes from ahead, shoots, and down into the water the damaged Stuka goes. But the Englishman does not live long to enjoy his cheap victory and glory and as he veers away after his attack he gets hit by a Me 109 and dives vertically into the sea.

"After thirty minutes flying, we at last see the coast of Normandy. We all sigh with relief. My formation comrades approach to the side of the aircraft, nod and smile. Everything in our squadron seems to be all right. We land at our base. Unbelievably, all of the aircraft from our Staffel have returned. Some had up to forty bullet holes in their fuselages and wings, but all landed safely despite this. Later, we heard that our commander, Major Plewig, is missing. Also, a Hauptmann and Unteroffizier as well. We cannot believe it. Nobody saw the CO go down."

Many Stukas that were hit in engagements over the British Isles managed to get back to France with astonishing levels of damage, albeit that they sometimes carried dead, dying or severely wounded crew members.

In its content, this broadcast is surprisingly informative and of particular interest is the comment that the formation had "no proper location" for the target ships. As we now know, this lack of clarity evidently caused the actual convoy to be missed. As for the name Puma, it is not certain that this was actually a codename used during that operation or if it was created for the purpose of the broadcast.

Apart from 145 Squadron, others were also mixed up in the fierce battle fought with the Junkers 87s and their escorts. For 43 Squadron this was the first time they had gone into action that day and its pilots had an exhausting and eventful time. The squadron had been led by its CO, Sqn Ldr J.V.C. 'Tubby' Badger and although many of the squadron pilots got involved with the Me 109 escort, Flt Lt T.F.D. Morgan, leading Blue Section, had found himself immediately among the Ju87 dive bombers. With him was Sgt C.A.L. Hurry (Blue 2) and Plt Off H.C. Upton (Blue 3). Engaging the rearmost Stuka in an echelon formation of five he fired short bursts of between two to five seconds whereupon the enemy machine immediately caught fire and dived into the sea. Morgan then tackled the next Ju87 which turned over emitting black smoke after a short burst before he then turned his attention on the remaining three Stukas. With Blue 2 and Blue 3 he moved in to attack, but the escorting force of JG27's Me 109 had different ideas.

Suddenly, each pilot in Blue Section was fighting the Messerschmitts, with Morgan claiming to have sent one of the enemy fighters into the water. During the dog fight, however, Morgan was attacked by a Hurricane although he could not identify who it was. Plt Off Upton, after claiming to have shot two Junkers 87s in the sea, and with another probably downed, found that his engine had been hit by return fire from the Stukas and was obliged to make a forced landing, unhurt, at Ford Farm, Whitwell, on the Isle of Wight. Sgt Hurry, too, had his Hurricane hit and beat a retreat back to Tangmere with numerous strikes. Hurry's attacker could have been

Lt Helmut Strobl of 5./JG27 who was certainly involved in that same combat, and who claimed hits on at least three Hurricanes. In an odd twist of fate it would be Alex Hurry who would shoot Strobl down over Appledore, Kent, on 5 September 1940 – the young Luftwaffe pilot remaining missing until his discovery exactly forty-six years later[4]. Writing to his family on 10 August about the action on 8 August Strobl told how he had added to his score of aircraft downed and went on: "…we only fly when there are ships on the water!"

Aside from the claim by Peter Parrott for the Ju87 downed at St Lawrence, the rest of 145 Squadron had also put in multiple claims for aircraft destroyed. The total squadron 'bag' for the late afternoon shoot was six Junkers 87s and two Messerschmitt 110s destroyed. One of the pilots who added to this claim was Plt Off J.E. Storrar who attacked a Stuka:

This image is testimony to the terrific punishment that the Junkers 87 could take. This aircraft got back with most of its tail fin torn away – the black outline illustrates what is missing!

"As I finished my ammunition with little obvious effect I suddenly became aware that there was a flame around his right undercarriage leg. I came up alongside. There was no sign of the rear gunner but the pilot was looking at me and I was no more than twenty or thirty yards away. I could see his face clearly and could virtually see his hand on the stick. The flame suddenly burst over the top of the wing. We both looked at it for what seemed like seconds when the Stuka's wing suddenly buckled – it turned over and smashed into the sea and exploded."

Flt Lt Roy Dutton, leader of 145 Squadron's A Flight was also in the thick of it. As he went into action, and to his absolute horror, Dutton's engine suddenly stopped. To be over the sea with a dead engine was bad enough, but to be over the sea and surrounded by enemy aircraft was a very dire situation to be in. As he fell away from the engagement and down to what he thought must surely be a ditching in the English Channel a Junkers 87 appeared in front of him. Firing off a burst, the enemy aircraft caught fire just as his own engine coughed back into life. Attacking and then claiming another Stuka, Dutton's engine finally packed up although by this time he had sufficient altitude to glide back over the coast and get into Westhampnett on a dead-stick landing. It was a creditable piece of airmanship with the inherent danger of a fatal result if the glide was extended for too long and flying speed decayed to the point of stall. Luckily for Dutton, he had got back home. All told, it had been a hard and bloody day for 145 Squadron who had five of their pilots killed. In fact, and taking into account the losses sustained by 43 Squadron,

4 See *Finding The Foe* by Andy Saunders, Grub Street, 2010.

the last engagement of the day had resulted in the loss of almost a quarter of the defending force involved in the battle off the Isle of Wight that afternoon.

When 43 and 145 Squadron had been ploughing into the massed formations to the south of the Isle of Wight, some of 152 Squadron's Spitfires had been headed down towards Weymouth Bay and there is little doubt that the controller had thought this was where the incoming attack was headed. After all, the remnants of CW9 Peewit were already in the bay, or else dispersing from there, and the small collection of ships that were still off the Isle of Wight were not of significance to the RAF controller – even if he knew about them. It made sense to him that the incoming raid was headed for the main concentration of CW9 Peewit ships and the expectation was no doubt that 152 and 238 Squadrons would engage the enemy above the convoy.

In the event, 238 Squadron did not even see the enemy on the operations that they flew between 16.20 and 18.05. Similarly, the nine Hurricanes of 213 Squadron haring down the English Channel from Exeter also failed to make it in time to see any action over the convoy, having taken off at 16.05. From the Spitfires of B Flight, 152 Squadron, who ran into the Messerschmitt 109s of JG53 over the sea some twelve miles south of Swanage shortly after 16.00, Plt Off D.G. Shepley was the only pilot to make a claim for a probable Me 109 but when the pilots of 152 Squadron broke off the engagement and returned home the battle of Convoy Peewit was over. By 16.45 the English Channel was clear of any further significant enemy air activity.

It had been the most sustained assault ever directed against a convoy in British waters by Stukas, and in summarising the air fighting over Convoy CW9, RAF Fighter Command was singularly up-beat in its assessment:

"Three engagements took place and considered as a whole may be reckoned from the point of Fighter Command the most successful battle of the war. Altogether eighty-four enemy machines were destroyed or severely damaged, at least sixty of these being confirmed, as against the loss of eighteen of our aircraft and fifteen pilots. The German High Command reverse the ratio and claim the score as forty-nine to twelve in their favour."

It was hardly an accurate or objective appraisal of events that day, with a gross over-estimation of the actual numbers of German aircraft destroyed. All the same, and notwithstanding the vessels actually sunk, things hadn't exactly gone according to plan for the Stukas, either.

CHAPTER 7

Eagle Day Debacle

R ECENT EVENTS IN THE ENGLISH Channel had seen the Stuka force exclusively employed against shipping targets, but that was about to change. Now, the whole focus of Luftwaffe attacks was about to shift dramatically and although one of the German war aims set out in July 1940 had been to "….strangle the supply of Great Britain by attacking its ports and its shipping", a further directive from the Führer would set the scene for future actions. In his Directive No.17, dated 1 August 1940, Hitler had ordered the intensification of the air war against England, with new specific objectives clearly set out:

"The German air force is to overpower the English air force with all the forces at its command, and in the shortest time possible. The attacks are to be directed primarily against flying units, their ground installations, their supply organisations and also against the aircraft industry, including that manufacturing anti-aircraft equipment."

Thus, the scene was set for the all-out offensive against the RAF. Once again, Stukas would spearhead many of the planned assaults over the coming days but on 12 August, and in preparatory raids carried out against south coast chain home radar stations on the eve of Eagle Day, the Stuka force was not committed. Instead, the stations at Dover, Dunkirk (Canterbury), Rye and Pevensey were dive-bombed by four groups, each of four Messerschmitt 110s, from Erprobungsgruppe 210 and the radar station at Ventnor on the Isle of Wight was hit by Junkers 88s. It was all part of the softening-up for the big day itself; a day when the Junkers 87 would be thrown, enmasse, against land-based targets in southern England for the very first time. However, the opening moves of Eagle Day itself would be carried out by the Dornier 17s of KG2. And it wasn't an auspicious start. It was the weather, though, that presented itself almost as much of an enemy as did the RAF – especially in relation to the Stuka force. Additionally, some disastrous failures in communications were equalled by utterly abysmal assessments in Luftwaffe intelligence appraisals. Against this background was set the scene for a shambolic event that was supposed to see the commencement of the RAF's destruction.

Before dawn, the Dornier 17 bombers of KG2 were being readied at their bases in northern France for a raid against the RAF airfield at Eastchurch on The Isle of Sheppey, which was to have been hit in two waves. Shortly after take-off, however, deterioration in the weather had been detected and the mission aborted not long after the fighter escort had joined up with the formation of Dorniers in the English Channel, and at around 06.30 the operation was cancelled. Unfortunately for the bomber formation, however, no recall signal was received and although

Aftermath of the Eagle Day debacle on 13 August 1940; one of the shot down Dornier 17s of KG2, alongside the railway line at Barham, Kent.

the fighter escort got the message, they were operating on different radio frequencies and were unable to communicate with their charges. Desperate measures like diving in front of the bomber formation and wing-waggling had no effect and the Dornier formations carried on, undeterred, puzzled by the strange antics of the circling fighters.

Frustrated, the fighter escort withdrew and left the Dorniers to their fate as they ploughed on to their target. As they came up the Thames Estuary the first formation was in four columns, line-astern, with about ten Dorniers in each column and they steadily approached RAF Eastchurch, above cloud, which was thickly layered between 3,000 and 4,000ft. In fact, it had been this bank of cloud, stretching along the Channel and merged with rolling sea-fog, that had caused the 'operation cancelled' signal. Just north of Whitstable, however, the bomber formation was clear of the cloud but ran into the waiting RAF fighters. With their fighter escort already back at their French bases, the unprotected Dorniers were torn apart and although at least one of the formations managed to hit Eastchurch and rain around 100 high explosive and incendiary bombs across the airfield, the second large formation was intercepted and scattered by the defenders before they could get through.

In that first attack, however, hangars and buildings were hit along with living quarters and the operations and administration blocks whilst the flying field was very extensively cratered. Sixteen had been killed, and another forty-eight injured. But this was a RAF Coastal Command airfield – and not one of the prime Fighter Command airfields that the Luftwaffe needed to take out. By sheer coincidence, though, there happened to be a visiting squadron of Spitfires at the time of the attack (266 Squadron) and one of their aircraft was lost when a hangar was consumed in flames. Doubtless, the sight of Spitfires on the ground at Eastchurch, glimpsed by some of the surviving Dornier crews, helped to cement the German belief about the importance of the airfield. So, not only had the attack gone in unprotected and vulnerable but it had done so against a target that was insignificant in the bigger scheme of things. In other words, a wasted effort and needless attrition to the Luftwaffe bomber force. It had set the tone for the debacle that was to continue to unfold throughout the day. And that bank of cloud and rolling fog, extending along much of the English Channel, was to play a hand in what should have been the first Stuka action of Eagle Day.

Much further to the south-west, out in mid-Channel and at around 06.40, another large force was detected approaching the south coast and about twenty miles out from St Catherine's Point. The official Air Ministry narrative of events noted that: "….as far as we know it took no aggressive action". The writer then went on to speculate that this may have been a fighter force waiting to cover the withdrawal of another shambolically executed bomber attack against airfields that had just been attempted by Junkers 88s of KG54 against Odiham and Farnborough (again, relatively unimportant airfields not assigned to Fighter Command) although those bombers had failed to reach their objectives. In fact, the large force that the RAF had noted taking no aggressive action most probably had deadly purpose, and was most likely the force earlier reported as 100 strong moving out from Dieppe and towards the Baie de la Seine sometime after 06.10. That force can only have been the assembled mass of Stukas from StG77, eighty-eight in total, that were headed for their airfield targets of Ford, Gosport and Thorney Island with no less than 173 Me 109 fighters and sixty Me 110s. A truly formidable armada of 320 aircraft.

Truly, Eagle Day was being launched with some panache and intent, but still the weather and ineffectual planning (based upon what we have already seen to be faulty intelligence appraisals) were conspiring to hamper the Luftwaffe's goal. In the case of the Stukas of StG77 it was that same troublesome bank of cloud and fog that was the enemy as for the Stuka force, a clear and uninterrupted view of the target was essential for any dive-bombing attack. Long before the English coast was reached it had become clear that meteorological conditions were way below the optimum requirements for any attack and the Stukas consequently wheeled about and returned home. Enroute, one of the Junkers 87s had developed engine problems and was forced to ditch its bomb load in the sea – although the others all returned with loads intact.

However, these same bombs would soon be used again in anger and the airfields at Ford, Thorney Island and Gosport had only gained a very temporary reprieve. Their turn would come, and all too soon. Indeed, the abortive attempts by StG77 were far from the end of Stuka operations on this day. By mid afternoon the weather had cleared sufficiently for the German high command to order that the 'attack of the eagles' should re-commence. After a false start to *Adler Tag*,

A Junkers 87 of the (St)/LG1 waits on an airfield in France with a bomb alongside ready to be loaded. Aircraft of this unit were involved in the devastating attack on RAF Detling of 13 August.

the Luftwaffe was yet to suffer more catastrophe and failure before the day was out.

As the frustrated crews of StG77 wound-down at their French bases after a fruitless and stressful two hours flying over the English Channel, other Stuka units were preparing for action over Britain further west, and also much further to the east. In total, eighty-six Stukas of I./StG1, II./StG1 and IV(St)./LG1 took off from their Pas de Calais bases at around 16.00 hours. (NB:- I./StG1, on the establishment of Fl.Korps VIII, had earlier that day ferried some of its aircraft up to Pas de Calais from their base at Angers to reinforce the Stukas of Fl.Korps II for this operation.) Respectively, the three units were allocated RAF Rochford, Gravesend and RAF Detling as their targets. Ahead of the Stukas, the skies were 'swept' by the Messerschmitt 109s of JG51 although close escort for the Stukas was undertaken by two Messerschmitt 110 Gruppen of ZG26. The escorts, though, were handled roughly by the Hurricanes of 56 Squadron, with one of their number sent plunging into the cliffs at Warden Point on the Isle of Sheppey by Fg Off Percy Weaver.

First of the Stuka Gruppen detailed to go in, but not by many minutes, was the formation of Hptm Anton Keil's II./StG1 with Gravesend on the north Kent coastline (presumably the RAF airfield there) as its objective. Whether it was Gravesend airfield or some other target in the vicinity that should have been in Keil's sights, it is all somewhat academic – although since the strategy was to go for airfields, the aerodrome was surely the logical target. As it transpired, Keil failed to find the intended objective despite the fact that, ironically, he had already built a considerable reputation in the Stuka force for being particularly skilful at navigating his way to pre-designated targets. Today, luck was with those on the ground at Gravesend rather than with Keil and his men.

That said, it must be recognised that for a Stuka formation leader, finding the way to an unfamiliar target with pinpoint precision was always a challenge. He alone would have been responsible for navigating the entire formation to its objective and any slight error or miscalculation along the way could easily result in the target being missed by miles. Additionally, the distraction of enemy fighters could be a real problem and Keil had only one chance to spot his target and to attack. There was no way of going around again for another look. That would have been suicidal and, in any case, the formation was too large and unweildly to even consider it. If the target was missed, then it remained so. In this case, the failure to find the target may have been partly due to residual cloud cover and there is certainly some evidence from the escorting Me 110 crews that the mission may well have been aborted when the formation reached the Canterbury area.

If II./StG1 had been struggling to get to their target, the participating aircraft of I Gruppe were having no luck, either, as they headed for RAF Rochford on the opposite side of the Thames Estuary. Quite why the target was not attacked is unclear, but this could have been for one of several reasons: inability to locate the airfield, unfavourable weather conditions (ie cloud base and visibility) and/or interference from RAF fighters. It is certainly the case that the Hurricanes of 56 Squadron did encounter the Me 110 escorts, but the RAF defenders were prevented from getting through to the bombers. Once again, the Me 110s were positioned so as to be the sacrificial lambs in the protection of the Junkers 87s and to take the defenders' punishment. So far in the distance were the dive bombers that the Hurricane pilots had mistakenly thought them to be He 111s.

The afternoon Stuka effort had, thus far, been rather a waste and the dive bombers fled southwards over Kent, apparently scattering bombs enroute. Gravesend and then RAF Rochford had been spared the attentions of the Stukas. Meanwhile, a free hunt across Kent by Messerschmitt 109s of JG26 was perfectly timed to add further confusion in the minds of the defenders. What were the attackers' true objectives? And where were all of these Stukas going?[5] After all, two large formations had swept up the Thames Estuary and then arched around southwards across Kent without attacking anything. At that moment, another force of Junkers 87 dive bombers were sweeping in across the county towards their target. These were the forty aircraft of IV.(Stuka)/LG1, led by Hptm Bernd von Brauchitsch, and their approach was witnessed by an astonished schoolboy, Richard Gardiner:

"In August 1940 I lived in Sutton Valence with my grandparents and my younger brother, Peter. I was fifteen years old and mad about anything aeronautical as well as being a keen cyclist.

"That particular summer holiday was to be by far the most exciting one I ever spent. Peter and I were soon experts at aircraft identification and this skill was given an easy test on Tuesday, 13 August.

"We had been over to Bearsted to have lunch with our aunt and cycling home that afternoon we had reached Langley when, away in the distance, we heard the sirens in Maidstone sounding the warning. I think we could hear them clearly from this far away because the weather was very overcast and still – unusual conditions for that particular August. Almost before the wailing of the sirens had stopped we heard the sound of many aircraft approaching from the south-east – and there, heading directly towards

Schoolboys Peter and Richard Gardiner (pictured left and right of the photograph) with their aunt at Maidstone during the Battle of Britain. In this photograph, Richard is holding a souvenir machine gun saddle-drum taken from a shot-down German aircraft.

us, flying below the cloud base came what to us seemed a vast armada of aircraft. Immediately we identified them as Junkers 87s – the dreaded crank-winged Stukas! The 'planes droned over us literally in an 'air-show' formation – low enough for us to make out the Luftwaffe markings and, to our great excitement (and not, strange as it may seem, fear!) the heads of some of the aircrew.

"We stood by the side of the road and gaped. One elderly lady was near us in her garden and asked us what she should do; I think we told her to go indoors!"

For the first time that day a Luftwaffe formation swept onwards, unhindered by either the RAF or the uncooperative weather. Amazed at what they had seen, and that the formation was not being set upon by swarms of Spitfires and Hurricanes, the Gardiner brothers had unknowingly

5 In respect of the plotting of German aircraft once they had penetrated inland, the RAF chain home and chain home low radar sites were wholly impotent and raids were lost to view because the radar only looked outward from the coast. Thus, radar was only useful for early warning . Once the coast was crossed, tracking lay entirely in the hands of the Observer Corps. As Dowding himself later pointed out in his post-war despatch on the Battle of Britain: "It is important to note that at this time the Observer Corps constituted the whole means of tracking enemy raids once they had crossed the coastline. Their work throughout was quite invaluable. Without it, the air raid warning systems could not have been operated and inland interceptions would rarely have been made."

Once German formations had passed 'behind' the coastal belt of CH and CHL radar stations they were no longer visible to the radar plotters and the tracking of raids like the one against Detling on 13 August fell to the Observer Corps. Here, observers man a post typical of the period.

been spectators to what was about to be the only successful Luftwaffe attack of Eagle Day. Richard goes on:

"As soon as the 'planes had disappeared we remounted our bikes and headed for home. Then, just as we reached the top of the hill and before descending into the village, all hell seemed to be let loose away to the north; we had never heard such a concentrated amount of explosions before. Obviously, somewhere was being really heavily attacked. So, home to tell the grandparents what we had seen.

"Well, we heard by rumour later that evening that it was Detling, a Coastal Command aerodrome, that had been the Stukas' target. It certainly gave me a lot to think and talk about – and to remember."

Certainly, Richard's recall of "all hell breaking loose" was pretty much correct regarding Detling, and it is to another contemporaneous report that we turn for an official accounting of events. This time, from the local Maidstone ARP controller:

"Shortly after 1600 hours and on receipt of a red warning, the Fire Observation Post on the roof of County Hall reported that a number of enemy dive bombers, believed to be about 15, had delivered a dive-bombing attack on an aerodrome.

"On receipt of this information I immediately ordered the Borough Control to have ready all available resources in First Aid Parties and Ambulances should they be required.

"Shortly afterwards a report was received from the Borough that the General Hospital had been asked by the Medical Officer to arrange for a reception of injured and for ambulances.

"On receipt of this message I immediately rang up the R.A.F. and obtained a rapid appreciation of the situation, which was to the effect that the number of casualties could not be definitely stated, but that they were certainly between 50 and 100 and that considerable damage had been sustained. I then ordered two First Aid Parties and four ambulances with four First Aid Parties and four cars for sitting cases. These were followed shortly after by two mobile units with doctors and nurses, five more ambulances, and two rescue parties.

"The Civil Defence services arrived very quickly and immediately commenced work on the casualties, assisted in the collection of the dead at a central point and the rescue parties were instrumental in the recovery of several more bodies.

"The living casualties were removed, the majority having received first aid and been evacuated to hospital within little over an hour from the time of the occurrence. Army ambulance

Detling was a RAF Coastal Command airfield and relatively insignificant in terms of Britain's front-line defences. Nevertheless, it was subjected to a devastating Stuka attack on Eagle Day and was then attacked again in follow-up raids on 30 and 31 August, twice on 1 September and again 2 September.

having meanwhile arrived, the Civil Defence ambulances and First Aid Parties, being no longer required, were withdrawn and the Rescue Parties continued their work until dark, when it had to be discontinued owing to the impossibility of using flares.

"On the 14th instant two rescue parties were again sent to the aerodrome and worked from approximately 07.30 hours to 15.00 hours, when they were returned to their depots.

"The co-ordination of the services was arranged by the Air Raid Precautions Officer, who accompanied the first parties and remained there until the Rescue Parties returned at night."

Bland and dry though this account is, it rather belies the true horror of what had taken place on the ground at RAF Detling where the situation was both grim and grisly. Over a period of several minutes, forty Stukas delivered with deadly precision around 200 high explosive and incendiary bombs on the airfield just as the station personnel were going to their main evening meal. Hell on earth, as Richard Gardiner had described the noise, was perhaps an under-estimation of the reality which in short order had killed sixty-seven service personnel and civilians and wounded numerous others. All of the buildings were badly damaged and many were wrecked, including hangars, and a direct hit had been achieved on the operations block, killing the station commander, Group Captain Edward Davis. (Note: Group Captain Davis's name is recorded on the Runnymede Memorial to RAF personnel who have no known grave. This has led to speculation that no trace of Group Captain Davis was found after the raid but this is not correct as it is known that a funeral service for him was held at St. Simon's Church, Chelsea on 20 August).

Quite apart from the loss of life, twenty-two aircraft (mostly Avro Ansons) were destroyed and many others had been damaged in the raid. Again, the Luftwaffe had blundered in selecting Detling for such a ferocious attack since it was yet another Coastal Command airfield and it was primarily Fighter Command whom the Luftwaffe needed to be targeting at this point in the battle. Had such devastation been visited upon, say, Biggin Hill, Hawkinge or Kenley at this stage of the campaign, and perhaps repeatedly, then the consequences for the RAF's fighter defence force would have been serious indeed. As it was, the virtual destruction of Detling mattered little in Britain's front line air defence. Nevertheless, bravery and fortitude shone through here as it had at Portland. At Detling the bravery of two WAAFs was ultimately recognised by the award of the Military Medal to each of them. The citation for the award to one of them, Acting Sgt Jean Mary Youle, tells her story:

"In August 1940 Sgt Youle was on duty in a station telephone exchange when the station was attacked and bombed by enemy aircraft. Part of the building containing the telephone exchange suffered a direct hit and bombs fell in very close proximity. The telephone staff were subjected to a heavy rain of debris and splinters and to the noise of the concussion of exploding bombs. It was solely due to the cool bravery of and superb example of Sgt Youle that the telephone operators carried on with their task with calmness and complete efficiency at a most dangerous time for them. She has at all times set an excellent example of coolness and efficiency to all."

It was this coolness and calm that no doubt enabled the lines to be kept open in order that outside ambulances and assistance could be summoned via County Hall at Maidstone to help those who had been injured – many of whom were tended by WAAF Corporal Josephine Robins, the other MM recipient at Detling that day. Cpl Robins had been in the parachute section when the first bombs began to fall and donning her tin helmet she dashed outside to be met with a vision of devastation; burning hangars, wrecked aircraft, collapsed buildings and an utterly horrendous noise. Rushing to the nearest air raid shelter she clearly glimpsed the large black and white crosses on a diving Stuka before hurling herself down the shelter steps and pushing into the crush of frightened airmen and airwomen huddled inside. Suddenly, one bomb landed directly outside her shelter dislodging the roof, with much of it falling onto the occupants at the far end from where Robins was crouched. After the racket of whistling bombs, explosions, gunfire, screeching aircraft and collapsing masonry had subsided there was another and yet more awful noise coming from the collapsed end of her shelter. Josephine Robins described it as "the noise of much distress".

Corporal Josephine Robins, whose portrait was painted by Dame Laura Knight.

This photograph of Stukas at low level over a British airfield is often ascribed to RAF Detling on 13 August, and although there is no absolutely firm evidence to suggest which location it was taken at it is, nevertheless, a good illustration of Stukas departing the target area at low level after an attack during 1940.

In reality, it was the terrible sound of the screaming, moaning and crying of the trapped, the injured and the dying. Not thinking of herself or her own safety, Josephine crawled in inky darkness, through brick dust and smoke and across jagged concrete, towards those who were calling out in terror and pleading for help. She continued to approach those needing her help, and although with cuts and bruises herself she rendered first aid, helped dig out the casualties and assisted in removing bodies. All the while, and as she worked, the smashed concrete roof threatened to collapse crushing her underneath its collosal weight. Only when she was satisfied that there was nobody left to help did she crawl out of the smashed shelter before making her way to one of the wrecked hangars to offer her services. Undoubtedly, her Military Medal was richly deserved. Others, too, retained some searing memories of the raid.

LAC David King worked in the Detling ops room, and was lucky to have survived the raid having been off duty during the day and not due on until 22.00 that evening.

"I had been to Maidstone in the morning and had noticed six Blenheims lined up along the perimeter fence. When I came back on the bus I noticed that where they had been was just a pile of metal and some engines. Nearly every building had been destroyed or damaged. How could this have happened without warning? Well, the system of air raid warnings was that air raid 'yellows' were telephoned over whenever enemy aircraft could pose a threat and a 'red' when an attack appeared imminent. In reality, we would get a 'yellow' whenever there was an enemy aircraft in the Channel and only a 'red' when they approached the coast. However, the CO realised that for everyone to run to the shelters each time we got

A terrible casualty toll resulted from the Stuka attack on Detling and many of the fatalities were later buried with full military honours in a mass funeral at Maidstone Cemetery.

a 'red' wasted precious time, and so he had arranged for the Observer Corps in Maidstone to 'phone if they had plotted a definite threat. That day they had seen the raid coming, and tried to 'phone several times but unfortunately all the 'phone lines were engaged. The observers could see the approaching Stukas but were powerless to do anything about it by warning us of the raid."

After the attack, a fleet of ambulances took the injured to Preston Hall Hospital but many were beyond any worldly assistance and these were left to local ARP casualty clearing officer, Wallace Beale. In civilian life, Beale was a Maidstone undertaker but the scale and awfulness of the whole thing was far beyond anything he ever imagined that he might experience. Even those of sterner stuff would have blanched at the scene that Beale found. He noted with a certain dispassionate tone that only five foot coffins were required for many of the deceased. The Detling incident depleted in one day Beale's local stock of smaller coffins that were reserved for unidentified remains.

At Detling, then,the raiding Stukas had approached the target without any warning being given, had attacked with impunity over many minutes and then departed southwards, unharmed, and out over the English Channel to France. Either the incoming raid had not been detected by radar or there had subsequently been a serious miscalculation at Fighter Command of the raid's size, composition and destination. For whatever reason, not a single RAF fighter had got anywhere near to the Stuka formation that attacked Detling in order to intercept it. No defenders were ever seen and some Luftwaffe observers were convinced that what few defenders were left had all been swept aside by the fighter escorts and the free-hunting Me 109s and that all of the other RAF fighters had doubtless been obliterated in the *Adler Tag* raid on airfields. This was a very dangerous supposition, as will be seen.

Further down the Channel, another Stuka operation was also underway at exactly the same time involving twenty-five Stukas from I./StG1, twenty-seven from II./StG2 and fifty-two from StG3. Of these, the StG1 element had been tasked with attacking Warmwell, those from StG2 were headed for Yeovil and those of StG3 were assigned to Portland. (NB: German records show the StG3 target to have been Portland but this is somewhat surprising given the direction of Eagle Day raids being focussed on fighter airfields since Portland was a naval base.)

The commander of I./StG1, Major Paul-Werner Hozzel recalled his part in the Stuka attacks that afternoon:

"The first strategic operations in the history of the Battle of Britain began with the codeword *Adler Tag* – or 'Eagle Day'. It was 13 August 1940. I./StG1, jointly with II./StG2, was put into combat action against the British fighter base of Warmwell, about eighty kilometres south of Filton which had been the allocated target for II./StG2. On the assumption that our attack would come as a complete surprise, we would be hitting the Hurricanes and Spitfires in their dispersal pens before they were given a chance to take off. We, as pinpoint dive-bombing specialists, were ready for our targets but we had not reckoned with what our host had in store for us, as will soon be seen. That morning we had taken off with about eighty [sic] Ju87s from Angers, landing at Dinard for our jump off to the coast. Assigned to us as fighter escort for the planned Stuka attack was the Me 109-equipped Jagdgeschwader 53, under the command of its young CO and my former training comrade, Major von Maltzahn, who was now a very successful fighter ace. There was also another Geschwader consisting of twin-engine heavy

Major Paul-Werner Hozzel.

Messerschmitt 110 fighters. The participation of the latter in that action was, unfortunately, only of symbolic value because the Me 110s were too clumsy and no match for the British fighter aircraft. Our heavy fighters actually needed their own fighter escort.

"We take off, picking up our fighter escorts over Guernsey. Then, climbing to an altitude of 4,000 metres, we headed for the enemy. The escort planes were buzzing around us—a comforting feeling. Above the English Channel the weather was quite clear, but when reaching the English coast we were met with a closed layer of clouds which extended over the country as far as we could see, at an altitude of about 3,000 metres. We could not guess the altitude of the cloud cover above the ground and hence it was really impossible to approach our target in clear sight of it. We had no alternative but to continue on our course for another 15 minutes after crossing the coast and then to dive blind through the cloud hoping that we would emerge above the target with sufficient altitude below the cloud base to carry out our attack. It was a most doubtful assumption, as we very soon realized.

"All of a sudden our British 'comrades' shot up like torpedoes through the clouds, each fighter vigorously firing from its eight barrels at our unit which was flying in wide open formation. With the 250kg bomb visibly suspended from our fuselages, each of our Stuka bomber crews sat, in the quite literal sense of the word, on a powder keg. Now, the first explosions were heard – a sudden fireball – and all was over. Our fighter (Me 109) and destroyer (Me 110) escorts dived on the enemy and so tied down a great number of the attackers, but many of them were still able to get through to us.

"We, with our weaker guns and burdened with our bomb loads, were unable to ward them off. We had no choice but to dive down and drop our bombs on the coastal areas, then to return in a hedge-hopping flight across the Channel to our home base. Thus we escaped further attacks, if only from below. With difficulty I was able to assemble my Gruppe, thus increasing our firepower in our defence against the British fighters pursuing us. Many a Stuka fell victim to pursuers in single one-to-one fights above the Channel. Having landed again in

Dinard we had lost about one-third of the 'planes sent out. [Sic. In fact, the total losses on this operation stood at six Ju87s of StG2, out of the total 104 Stukas committed]. The rest of us were pretty heavily damaged by the enemy fire. The German command had profoundly erred in judging the strength of the British fighter forces which, at that time, were twice as strong as had been assumed. Our Stuka Gruppen were, all the same, thrown into battle again, twice or even three times, with the result that they suffered further terrible losses."

Whilst none of the Stukas either found or got through to their targets, they were still given a mauling by defending fighters. These were the Spitfires of 609 Squadron, and in his book *Spitfire Pilot*, Flt Lt David Crook took up the story:

"At about 4 p.m. we were ordered to patrol Weymouth at 15,000 feet. We took off, thirteen machines in all, with the CO leading, and climbed up over Weymouth. After a few minutes I began to hear a German voice talking on the RT, faintly at first then growing in volume. By a curious chance the German raid had a wave-length almost identical with our own and the voice we heard was that of the German commander talking to his formation as they approached us across the Channel. About a quarter of an hour later we saw a large German formation approaching below us. There were a number of Junkers 87 dive bombers escorted by Me 109s above, and also some Me 110s about two miles behind, some sixty machines in total.

"A Hurricane squadron attacked the Me 110s as soon as they crossed the coast and they never got through to where we were.

"Meanwhile the bombers with their fighter escort still circling above them, passed beneath us. We were up at almost 20,000 feet in the sun and I don't think they ever saw us till the very last moment. The CO

Flt Lt D.M. Crook.

gave a terrific 'Tally ho' and led us around in a big semi-circle so that we were now behind them, and we prepared to attack.

"Mac, Novi (one of the Poles), and I were flying slightly behind and above the rest of the squadron, guarding their tails, and at this moment I saw about five Me 109s pass just underneath us.

"I immediately broke away from formation, dived on to the last Me 109, and gave him a terrific burst of fire at very close range. He burst into flames and spun down for many thousands of feet into the clouds below, leaving behind him a long trail of black smoke.

"I followed him down for some way and could not pull out of my dive in time to avoid

One of the downed Stukas of 5./StG2 fell at Rodden, Portesham, resulting in the death of Uffz Lindenschmid and Fw Eisold and this was the scene as villagers flocked to view the scattered wreckage.

going beneath the clouds myself. I found that I was about five miles north of Weymouth, and then I saw a great column of smoke rising from the ground a short distance away. I knew perfectly well what it was and went over to have a look. My Me 109 [sic[6]] lay in a field, a tangled heap of wreckage burning fiercely, but with the black crosses on the wings still visible. I found out later that the pilot was still in the machine. He had made no attempt to get out while the aircraft was diving and he had obviously been killed by my first burst of fire. He crashed just outside a small village, and I could see everybody streaming out of their houses and rushing to the spot."

Illustrative of the difficulty faced by Observer Corps posts in sometimes accurately plotting what was going on, especially when it was cloudy or the visibility was poor, are the log books for two of the posts in Dorset for that afternoon; R.4 at Poundbury Camp, Dorchester, and R.3 at Yetminster. At 16.35 hours, the R.3 site reported: "Raid approaching post R.3. Dorchester alert. (*Public air raid warning*) Fighters up from aerodrome (*RAF Warmwell*). Ten hostile "planes advised twenty miles south of R.3." Then: "Large number of hostile aircraft advised to the south of post R.4."

Neither post was aware of the scale of the huge armada of German aircraft approaching them, right on their door step, and neither did they know its composition, height or its track. Luckily, it would transpire that on this occasion it didn't greatly matter.

6 In fact, there were no Me 109s shot down that day at the spot described by Flt Lt Crook and it would seem that when he had emerged from the cloud and saw wreckage burning on the ground he concluded it was 'his' Me 109. In fact, from the location given, it is very clear that he had seen the wreckage of one of the two Junkers 87s of 5./StG2 that were downed at Rodden and Grimstone. Either of these locations is not too far adrift from the "five miles from Weymouth" that Crook describes. Three Me 109s of JG53 were brought down into the sea by 609 Squadron, and one that crashed into Poole Harbour may well have been the fighter claimed by Crook.

Flt Lt Crook claimed one of the escorting Me 109s of JG53 as destroyed and his victory may well have been over the 5th Staffel aircraft that crashed into Poole Harbour. The pilot, Uffz Hohenseldt, was captured unhurt and his Messerschmitt later fished from the water to be exhibited at a local sports ground.

Collosal effort had truly been expended by the Stuka crews on 13 August, and all of it had either been wasted or was for very little return; aborted operations during the early morning, failures to find two targets in the afternoon, one objective hit at Detling but not of 'high value' and three further afternoon operations which had been thwarted by weather conditions and the appearance of RAF fighters. In the latter three missions, the Junkers 87 losses had caused Hptm Walter Enneccerus, the commander of II./StG2, to comment that RAF fighters had "...ripped our backs open up to the collar". The next few days were not going to get any easier.

The 609 Squadron 'state' board on 13 August 1940, showing the numerous claims against Ju87s and Me 109s by squadron pilots at the end of that day's fighting.

90

CHAPTER 8
Hellfire Corner

T HE RATHER MUDDLED AND DISAPPOINTING outcome for the Luftwaffe on Eagle Day must have caused commanders to draw breath overnight and to consider their next moves. The day's operations had been ordered with great optimism and yet the result could really only be described as an abject failure. It had, though, only been the opening day of the campaign to empty the skies of the Royal Air Force and there was much work yet to be done. Still on the target list were several objectives that had not been hit, as planned, on 13 August and they would be re-allocated in due course. For now, on 14 August, there needed to be some rationalisation of the situation then extant and a re-scheduling of attacks across the next few days. Very much part of the continuing campaign to eliminate the RAF as an effective fighting force would be the further commitment of the Stuka Gruppen, and although the weather on 14 August 1940 was not ideal for the full range of operations that the Luftwaffe needed to undertake, it was at least sufficient perhaps to allow an attempt for some objectives on their target list to be eliminated. However, the only target successfully attacked that day by the Stuka force was wholly unrelated to RAF Fighter Command. Militarily, it was utterly insignificant.

Spitfires K9911, K9907 and L1094 of 65 Squadron sit at dispersal whilst at readiness.

The morning was almost over before there was any sign of important enemy movement and then, at 11.40, a force of thirty or more was plotted over the Strait of Dover a few miles south-west of Calais. Between 11.43 and noon three more formations were detected in the Strait, each one of them at least twenty strong. The controller, therefore, sent three squadrons into the air; 65 Squadron (Spitfires), 615 Squadron (Hurricanes) and the Hurricane-equipped 151 Squadron, albeit with only six aircraft. All three squadrons were airborne by 11.55, by which time the German formation was about to cross the coast. Accordingly, another squadron was scrambled; this time, the Spitfire-equipped 610 Squadron from Biggin Hill. As it happened, another non-Stuka unit with dive-bombing intentions was also part of the incoming formation, this being a force of nine Me 110s from ErprGr 210 who carried out a short sharp attack against Manston at 12.05 with four hangars either destroyed or damaged. Neither 65 nor 151 Squadrons, who were both in the vicinity, interfered with this attack and it actually seems that 65 Squadron were directed away from Manston towards Dover just before the attack went in. However, 151 Squadron engaged with the escorting Me 109s at higher altitude above Manston, but were quite unaware of the bombing that was going on below them due to 7/10 cloud cover that was now creeping across the region at between three to four thousand feet and was shielding

During the Stuka operations towards the Dover area on 14 August the escorting Me 109s took the opportunity to shoot up the Dover balloon barrage. Here, a press photographer has snapped one of the marauding Messerschmitts machine-gunning one of the balloons.

Manston from their view. It was instead left to the Bofors ground defences at Manston to counter the raid and the gunners managed to bring down one of the raiding Me 110s. In all probability, there was an intention to carry out a two or three-pronged dive-bombing attack and it is likely that the force that had approached the Kent coast out in the Channel was part of that plan.

By 12.20, just as it turned west towards Folkestone, it was realised that the force was much larger than the original estimate of 'thirty plus' and just before 12.30 it crossed the coast near Folkestone and was tracked by the Observer Corps heading towards Dover. Almost certainly, this raid included a force of Stukas, amongst them elements of (St)/LG1. As the formation swung towards Dover some of the escorting Me 109s peeled away and set about attacking the Dover balloon barrage, shooting down seven in a matter of minutes. By this stage, though, it would seem that the Stuka force had typically split into two groups and it may well be that one formation was headed for Hawkinge and the other for Lympne involving twenty-four Stukas. However, the increasing and lowering cloud cover resulted in the mission being aborted as the conditions were rapidly becoming less conducive for dive-bombing attacks. Indeed, it was reported that the formation was departing by 12.45 "having done practically no bombing".

However, nine of the Stukas of 10.(St)/LG1 carried out a dive-bombing attack against the South Folkestone Gate Light Vessel, ten miles south-east of the town, sinking it shortly before 13.00 with the loss of two Trinity House staff, Seaman Harry Edgar and Lamplighter John Wade. It is difficult to imagine that the light vessel was specifically the Stukas' intended target for that sortie, but with conditions for attacks better over the Channel perhaps the Staffel attacked this target of opportunity out of frustration once their main mission had been called off. Whatever, it brought down the attentions of 610 Squadron's Spitfires and the Hurricanes of 615 Squadron and resulted in one Stuka being sent into the sea with the loss of both crew and another getting home damaged and with an injured radio operator.

The Stuka operations on 14 August had been a rather half-hearted affair, with only the militarily insignificant sinking of the South Folkestone Gate Light Vessel to show for their efforts. It was with renewed vigour, though, that (St)/LG1 returned to the same area the very next day – almost as if the sortie just twenty-four hours previously had been a full dress rehearsal for the main event. And one of those on the mission list for 15 August was again Target No. 1157; Lympne airfield in south-west Kent. Already, the airfield had come in for an exceptional battering and had been subjected to two raids by Junkers 88s on 12 August. First, nine Ju88s in three vics of three bombed the airfield at around 08.15 that day and caused extensive damage to hangars, offices and landing grounds as 141 high-explosive bombs were scattered across the airfield in a matter of seconds. In the late afternoon, moreover, another bombing attack was made on Lympne and this time 242 bombs were dropped rendering the landing ground unserviceable through cratering and UXBs. In this raid, one RAF airman was killed and two were seriously wounded. Although the airfield was administratively part of RAF 11 Group, Fighter Command, and was occasionally used as a landing ground by fighter aircraft, it was not an operational airfield as such, and no squadrons were based there. Thus, singling out RAF Lympne for such concentrated attention was another futile effort and aside from considerable damage to infrastructure and the resulting casualties, the only other result of the raid was widespread destruction amongst the pre-war

Oblt Kurt Gramling of 10./(St)LG1 sits astride a bomb during the early summer of 1940. On 14 August 1940 he was lost with his radio operator, Uffz Franz Scwatzki, during the sinking of the South Folkestone Gate Light Vessel.

civilian aircraft of the Cinque Ports Flying Club that had been grounded for the duration and remained hangared there. The same day, 12 August, had again seen a Stuka force attempt to hit traffic in the Channel and the raid at around 11.30 that morning had seen some fifteen Ju87s of (St)/LG1 attacking shipping. The Stukas, escorted by a force of Me 109s, had been intercepted by RAF fighters who had been scrambled to meet the threat and it was 151 Squadron who reported seeing a single ship being bombed that was some distance away from the convoy. In all probability that ship was either HM Trawler *Pyrope* or *Tamarisk*, both of which were sunk by Stukas off North Spit Buoy. Although only one Stuka was shot down there was yet more overclaiming by 501

Squadron who reported six Ju87s destroyed, two probables and three damaged. However, after this brief diversion, let us now move forward again to the 15th.

As we have seen, and to all intents and purposes, the airfield at Lympne had effectively been put out of commission during the two raids carried out on 12 August. However, the Luftwaffe decided that Lympne needed some further treatment along with RAF Hawkinge, the operational fighter airfield just along the coast above Folkestone.

At around 10.45, radar tracks were being picked up which showed large build-ups of activity in the Pas de Calais region with the raid calculated at 'thirty plus' as it neared Cap Gris Nez. (In fact, the formation turned out to be very much larger than that.) Accordingly, in the next quarter of an hour, 501 Squadron's Hurricanes were ordered up from Hawkinge, 54 Squadron's Spitfires from Manston, 56 Squadron and their Hurricanes from Rochford and 615's Hurricanes from Kenley, although the latter two squadrons were only ordered up just ten minutes or so before the large German formation crossed the coast near Dungeness at exactly 11.29. The enemy raid comprised an escorting umbrella of Me 109s who were shepherding the Ju87s of II./StG1 and IV.(St)/LG1, and as soon as they were past Dungeness the Stuka formation split in two. Hptm Keil led his group of twenty-six Stukas of II./StG1 the short distance to Lympne to finish off the already battered and badly wrecked airfield while Hptm von Brauchitsch led a similar number round in a wider arc to attack Hawkinge.

High above Lympne, the Stukas lined up for a text-book attack; out of the sun and into the wind. One after the other they swooped down to deliver their deadly cargo and decimated what little was still left standing or was undamaged. Amongst the buildings hit were the hangars, with two wooden buildings used as paint stores struck and burnt out and the station sick quarters wrecked. All power and water services were cut. In the event that Lympne had been required for operational use it was, at least for now, beyond any such capability and the traumatised ground personnel were dispersed from what was left of the station to outlying houses near the airfield which had been hastily requisitioned. All the same, and notwithstanding the fact that the airfield was so very badly knocked about, the operations record book of Fighter Command noted that Lympne was serviceable again forty-eight hours later. As for the raiders, it was almost a re-run of the IV.(St)/LG1's attack on Detling just three days previously when the airfield was flattened with absolutely no opposition. The Hurricanes of 501 Squadron and Spitfires of 54 Squadron were just too far east to intervene at Lympne and, in any case, what was going on there was lost in the

RAF Lympne, whilst nominally a Fighter Command airfield, housed no fighter squadrons and was not a key airfield. Nevertheless, it was devastated in an attack by Stukas of II./StG1 on 15 August 1940 and this aerial photograph shows to advantage the massive scale of destruction and a profusion of bomb craters.

During the attack against RAF Hawkinge on 15 August the station's anti-aircraft Bofors guns put up a spirited defence against the raiders, albeit that none of the dive bombers were hit by the gunners.

summer haze. Haring towards the area, though, were the Hurricanes of 615 Squadron from Kenley but, by the time they were anywhere nearby, the Stukas were back out over the Channel and heading for home, leaving the squadron to tangle with the Me 109s who were covering the Stukas' withdrawal. Things were a little different further east, though, as nine of von Brauchitsch's Stukas lined up on Hawkinge and began their attack.

At first, the leader of IV.(St)/LG1's modestly sized Ju87 force must have thought he would meet no resistance, just as had happened at Detling. Almost immediately, though, the four defensive Bofors guns of the 11th AA Regt, 35 Bty, opened up on the approaching Stukas as they entered their dives. Also firing doggedly were the Lewis guns associated with each of the Bofors. Initially, the dive bombers were unseen by the Hurricane pilots of 501 Squadron who were much higher and didn't notice the start of the attack on their home airfield. No doubt it was the exploding bombs and bursting AA shells that drew their attention, and in no time at all the pilots were down and amongst the Stukas with 54 Squadron's Spitfires not far behind.

Although the fighters were too late on the scene to prevent Hawkinge being hit, the damage was surprisingly light when considering what had been achieved at Detling and, just moments earlier, at nearby Lympne. However, the Hurricanes that had suddenly roared down on the Stukas as they were either pulling out of their dives or preparing to go into them must surely have un-nerved the dive-bomber crews. If nothing else, the sight of the rapidly closing fighters and the barrage put up by the ground defences may well have had a detrimental impact and it certainly seems to be the case that a number of the forty-five bombs found their way outside the target area. All the same, some of the airfield buildings were hit and vital electric cables severed.

On the plus side, however, Sgt D.A.S. McKay of 501 Squadron latched onto one of the attacking Stukas of 10.(St)/LG1 and chased it until it crashed through power cables at More Hall, Folkestone, before smashing itself to pieces amongst the houses in nearby Shorncliffe Crescent. Somehow,

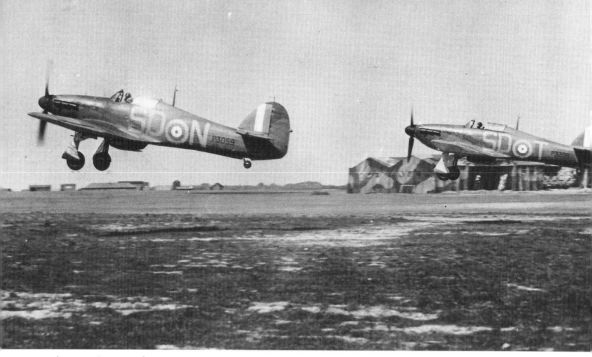

The Hurricanes of 501 Squadron were scrambled from RAF Hawkinge to counter the incoming raid by Stukas of IV./(St)LG1 and although they were unable to prevent the attack on the airfield they nevertheless managed to account for two of the raiders destroyed with another two damaged.

the radio operator, Uffz Franz-Heinrich Kraus had managed to bale out and landed outside 81 Harcourt Road but was severely wounded in the head and leg and died later in hospital. The mutilated body of the pilot, Uffz Herman Weber, was found amongst the shredded wreckage that was scattered over and amongst the semi-detached houses where the Stuka had come to rest.

Meanwhile, Hptm Rolf Munchenhagen who was leading the Staffel was shot down into the sea off Folkestone. Badly wounded, he felt that he was rather reluctantly rescued from the water, but given that he was fished out of the sea almost exactly at the very spot where his unit has sunk the South Folkestone Gate Light Vessel just the day before, perhaps his cold reception was understandable. His back seater, Fw Herbert Heise, was not so lucky and lost his life in the crash. Post-war, Munchenhagen was to serve with the 'new' Luftwaffe and worked with RAF officers in a senior NATO role during the late 1960s. Even so, he was reluctant to discuss this escapade when writing to the author in 1979, although he nevertheless replied with a hint of humour:

> "I'm afraid I can't help you with information. All I can say is that I flew to England with many other Germans on 15 August 1940. Unfortunately, we were not tourists and the main difference was that we were carrying bombs, not suitcases. A Hurricane pilot evidently didn't like me carrying bombs to the UK and shot me down – which I can understand entirely. So, I spent the rest of the war as a guest of His Majesty."

Although the attackers had withdrawn across the Channel from Kent the danger to Fighter Command had not yet passed. Further west, more Stuka formations were preparing for yet another operation directed towards the Dorset coast. The operation during the late afternoon involved approximately forty Stukas of I./StG1 and II./StG2, escorted by approximately sixty Me 109s of JG27 and JG53 and twenty Me 110s of V./(Z)LG1. In all probability, the raid was a diversionary one rather than aimed at any specific target but Portland seemed to be the landfall for which the huge formation was headed, although surviving Luftwaffe records relating to the dive-bomber losses would seem to indicate that the Stukas were assigned to attack Warmwell (StG1) and Yeovil (StG2). Given the failure of Stuka raids to reach these very same targets on 13 August, it may well have been likely that the two Stuka Geschwadern were coming back to finish the job. They were to be thwarted once again.

As the threat became apparent on the radar screens, so the largest force of RAF fighters to meet a single German raid thus far was put in to the air between 17.00 and 17.50: 152 Squadron (Spitfires), 234 Squadron (Spitfires), 601 Squadron (Hurricanes), 111 Squadron (Hurricanes), 43 Squadron (Hurricanes), 213 Squadron (Hurricanes), 249 Squadron (Hurricanes), 32 Squadron (Hurricanes), 501 Squadron (Hurricanes), 87 Squadron (Hurricanes), 609 Squadron (Spitfires), 1 Squadron (Hurricanes) and 602 Squadron (Spitfires). In total, an impressive thirteen squadrons. And an equally impressive 150 fighters. Not all, though, were vectored directly towards the incoming raid that included the Stuka formation, and the post-war Air Historical Branch narrative of the action is perhaps the best summary of events:

"The great air battles that resulted were fought principally in two areas; near Portland and near Portsmouth. Three or four raids totalling over a hundred aircraft had been plotted as they approached Portland. Nine Spitfires of 152 Squadron first came into action with them. Taking off from Warmwell at 17.00 our pilots had ample time to intercept before the enemy crossed the coast. At 17.20 they saw a formation of about thirty Ju87s some five miles south of Portland at 12,000 feet with an escort of nearly a hundred fighters (in their estimate) stepped up to 14,000 feet (Me 110s) and up to 16,000 feet (Me 109s). The Spitfires dived out of the sun to attack the dive bombers and then climbed to engage the first layer of fighters, the Me 110s. One Spitfire was lost (with pilot saved) and the squadron claimed to have destroyed three fighters and two dive bombers. Against odds of over ten to one, however, the squadron could hardly break up the enemy formation.

"Meanwhile, the Hurricanes of 213 Squadron (RAF Exeter) had arrived and encountered the same enemy formation. It was by far the squadron's largest engagement up to that date, but it was principally with the enemy fighters, for the bombers disappeared 'as soon as the fight started'. Many of the fighters apparently went into a 'great cylindrical wall' which 'it was almost impossible to attack without placing oneself in a vulnerable position'. Some of the dive bombers were apparently destroyed but these were stragglers found low down near the sea. The squadron, which lost one aircraft, put in an extremely large claim of successes (including fourteen Me 110s and five Ju87s definitely destroyed); and the last pilot to take off, who arrived after the combat had started, reported 'burning aircraft falling into the sea south of Portland'.

"87 Squadron (also up from Exeter) arrived on the scene apparently a little later, but it was obviously with the same enemy formation that they were engaged. They, too, put in much heavier claims than usual – nine fighters and four [in fact three; Author] dive bombers at a cost of two Hurricanes and one pilot."

Typically, in large-scale encounters like this against escorted Ju87 formations, overclaiming by the RAF pilots was rife. Against the eight Ju87s claimed as definitely destroyed by 152 and 213 Squadrons, the actual total was four Stukas lost and one damaged. The claims for fighters shot down were also wildly inflated. However, and whether it was by design and intent or through

The houses at Shorncliffe Crescent, Folkestone after being hit by Sgt McKay's victim. In the distance, Hurricanes can be seen returning to Hawkinge.

the defence put up by the RAF fighters, the Stuka formations turned and broke for home without attacking any target and, as 213 Squadron had observed, they seemed to disappear as soon as the fight started. Further eastwards, though, escorted formations of Junkers 88s were heading inland from The Solent to attack RAF Middle Wallop, Worthy Down and Odiham but these formations, too, were roughly handled by 43, 249, 601 and 609 Squadrons. If the Stuka sortie a little further to the west had been diversionary, it had not succeeded in keeping RAF fighters off the backs of around the sixty-odd Ju88s of LG1 and their swarming ZG2 Me 110 escorts.

It had not exactly been a day of crowning successes for the dive bombers; less than dramatic results at Hawkinge, an unimportant airfield temporarily knocked out at Lympne and no return for the late afternoon effort off Portland. A pretty dismal Thursday. Tomorrow, it would be another dark day.

CHAPTER 9 Black Friday

AFTER THE RATHER CATASTROPHIC START for the Luftwaffe in its launch of *Adler Tag* on 13 August, the following two days, as we have seen, had witnessed the Germans keenly trying to get some direction and momentum back into what was supposed to be a major air assault. After the somewhat limited air operations on Wednesday 14 August, and then the increase in tempo the next day, the Luftwaffe seemed to have surely made up its mind for a plan of action on Friday 16 August. And this time the weather was being rather more co-operative; little or no cloud and just light haze over the English Channel. Once again there was more than one 'prong' of activity, with incursions over Kent and the Thames Estuary area involving Me 109s and large formations of Dornier 17s that had resulted in large-scale engagements with British fighters. For the most part, though, the Dorniers did little damage with one of the formations ending up dropping their bombs on Tilbury Docks and Northfleet. It is likely that these were unintentional targets, and that the Dorniers had ditched their bombs as a result of being unable to locate their intended targets because a bank of Thames fog that had rolled up the river had obscured their vision. On the other hand, another formation of eighteen Do 17 bombers had got through to the airfield at RAF West Malling, Kent, and carried out an attack at around 12.30. The station was already unserviceable as a result of a bombing raid the previous day, but this new attack did not materially worsen the position. The raid, however, saw the end of that morning's activity over Kent. It was activity that had thus far been devoid of any Junkers 87 Stuka involvement, but that situation was about to change as the radar stations along the western edges of No 11 Group, RAF Fighter Command, began to pick up large hostile formations around 12.30 making their way across the central Channel area. This time, it was clearly apparent that the Luftwaffe meant business and radar stations had detected one hundred plus raiders heading towards The Solent area.

This estimation had resulted in five full squadrons being scrambled and in the air by 12.45 (Numbers 1, 43, 213, 152 and 601 Squadrons) but the fifty-odd RAF fighters were, on the face of it, still outnumbered by the incoming German force. In fact, the estimation of the raid size gleaned from the radar plots was very considerably under the actual number involved. Inbound toward the Sussex and Hampshire coasts were no less than 347 enemy aircraft; seventy-nine Ju87s, fifty-four Me 110s and 247 Me 109s. First in, sweeping ahead as top cover for the Stuka force, was a wave of Messerschmitt 109s and above the Selsey peninsula at 20,000ft they became embroiled in combat with the Hurricanes of 1 Squadron. To a very large extent the combat was inconclusive on either side, but an exception to this was the shooting down of Plt Off Tim Elkington (Hurricane P3173, JX-O), probably by the high-scoring 'ace' Major Helmut Wick who was leading the sixty-two Me 109s of JG2. Almost as soon as the Messerschmitts had engaged, however, they were having to be mindful of their fuel states. Soon, they were turning about and heading back across the Channel. Nevertheless, 1 Squadron had perhaps facilitated the task of the Hurricanes of 43 Squadron by diverting some of the escort away from their charges, the Junkers 87s. Perhaps 43 Squadron's account of its part in that engagement is best told collectively in the words of Fg Off F.J. Cridland, the squadron intelligence officer:

"Eleven Hurricanes took off at 12.45 hours and intercepted fifty to one hundred Ju87s travelling north off Beachy Head [sic: this is in error and the formation was off Selsey Bill, not Beachy Head; Author] at 12.55. The squadron was at 12,000ft and the enemy aircraft were at 14,000ft in flights of five, seven in close vics, and with the vics stepped up. A head-on attack was made and it seems to have been very successful. Formation of enemy aircraft broke up at once and some turned straight back to France, jettisoning their bombs. The leading aircraft was shot down by Sqn Ldr Badger, who was leading the squadron as Green 1, and two people baled out. There were escorting Me 109s at 17,000ft or higher, but they took little

The Stuka operations against targets in the Solent area on 16 August 1940 were covered in part by the Me 109s of JG2 under the command of Major Helmut Wick and during this sortie he accounted for his twenty-second aircraft destroyed. This was almost certainly the Hurricane of Plt Off Tim Elkington of 1 Squadron. Here, Helmut Wick proudly displays the victory tally on the rudder of his Me 109.

part in the engagement. Some of the pilots never saw them at all. The squadron then turned and attacked from astern, whereupon the combat developed into individual affairs and lasted eight minutes. Some of the enemy aircraft made no attempt at evasion, while others made use of their manoeuvrability by making short steep climbing turns and, on account of their slow speed and tight turns, one pilot at least made use of his flaps to counteract this."

Although 43 Squadron had believed they had 'broken up' the formation of Ju87 Stukas, this was almost certainly not the case and it is necessary to understand the precise situation in the large formation of Stukas when the squadron engaged them, head-on, just to the east of The Isle of Wight. This was just at the point in the flight when the large formation of seventy-nine Stukas *did* split up to head for their individual targets. Just as planned. Twenty-nine of the dive bombers continued straight ahead towards RAF Tangmere, and these were the aircraft of I./StG2, with another twenty-two (of I./StG3) veering north-westwards in the direction of Portsmouth. Meanwhile, another twenty-eight of III./StG1 made off toward the Isle of Wight and then immediately split into another two formations; one of twenty and another of eight, respectively heading toward Southampton and the smaller group south-westward toward Ventor. As they split, the pilots of 43 Squadron must have thought that they had scattered the Stukas across the skies in the face of their head-on attack. Nothing could have been further from the truth.

As individual engagements took place, there were certainly Stukas in trouble that would have been jettisoning their bombs and heading for home – just as the pilots of 43 Squadron had observed. In fact, and although the 43 Squadron Hurricanes were 'mixing-it' with the Stukas off Selsey Bill, they had failed to realise that one of the elements of the formation had, in effect, broken through and were on a direct bearing toward Tangmere, their squadron base and almost the ancestral home of the 'Fighting Cocks' squadron. Moreover, the ground elements of 43 Squadron back at Tangmere were also about to meet the Stukas head-on!

Having got both A and B Flights away at around 12.45, the groundcrews of 43 Squadron had little to do but sit it out and await the return of their aircraft. However, as the departure of the Hurricanes from Tangmere had come conveniently at around lunchtime it was inevitable that the crews would take time out in the summer sunshine to have a bite to eat, and it had been the turn of Aircraftsman Bill Littlemore to go to fetch the 'wads' (service slang for sandwiches and rolls) from the Naafi canteen van. Bill takes up the story:

> "The NAAFI van used to pull up between Number 1 & 2 Hangars, and on that day I had gone a little earlier than usual and left the wagon just before 12.45 to take the short cut back across the grass rather than around the perimeter and back to B Flight dispersal. I had just dished up the grub when there was a kerfuffle on the Tannoy and one of the lads said 'That'll be the boys back now'. I replied: 'That's not ours… that's Jerry!' I went to the door of the dispersal hut and looked up. There was a Stuka with its nose pointed right at me and with a bomb just leaving it. It landed right between the two hangars and killed a young lad who had been standing right where I had just been. He was buried in Tangmere churchyard – but it ought to have been me."

Equally thankful was AC2 James Beedle, an engine fitter with 43 Squadron who later became the secretary of the 43 Squadron Fighting Cocks Association, compiler of the squadron's published history and, together with the author of this book, one of the founders of the Tangmere Military Aviation Museum. Jimmy had changed duties that day with another young aircraftsman, nineteen-year-old AC1 James Young. This was the same aircraftsman of whom Bill Littlemore had said "….it ought to have been me". Such was fate, although that same fate was about to catch up with a number of the Stuka crews, too; among them Heinz Rocktäschel and Willi Witt who had taken part in their first operation over the Channel on 4 July but, in total, had flown no less than seventy-nine operational flights[7] since the very start of the war. Together, they had survived a number of operations over the Channel since 4 July and had also come through the attacks on Convoy Peewit unscathed.

Having survived the gauntlet of the 43 Squadron Hurricanes on the run in to target, the twenty-nine Stukas of the first Gruppe, StG2, had settled into their attack on RAF Tangmere at almost precisely 13.00 hours and pretty much just as the Hurricanes of 601 Squadron had arrived on the scene. Originally, 601 Squadron had been instructed toward Selsey at 10,000ft, but then received orders to attack the high guard of Me 109s and told to climb to 20,000ft over Bembridge. However, and since the fighters had already been tackled by 1 Squadron's Hurricanes, 601 Squadron dived down to take on the Stukas that were seen way below them and already in their attack on Tangmere. As we know, attacking the Stuka in its dive was nigh-on impossible

---

7 See Appendix VIII.

Although a pre-war image, this was very much how RAF Tangmere appeared before the raid by the Stukas of StG2 on 16 August.

but the RAF fighter pilots knew that they could catch them on the pull-out and it was with some gusto that the pilots of 601 Squadron tore into the Stukas as they levelled out and ran for the sea. Just at that moment the Hurricanes of 43 Squadron were turning back home for Tangmere after having engaged the main formation off the coast just a few minutes earlier.

Together, the two squadrons set about the retreating Stukas as massive palls of oily black smoke rose ominously, ever higher into the bright summer sky, emerging from bright pillars of flame that were now dotted across the airfield. However, so confused were the engagements that ensued that in most cases it is difficult with any certainty to attribute specific Stuka losses to specific RAF pilots. Certainly, the fighter pilots managed to inflict a good deal of damage and were able to exact some just revenge, although the claims made for the numbers of Stukas destroyed or damaged bore little relation to the actual totality of the Luftwaffe's losses.

In fact, a total of nine Ju87s were lost and seven damaged, wheras 43 Squadron claimed seventeen destroyed, five probably destroyed and three damaged with 601 Squadron additionally claiming ten destroyed, two probably destroyed, three damaged and another shared as damaged with another unidentified pilot. This was over-claiming on a grand scale, and the majority of those that were claimed as destroyed, probably destroyed or damaged were from among the Tangmere attackers. Thus, the number actually claimed as destroyed exceeded by *twelve* aircraft the actual number of aircraft (twenty-nine) that had been engaged in the raid. Little wonder that the official historian of the Air Historical Branch was moved to write of 43 Squadron's part: "There ensued a combat in which a heavier toll of enemy aircraft was claimed than in any previous engagement by a single British squadron."

One of the Stuka losses, though, can easily be attributed to one particular pilot through the specific detail contained in his combat report. Factually, and geographically, there can be no doubt about that pilot's claim. He was F/O Carl Davis of 601 Squadron:

Top left, clockwise: The funeral pyre of a burning Tangmere rises in the distance and is caught by photographer Frank Lalouette from Bognor Regis.

Black smoke rises from the burning hangars at Tangmere on 16 August.

Wrecked vehicles and motor cycles were also destroyed in considerable numbers during the Stuka attack on RAF Tangmere.

"We took off and patrolled base at 10,000ft and then were ordered to Bembridge at 20,000ft. We were then told there were bandits coming from the south and to take the top layer. Bandits were seen below coming in at about 10,000ft but we could see no escort, so dived to attack. Just at this point the enemy aircraft dived for Tangmere. By the time I reached them they were at about 2,000ft, had delivered their attack and were making for the south. I closed with one Ju87 and after several bursts he went down under control and landed between Pagham and Bognor, crashing through some trees and a hedge. No one got out. Heavy fire, fairly accurate, and violent evasive actions were employed by the Ju87. My aircraft was hit in the radiator, so I returned to Tangmere and landed at about 13.05 hours."

The Stuka that he had brought down was certainly the machine that had ended up crashing through trees at Bowley Farm, South Mundham, which is situated mid-way between Pagham and Bognor just as Carl Davis had described. The aircraft was one of the Tangmere raiders, a Junkers 87 of 3./StG2, W.Nr 5618, T6 + KL.[8] The pilot, Fw Heinz Rocktäschel, had been hit and mortally wounded but managed somehow to bring his Stuka in for a hasty forced-landing under

8 This aircraft was immortalised in the 1970s Airfix 1/24th scale model kit, and particularly through the dramatic illustration for the box lid by artist Roy Cross.

Fg Off Carl Davis, a victor on 16 August 1940.

some sort of control – albeit that it went careering through trees and a hedge as it did so. Local schoolboy Laurie Penfold was one of the first on the scene, and he recalled that when it came to rest the Stuka had tipped up onto its nose with the motionless bodies of the crew slumped inside and smears of blood streaking the Perspex of the cockpit canopy. The radio operator, Obfw Willi Witt, was already dead. His bullet-riddled body was arched backwards in his seat with a lifeless face staring, unseeing, at the sky. Rocktäschel, the pilot, was gently lifted from the cockpit and taken to the Royal West Sussex Hospital in Chichester where he died later that same day. The hard war fought by Heinz Rocktäschel and Willi Witt was over. After a long innings, they had flown their last mission but they must have known, perhaps with growing certainty, that they had been living on borrowed time.

Another aircraft flown by Uffz Paul Linse was sent spearing into the ground not far away at High Piece Field, Honor Farm, Pagham. The aircraft was W.Nr 5138 T6+LL. On impact, the aircraft had smashed itself to pieces and burst into flames before Linse or Messerschmidt had any chance of escape. Obgf Messerschmidt, it seems, was thrown clear of the wreckage but killed instantly although the badly burned body of his pilot, Paul Linse, was caught up in the mangled remains of the Stuka. Unusually, a press photographer took pictures of both bodies at the crash site and the images were later widely published and circulated. For reasons that are not clear, but possibly due to adjoining local authorities not wishing to take responsibility for the burials, the two German airmen were left where they lay for many days. Out of some respect, the body of Messerschmidt was apparently turned over, face downwards, and the body of Linse partially covered over with sections of wreckage from the aircraft. Meanwhile, as was customary, a steady procession of sightseers converged on Honor Farm to gape at the wreckage and at the bodies of the two dead Germans. In effect, they were left openly on public view. During this period the wreckage was literally picked over for souvenirs as the bodies of the two crew members still lay in the summer heat alongside the shattered Stuka. It cannot have been a pretty sight. Unfortunately, it turned out that not only was what was left of the Stuka robbed of parts but that little respect was similarly shown for the dead, and over the days that followed the bodies that lay in High Piece were thieved of all personal effects. In the end, and by the time the authorities finally got around to burying the two airmen, there was nothing left by which to identify them and they therefore had to be laid to rest as 'unknown' German airmen. An injustice that was felt strongly by the family of Paul Linse many decades later.

The *Bognor Regis Observer* of 24 August, 1940, reported critically on the habit of souvenir hunting from crashed German aircraft and without giving details or locations it made a very clear reference to the ghoulish behaviour that had been shamelessly exhibited at Honor Farm. In its article, the newspaper commented: "…we have been told that some collectors have even descended to cutting the buttons from dead men's clothes" and went on to justifiably call such

The 3./StG2 Junkers 87 Stuka downed by Carl Davis undergoing examination.

actions "disgusting". However, and whilst the two men were buried at St Stephan's Churchyard, North Mundham, under a grave marker that gave them no identity their grave was one of those exhumed during the 1960s for re-burial at the German Military Cemetery, Cannock Chase. Upon exhumation, the two men were positively identified and given named headstones at Cannock. All of this, though, came too late for the Linse family.

When the two men had failed to return to their base on 16 August 1940 they were posted as missing, and in common with all families in that same situation many months were to pass as they hoped for positive news that would mean their loved ones were either prisoner of war or injured. No such news was ever forthcoming, and eventually it was presumed that both men had lost their lives over the English Channel. Since neither had been reported as POW, nor the International Red Cross informed that their bodies had been found in England, it was the only conclusion that the families could reach. Unfortunately, when the German War Graves Service (VDK) identified the two men in the 1960s prior to their re-burial at Cannock all trace of the current whereabouts of the families had been lost as a result of the post-war chaos in Germany and, unknowingly, Paul Linse's mother decided to apply to the German courts for a certificate that officially pronounced him dead. To her, it gave some comfort and closure. Sadly, she could also have had the comfort of knowing of the existence of Paul's grave, but a connection was never made.

She eventually passed away unaware that her son lay buried in England, and it was not until 2013, during the production of this book, that the Linse family traced the author and discovered the truth. Asking to see the photograph, distressing though it was, Paul's sister was certain: "I recognised him in the first second", she said. The family mystery had been solved. Ever since the Battle of Britain, the removal of any means of identification in 1940 had continued to have repercussions, the consequences of which had been felt in the Linse household for more than seventy years.

Only one other Stuka from the Tangmere force was brought down on land, and this was another 3 Staffel machine, W.Nr 5580, T6+HL, probably shot down by Sqn Ldr J.V.C. Badger, the CO of 43 Squadron. The aircraft put down rather heavily on the east side of the B2145 Chichester to Selsey road at the Church Norton junction, and close to Park Farm. The stricken dive bomber bounced and wobbled across the first field before eventually careering across the roadway, wiping

Above: At Honor Farm, Pagham, another 3rd Staffel Stuka was shot down, the aircraft badly breaking up, burning on impact and killing Uffz Paul Linse (*top right*) and Ogefr Rudolf Messerschmidt.

Right: A contemporary yet grisly photograph of the wreckage at Honor Farm with the body of Paul Linse clearly visible under smashed-up pieces of his aircraft. Such photographs, taken by the British press, were considered quite acceptable at the time and this image is by no means unique.

off both undercarriage legs and abruptly coming to rest on its belly on the west side of the carriageway. Home Guardsman Frederick Barnes was at his post just across the road, and had been startled by the sight of the Stuka heading straight for him.

Grabbing his rifle, he dashed to the aircraft as it came to rest in a cloud of dust as steam hissed from the radiator that had been punctured by Badger's bullets. Slowly, under the watchful gaze of Barnes, the two unwounded but shaken crew members clambered down from their cockpit and as Barnes ordered "Hands up!" The two Germans willingly obliged, but Barnes then asked for their pistols and, in a comic moment, rested his rifle against the trailing edge of the wing and went forward to take their weapons. Only then did the horror of the situation dawn upon him; he was alone, had put down his rifle out of reach and now the two Germans were advancing on him and unholstering their pistols! The airmen, though, were in no position to cut up rough and both of them came quietly. For Uffz Paul Bohn and Obegfr Johannes Bader the war was over. Inexplicably, when Bader was searched, he was noted to have had in his possession a bag containing a small Stars & Stripes flag measuring approximately twelve inches by six inches.

Further raiders from this Stuka operation were downed in the English Channel, of course, and one other 3 Staffel machine that had been hit and damaged ditched just east of the Isle of Wight

The Selsey 3./StG2 aircraft was most likely hit by a Hurricane of 43 Squadron before ending up in a roadside hedge with its two crew members taken prisoner.

when its engine seized after an attack by Hurricanes of 43 and 601 Squadron. With its fixed undercarriage, the Stuka was a dangerously unsuitable machine to put down on water but Uffz Ernst König had no choice. As soon as the wheels dug into the wave tops the Junkers 87 flipped over, and although König and Uffz Josef Schmidt were both badly injured they were fortunate to be picked out of the water by a Royal Navy launch, eventually being transferred to the Royal West Sussex Hospital at Chichester. Here, the pair languished for some days before RAF Intelligence became aware of their existence – although it was noted that not until December 1940 was the gunner released from hospital whilst the pilot was still detained there. Despite his earlier release from hospital, so serious were Schmidt's injuries that he was eventually repatriated to Germany in 1943.

These, then, were some of the victims of the intervention of 43 and 601 Squadrons, but just along the road at RAF Westhampnett the Spitfire pilots of 602 Squadron had been stood down for the morning. Their CO, Sqn Ldr 'Sandy' Johnstone, had spent the time sitting in his office catching up on tedious paperwork and later inspecting the airmen's billets which, he complained, "…smelt of dogs". This, though, would soon be the very least of Johnstone's worries:

"It was as we sat down for lunch that the fun and games started.

"We were surprised to be given the order to scramble from a 'Released' state, but the reason was all too apparent as we rushed helter-skelter from the Mess to see thirty Ju87 dive bombers screaming vertically down on Tangmere. The noise was terrifying as the explosions of the bombs mingled with the din of ack-ack guns which were firing from positions all around us. We could hear the rattle of spent bullets as they fell on the metal covered Nissen huts where we hurriedly donned our flying kit. Chunks of spent lead fell about us as we jinked our way to our parked aircraft. Our crews, wearing steel helmets, had already started the engines and sped us on our way with the minimum of delay. It was a complete panic take-off, with Spitfires darting together from all corners of the field and it was a miracle that none collided in the frantic scramble to get airborne.

"I called the boys to form up over base at Angels 2 (two thousand feet). A Flight was already with me, but there was no sign of B Flight. However, there was no time to stop and look for them! The air was a kaleidoscope of aeroplanes swooping and diving around us, and for a moment I felt like pulling the blankets over my head and pretending I wasn't there! I had no idea it could be as chaotic as this. A Hurricane on fire flashed past me, and I was momentarily taken aback when the pilot of the aircraft in front of me baled out. Then, it was all over. No one else was about.

"Boyd, Urie, McDowall and Rose and myself[9] all claimed victories. I think Boyd's effort was the best of the bunch, for a Stuka pulled out of its dive straight in front of him just as he became airborne, and when he pressed his firing button it simply blew apart. He said that he was so surprised he merely completed a circuit and landed, without even retracting his landing gear! I don't suppose he had been airborne for more than a couple of minutes."

Surprisingly, very little detail about the raid is entered in the operations record book for RAF Tangmere with the commentary being limited to just a few lines, thus: "The depressing situation was dealt with in an orderly manner and it is considered that the traditions of the RAF were upheld by all ranks." Astonishingly, the record book then goes on to state: "It must be considered that the major air attack launched on this station by the enemy was a victory for the RAF!"

This was surely a statement of breathtaking exaggeration and it bears not one ounce of credibility when considering the circumstances of the raid and the damage that had been inflicted. In total, thirteen RAF personnel had been killed and a large number injured with six Blenheims, seven Hurricanes, two Spitfires and one Magister either destroyed or damaged. During their attack on Tangmere the dive bombers had hit all of the hangars and totally destroyed two (one of them by fire) and the station workshops, fire hydrant pump house, sick quarters, officer's mess, motor transport depot, stores, Salvation Army hut, Y-Service hut and many other buildings had all been hit and damaged – many of them severely. Around forty motor vehicles were also destroyed along with several motor-cycles, and lorries and equipment belonging to the RAF Faygate-based 49 Maintenance Unit were also lost. A number of private cars, too, were destroyed with some of them being hurled high into the girders that supported the roof of the 'garage' hangar. But if the RAF's own assessment of the situation in its operations record book was somewhat under-played, then so was the report in the local *Chichester Observer* newspaper. In its edition of 23 August the paper reported: "The damage was only slight. One of the small buildings that received a direct hit was being used as a sick bay." It also went on to quote a local resident who told the *Observer* "It is amazing that the raiders did no substantial damage". Clearly, newspapers were subject to censorship controls but those who lived locally and knew the truth must have thought they were reading of an attack on some other airfield.

Such was his concern to get at the truth of things, and far removed from the tittle-tattle of provincial newspapers, that Prime Minister Winston Churchill signalled the Chief of the Air Staff on 17 August and specifically mentioned what he referred to as "...twenty-one destroyed on the ground – the bulk at Tangmere. Let me know the types of machine destroyed on the ground."

9 The victories mentioned by Johnstone, presumably over Ju87s, are not reflected in RAF Fighter Command combat claims with the exception of one credited to Fg Off R.F. Boyd. Given the circumstances of Boyd's combat as reported by Johnstone, he must have fired at the Ju 87 that crashed at Honor Farm carrying Linse and Messerschmidt to their deaths. In his original account, Johnstone muddles up some elements of this engagement with another later that day against Me 110s. Additionally, Johnstone fails to mention that two aircraft of 602 Squadron landed back at Westhampnett damaged after the engagement with the Stukas; Plt Off T.G.F. Ritchie (Spitfire K9881) and Plt Off H.W. Moody (Spitfire P9463). Both pilots were unhurt and their aircraft repairable.

Churchill, it seems, was also somewhat exercised by what might be optimistic claims about the numbers of German aircraft downed, but in a memo to the Secretary of State for Air on 21 August he railed at American newspaper correspondents who were casting considerable doubt on the RAF's figures. "I confess that I should be more inclined to let the facts speak for themselves", he said, and went on to state: "They will find out quite soon enough when the German air attack is plainly shown to be repulsed." There was some way to go yet, though, before any obvious state of repulse would be reached, and given what we now know to be the hugely over-inflated claims made by the RAF against the Stukas on 16 August, the prime minister had good reason to show some anxiety.

The scene at Tangmere that had occasioned the prime minister's interest was, of course, one of utter devastation and is ably described by some of those who were there to witness it. One of those was Aircraftsman Peter Jones, an airframe fitter serving on 43 Squadron:

> "When the raid was over, the place looked like a sorry mess. I remember looking at the broken aircraft and saying to myself 'There's a hell of a lot of work to be done'. Later, we heard a rumour that the Group Captain [Jack Boret, the station commander] had floored a stroppy German prisoner with a good right hook. That cheered us all up no end! Then the WVS turned up, armed with churns of tea. I had a mug of tea thrust into my hand and a Woodbine cigarette was lit and stuck in my mouth. That was my very first cigarette, and I've been an addict ever since. I blame my addiction on the Stukas!"

Another perspective was added by Sqn Ldr 'Sandy' Johnstone, the CO of 602 Squadron, just down the road from Tangmere at RAF Westhampnett:

> "I drove over to Tangmere in the evening and found the place an utter shambles, with wisps of smoke still rising from the shattered buildings. Little knots of people were wandering about with dazed looks on their faces, obviously deeply affected by the events of the day. I eventually tracked down the station commander, standing on the lawn in front of the officer's mess with a parrot sitting on his shoulder. Jack was covered with grime and the wretched bird was screeching its imitation of the Stukas at the height of the attack! The once immaculate grass was littered with personal belongings which had been blasted from the wing of the mess that had received a direct hit. Shirts, towels, socks, and a portable gramophone – a little private world for all to see lay in profusion around our feet. Rubble was everywhere, and all three hangars had been wrecked [sic]. Alas, a heavy girder had crashed on top of my aircraft [LO-Q[10]] breaking her back and severing one of her mainplanes. Tommy Thompson, the station adjutant, showed me the remains of the neighbouring hangar and, pointing to its massive door lying flat on the ground, remarked wistfully: 'My Triumph Dolomite is under that little lot. I only bought it last week!'
> "What could I say?"

These testimonies add colour to the somewhat impersonal and incomplete account of events as covered in the station operations record book and give the lie to the contemporary local newspaper reports. They also give us some idea as to the scale of the devastation suffered by

---

10 Spitfire L1004. Incredibly, and despite the damage, L1004 was subsequently re-built and converted to a Spitfire Va. One other Spitfire of 602 Squadron, P9463, received Category 2 damage at Tangmere during this raid.

Tangmere that day. An equally colourful account was provided by LAC Len Swift who was fortunate to miss the raid but arrived back at Tangmere on Sunday 18 August when he wrote home to his mother about the scene that he had found there, and of the atmosphere of nervousness that prevailed:

"Sunday, 2.30pm, 18th August 1940
Dear Mother,
"I arrived on time yesterday and was astounded to find that the aerodrome had been bombed to hell at dinner time on Friday. Everybody is now air-raid conscious and when the alarm goes you should see them run! I am writing this in a field outside the 'drome during our third raid today. All those not on duty jump the boundary wire when the alarm is given, and having seen the damage done by the raid on Friday, I am content to get outside the aerodrome as quickly as I can.

"While sitting here we have heard at least a dozen bombs drop a bit too near for our liking, but far enough away to prevent our seeing any effects of it.

"There is not a building on the Aerodrome which does not show some effect of the bombs, and it is a miracle there were not more killed than 12 and 60 injured. Out of the 54 fellows I came here with, only one is dead, but several had near escapes. They tell me that all the bombs were dropped within six minutes.

"I have discovered a peculiar smell like sh-t in this ditch, and on investigation I have discovered I have been sitting in some much to my disgust and my two pals' amusement. It seems that the Stuka is a good laxative!

"It is now 6.00pm Monday night, and I have been on fatigues all day long cleaning up some of the mess around the 'drome and we have had two alarms this afternoon, but no 'planes got very near although one machine dropped four bombs outside the 'drome and was immediately shot down by a Spitfire.

"I am due to go on duty again at eight pm and rather welcome the idea of being outside these days. The fellow that was killed among our lot on Friday dinner time was going home at four pm that same day. I told him on Thursday that I had my leave from eight am and he said it was a pity we could not go together as he lived at Enfield. He was married and had two children.

"There has been a spot of bother over the airmen taking cover outside the 'drome, by the way, and we are now supposed to go to our shelters inside.

"As you can imagine it has upset a lot of things here; there is still no electric light on yet and the water is only on in some places. I was rather annoyed when I was moved last Thursday to my present billet, because it is so far from the cookhouse but I don't mind the distance now and am quite thankful to be away from the flying field.

"They tell me that on Friday the bombs started to drop at once after the warning was given, and everyone seems to think they got too close by a mistake.

"Every hangar here bar one had a direct hit and a lot of 'planes on the field were disabled and when they had dropped the bombs, they machine-gunned the men as they ran for shelter and did the same to one of our ambulances, too. You should see the huge craters made by the bombs.

"If this letter seems a bit sketchy you should remember that I am jotting things down as I think of them. Oh yes, all of the bombers were brought down and none got back to tell the tale. All together there were 28 bombs dropped [sic].

"Well Mother, that's all for now and don't worry because they have done the damage now.
With Love from
Your loving son,
Len."

For once, the Stuka force had hit and badly damaged a principal RAF Fighter Command sector station. What they had failed to do, though, was to put it out of action or significantly dent the armour of Britain's defence. Despite the devastation that had been caused, the Stukas had left untouched the vital dispersal areas and, although cratered, the flying field was still usable and the holes quickly filled in. Crucially, the operations room and telecommunications were not disrupted. The resident fighter squadrons, too, had been airborne and thus avoided being caught and hit on the ground and their home station had not even been non-operational for an hour. Aircraft were returning moments after the attack, and simply landed and taxied in amongst the bomb craters. In fact, after 43 Squadron were back on the ground it sent off another sortie, at flight strength, within twenty minutes of the raid.

Whilst the Stukas had once again demonstrated the pinpoint damage and destruction they could cause to an airfield (none of the approximately 145 bombs that had been dropped fell outside of the airfield), it perhaps highlighted the deficiences in using a tactical weapon to bring about a strategic objective. In France, for example, attacks were carried out by the Stukas with the Panzers then immediately following up on the ground to take advantage of the softened-up targets to prevent them being repaired and put back into service. In Britain, and once the Stukas had left, the defenders could repair and re-organise and the raiders rarely came back to consolidate their successes.

Additionally, of course, it is the case that part of the defenders' failings in France had been a complete lack of any integrated command and control structure for fighter operations and raid interceptions. In Britain, one of the main strengths of Fighter Command had been its command and control system, and if a more offensive effort had been directed at this system (including radar sites), the Stukas *may* have achieved much more than they did. Indeed, the Germans attacked airfields not so much to destroy or even to render areas unserviceable, but to destroy the nodal points of communication and control. It was damage to the telecommunications and operations rooms, rather than to landing grounds and hangars, that most interfered with the proper workings of 11 Group. Thus, and whilst the attack on Tangmere (an important RAF sector station) was well chosen, the failure to knock it out of use was significant. But it wasn't just Tangmere that the Stuka force attacked on 16 August 1940.

When the massed Stuka formation had split up just short of the English coast, Hptm Helmut Mahlke led his III./StG1 towards the Isle of Wight; eight aircraft of 8 Staffel peeling off to attack the Ventnor radar station and twenty Stukas of 7 and 9 Staffel streaking for the Fleet Air Arm airfield at Lee-on-the-Solent, HMS Daedalus. Housing a motley collection of non-frontline naval air units and aircraft this was yet another airfield target for the Stukas that was just not worth the Luftwaffe's attention. However, at around 13.00 Mahlke led his Stukas down in an attack which wrecked three hangars and burnt down an airfield store. Several houses adjoining the airfield were also destroyed, but the landing field itself was undamaged in a futile attack. There were no fatalities, although two Royal Marines manning a searchlight on the control tower escaped with their lives when two heavy bombs exploded each side of the tower, albeit leaving one of the marines injured. During the attack, however, one of Mahlke's pilots had forgotten to unlock his bomb-release and pulled out of the dive with his load still on board. It was an error

This scene of the interior of the Tangmere ops room was sketched by one of the WAAFs who worked there.

that had unfortunate consequences for an armed RN trawler that just happened to be going about its duties in The Solent.

In his pre-attack briefing Mahlke had arranged that the Stukas should head out back across the Isle of Wight, hard on the heels of 8 Staffel, and at extremely low level. The idea behind this tactic was that any anti-aircraft guns would have been alerted by the attacks on Ventnor and Lee-on-the-Solent, and thus would be ready to engage any raiders. At such a low altitude, Mahlke reasoned, there would be insufficient time for gunners to spot the Stukas and get a bead on them and they would be gone before any of the light anti-aircraft guns could do very much about it. Across the island, it was a tactic that worked. However, as they over-flew The Solent, the Stukas were engaged by gunfire from the naval trawler and the hapless pilot who was doubtless cursing himself for his stupid error over the target had suddenly found that he had the means and wherewithal to tackle the impertinent little trawler, and set about doing so with some enthusiasm and purpose! Although he didn't manage to sink the vessel with his bombs, he did damage it sufficiently to cause it to be beached with seven of the crew reported as being helped ashore by the 543/42 Searchlight Battery at Stokes Bay Pier.

Streaking out over the island the scattered Stukas raced to form-up on Mahlke's Junkers 87 with its distinctively marked bright yellow wheel spats – recognition markings he had specifically designed to help his men formate on him. As they raced southwards, the Stukas passed columns of black smoke rising from the battered radar station at Ventnor that plainly signaled the 8th Staffel's success just moments earlier. Off to port, another ragged formation of Stukas was also racing southwards not far above the waves, and these comprised the twenty-two Ju87s of I./StG3 home-bound after striking Grange airfield at Gosport. Here, the level of damage at what was again another insiginificant airfield in the air defence of Great Britain (Grange housed 22 Squadron's Beauforts, the Air Torpedo Development Unit and the FAA Maintenance Unit) was similar to that sustained at Lee-on-the-Solent; one hangar and a house both being reported as

One of the targets for Stukas on 16 August was the radar station at Ventnor on the Isle of Wight. Here, distant smoke rises from the station as tin-hatted RAF personnel peer from the undergrowth. They are salvaging the Junkers 87 that had crashed on St Martin's Down on 8 August 1940. (see page 71)

"seriously damaged". Nine aircraft were destroyed and another ten damaged, and it was further reported that one of the bombs dropped in front of No 2 gun at Holbrook gun position and large splinters penetrated the gunshield of No 3 gun. One of the gun crew was killed and the splinters wounded several others, with a gun crew member on No 4 gun having a hand blown off. Despite all of the mayhem it was noted that: "Tribute is paid to the way in which the NAAFI girls assisted in treating the injured personnel."

By the time Lee-on-the-Solent and Grange had been hit, Oblt Skambraks' pilots of 8./StG1 had already delivered something like thirty-two high-explosive bombs with deadly accuracy onto the Ventnor chain home radar station. Already badly damaged and out of action following a raid by Junkers 88s on 12 August, the station was being repaired when at least seven bombs hit the main compound causing fires to break out that destroyed most of the remaining structures, the heat from those fires actually damaging the radar towers. Ventnor was now declared effectively destroyed and had to be replaced by a mobile reserve station which was not up and running until 23 August. Of all the bombs dropped during the Stuka raids of 16 August, the few that were delivered by Skambraks and his men at Ventnor were perhaps the most significant in terms of the operational capability of 11 Group, Fighter Command. They were also demonstrative of what could be achieved by Stukas acting against well chosen targets. There is, however, one last action directly related to the Stuka attacks of 16 August that is legendary in the history of the Battle of Britain.

Although the Stukas of StG2 that had gone for Tangmere had suffered significant losses, those of both StG1 and StG3 were unmolested by defending RAF fighters and, in part, this may well be attributable to the actions of the Messerschmitt 110s of ZG2 and V.(Z)/LG1 who circled protectively between potentially incoming RAF defenders and the Stuka forces going for Grange, Lee-on-the-Solent and Ventnor. No RAF fighters got at these particular Stukas, but a section of

The airfield at Gosport targeted on 16 August 1940.

Hurricanes from 249 Squadron, RAF Boscombe Down, were detached from their patrol line between Ringwood and Poole to investigate enemy air activity in the area to the north of The Solent. In fact, this 'activity' had been the two-pronged air attacks against Grange and Lee-on-the-Solent and as Flt Lt James Nicolson led his two Hurricanes down towards the Hamble heavy smoke was already rising from the dive bombers' efforts. Out of sight, and now out to sea, the Stukas were already out of reach of the Hurricanes and the heavy Me 110 escort also stood in the way of any pursuit.

As Nicolson's Red Section (comprising Nicolson with Sqn Ldr Eric King and Plt Off Martyn King) headed off to investigate, they spotted Spitfires in the distance which were apparently dealing with the raiders and the three Hurricanes thus began to climb over Southampton Water to rejoin their squadron. What they had probably seen, off to the west of the Isle of Wight, were the Spitfires of 152 Squadron doing battle with Me 109s. As they climbed to re-join, so the three Hurricanes were 'bounced' by unseen Messerschmitt 110s. Plt Off Martyn King was shot down and killed when his parachute collapsed and Sqn Ldr King beat a hasty retreat to Boscombe Down with a damaged aircraft. Meanwhile, Nicolson's aircraft had been set ablaze and just as he was about to vacate the cockpit he was overtaken by what he presumed to be his attacker. He continued to sit in the inferno of the cockpit for a few moments more in order to shoot down his attacker before baling out, badly burned and peppered with shell splinters. To add insult to injury, quite literally, he was then fired on by Home Guardsmen who thought he was a German parachutist. For his actions that day Flt Lt James Brindley Nicolson was awarded the Victoria Cross, the only VC awarded to RAF Fighter Command for the entire duration of World War Two.

Although not 'close cover' at the time of the brief engagement with the Hurricanes of 249 Squadron, or the Spitfires of 152 Squadron off to the west, the Messerschmitt 110s of ZG2 and V./(Z)LG1 and the Me 109s of JG2, JG27 and JG53 had seemingly held off the approaches of any RAF fighters for the Stukas of StG1 and StG3 to do their work unhindered. None of these Stukas were even seen by the RAF fighters, and whilst this may have been largely due to the retreating aircraft being lost in haze off to the south, the RAF Spitfires and Hurricanes were too late to intercept as all three objectives had been bombed by 13.15 and only just as the RAF squadrons were approaching the scene.

For the men of StG2, and for those on the ground at Tangmere, it had been 'Black Friday'. Once again, we also had a day where huge effort was expended by the Luftwaffe Stuka force against airfield targets that were wholly inconsequential in the grand scheme of the overall objective. Only one important RAF Fighter Command airfield had been attacked, and that had not been put out of action nor its resident fighter squadrons much harmed. The few bombs that had been rained on Ventnor were the only ones that had had any real impact that day by having some small effect on degrading the RAF's early warning capability.

Flt Lt James Nicolson (*centre*) of 249 Squadron seen here with the CO, Sqn Ldr John Grandy (*left*) and the squadron adjutant Fg Off Lohmeyer (*right*) shortly before the combat on 16 August.

CHAPTER 10 'He Died That England Might Live'

FLIGHT LIEUTENANT JAMES NICOLSON, VC, was not the only fighter pilot embroiled in events connected to the Stuka attacks of 16 August, 1940, who would go down in the annals of Battle of Britain history. Another was Plt Off William Fiske, or Billy Fiske as he was better known. His story is inextricably linked to some exceptional bravery on the ground by RAF personnel, and these acts of courage would see the award of two Military Medals and one Military Cross. Despite the outstanding behaviour of two airmen and one officer, this all proved sadly insufficient to save the life of Billy Fiske. No account of the Stuka attacks against Britain would be complete without his story, a telling of the circumstances of his rescue and of his subsequent death – all of it the consequence of being caught up in one of the most notorious raids against Britain carried out by Junkers 87s.

William Meade Lindsley Fiske III was born in Chicago, Illinois, on 4 June, 1911, to successful financier William Fiske and his wife Beulah. The Fiske family had emigrated from Suffolk in the 17th century and thus had strong links with England. A privileged childhood saw him schooled privately in the USA and France, and it was to Paris that the family eventually moved in 1922.

In France young Billy grew to love the European winters and all they could offer and before long was a fearless, world-class skier and had soon progressed to bob sleighing. At sixteen he drove one of the two American bobs in the Winter Olympics at St Moritz, and took his team on to win. He remains the youngest Winter Olympic contestant ever to win Gold. After he had finished schooling at Sutton Courtney, Fiske won a place at Trinity College, Cambridge, where he read history and economics. A contemporary at Trinity was Carl Davis, another American citizen, whose path would again cross Fiske's during the Battle of Britain.

Around 1933-34 Fiske ventured into the Hollywood film industry, an industry that has recently shown itself keen to immortalize his story. *White Heat*, starring Virginia Cherrill, Cary Grant's wife, the first film Fiske produced, opened up another exciting adventure.

Winters, however, were always spent at St Moritz. Here, Fiske fostered friendships with 'Mouse' Cleaver, 'Willie' Rhodes-Moorhouse, 'Little Billy' Clyde and Roger Bushell, the 'Big-X' of Great

Escape fame. All, Carl Davis included, would later join 601 Squadron, Auxiliary Air Force, that with good cause came to be dubbed 'The Millionaires' Squadron'.

After university, Fiske had worked for his father's employers, the bankers Dillon Read. Although the slopes still beckoned, he flatly refused to enter the 1936 Winter Olympics in Germany. Billy soon acquired his pilots 'A' Licence and is said to have been a natural pilot. Speed remained the drug that Fiske craved, and he raced his Stutz car in the 1930 Le Mans 24-Hour event to complete the playboy image that had inevitably been cultivated around him. It has been reported that Fiske had it all: good looks, money, fame, fast cars, girls, and an infectious personality. In 1938 he met Rose Bingham, the former Countess of Warwick, and in September of that same year they were married in Maidenhead.

The couple then returned to the USA along with Rose's young son, David. Here, Billy met up with another English friend, William Pancoast 'Billy' Clyde, who was working as a corporate pilot and also in 601 Squadron. The two men could see that war was coming, and by the end of August 1939 Clyde was recalled to his squadron in England. Not wishing to be left out of the war, Fiske investigated how he might get to England to join up but was alarmed to discover that, upon declaration of war, it would be impossible to obtain a visa for England. Impulsively, he left at once with Clyde, the two sailing on the *Aquitania* on 1 September and arriving in Britain on 9 September, just six days after the war had begun. In his diary, Fiske wrote of his new adventure and of his burning desire to join the RAF.

> "I believe I can lay claim to being the first US citizen to join the RAF in England after the outbreak of hostilities. I don't say this with any particular pride, except perhaps insofar as my conscience is clear, but only because it probably has some bearing on the course of my career. The reasons for joining the fray are my own."

Enviously, Fiske watched Clyde fly off to war with 601 Squadron while he was left to plot his enlistment. His connections in high places paid off almost at once and he was invited to lunch at the Savoy with the son of Lord Bledisloe at which Billy found that his lunch companion was an AAF pilot who had also brought along a friend from the Air Ministry. He was soon fixed up with an interview with someone he would describe as "a very senior RAF officer". The identity of this man remains open to doubt but some sources name him as Air Chief Marshal Sir William Elliot although no such officer appears in the Air Force List of the period. Instead, there is a reason to suppose that Billy's contact was Gp Capt William Elliot, though it remains unclear who this man was or the position he held within the RAF or Air Ministry. Suffice to say, though, that strings were pulled and the wheels oiled to enable Fiske to enlist on 18 September and go to No 10 Elementary Flying Training School (EFTS) at Calne, Wiltshire, for training on Tiger Moths. With ninety hours of flying time already under his belt, Billy probably had the edge on many of his contemporaries there.

At this period, the official view in England was that it was not yet in the interests of the RAF to enlist American citizens and the official American viewpoint was that it was strictly illegal. Nevertheless, Billy had cut through the red tape and got himself accepted as an RAF pilot under training. From 10 EFTS he went to No 2 Flying Training School (FTS) at Brize Norton, Oxfordshire, on 20 March, 1940, and three days later he was granted his commission as acting pilot officer. At Brize Norton he flew Harvards, gaining experience for the first time on a high-performance aircraft.

Billy's contact with his friends on 601 Squadron increased his frustration as he heard about their battles in France and over the Channel. By 10 July, 1940, the Battle of Britain was underway, and on the 12th Billy had completed his training. That day he rang his friend Flt Lt Archibald

Hope, commanding A Flight of 601 Squadron at RAF Tangmere, flying Hurricanes. He could not endure the prospect of wasting further time at an OTU. "Stay where you are", Hope told him. "Say nothing to anybody about postings. We'll fly up and get you!" Later that day, Plt Off William Fiske 78092 formally became part of the establishment of 601 Squadron in what may well have been the most unorthodox posting of a RAF officer ever undertaken.

With no experience on Hurricanes, it might be thought that Billy's impetuosity could only spell disaster. The life expectancy of properly trained and experienced pilots was not high, and so the odds were stacked against him. Later, Sir Archibald Hope, Bt, recalled: "He was the best pilot I've ever known. It was unbelievable how good he was, and how fast he picked it up." Billy felt that he had been infused with the lifeblood he needed; speed, danger, purpose and his friends around him. To his wife Rose, he said: "Life has never seemed so good". Sadly, it would also be very short.

The day after his arrival at RAF Tangmere he had his first flight in a Hurricane, but managed to burst a tyre on landing. From 14 to 19 July he made nine practice flights before flying his first operational patrol on the 20th. Up for a mere 20 minutes in Hurricane UF-M on 20 July, he wrote in his logbook: "Saw men picking teeth in Cherbourg!" This, then, was the colourful character who was to lose his life whilst caught up in one of the Stuka's deadliest attacks.

Long before the Junkers 87 formation was plotted in-bound to the south coast at lunchtime on 16 August 1940, the Hurricanes of 601 Squadron had already been airborne and busy that day. Led by Flt Lt Archibald Hope (*right*), the squadron was first airborne at 08.10 for an

uneventful thirty-five-minute patrol, and then again at 10.10 the whole squadron, including Fiske in Hurricane UF-H, was ordered off on yet another uneventful operation. Back on the ground before 11.00, the Hurricanes were quickly re-fuelled and turned around for the next call to duty. It wouldn't be long in coming, and it was to be a busy day. At 12.25 the squadron was scrambled to patrol base and then ordered to climb to around 20,000ft, apparently with Archie Hope leading. Fiske was again in UF-H, P3358.

Hurricanes of 601 Squadron re-fuelling at RAF Tangmere. Airborne from their home airfield on 16 August 1940, 601 Squadron were scrambled against the attacking Stukas.

During the raids against British targets on 16 August 1940 (and again on 18 August) massed formations like this one of Junkers 87 Stukas were encountered by the defending RAF fighter pilots.

After being airborne for a while the squadron, still climbing, was vectored towards Bembridge on the Isle of Wight before being given a steer back to Tangmere again. As they approached they saw large numbers of Ju87s below them to the south at 12,000ft and heading toward their home airfield. However, the controller warned of the danger of fighters above and told the unit to maintain height. After the war, Archie Hope recalled this mission and said:

"I think the fighters were a myth, because I never saw them. Although the controller ordered otherwise I decided to go down to attack the Stukas when I saw them go into their dives, but we were by then too late to do anything about it. The bombs were falling already, and it was impossible to get the Stukas in their dive. I recall seeing a bomb burst very close to my car on the ground at Tangmere, and this made me feel even more justified in my decision to defy the controller!"

Hope went on to describe how the squadron then individually pursued the Ju87s back out to sea around Bognor, a number of the raiders being dispatched. Certainly, that happened. Oddly, though, the squadron operations record book indicates that Hope did not actually participate in this interception and, as we shall see, his testimony introduces further confusion as to his part in events – although his post-war account of things was clear. As for the fighter escort, they were certainly there in the form of the Messerschmitt 109s of JG27 and they were certainly seen by the pilots of 43 Squadron who were also engaged against the same Junkers 87 formation. That said, the 43 Squadron pilots did concede that the Me 109s "took little part in the engagement".

Of the raiders, we know that one bullet-riddled Stuka, with its dying crew on board, was sent crashing through trees at Bowley Farm, South Mundham, by the other American on 601, Fg Off Carl Davis. Another of the Tangmere raiders ended up in a road-side hedge at Selsey, and a funeral pyre rose for yet another wreck at Pagham. (All of these events are detailed in the preceding chapter.)

Meanwhile, Fiske was already in very serious trouble and heading back for the airfield. If the timings of events are accurate then it would seem likely that his problems began before the squadron had got anywhere near to the Stukas to engage them. Maybe he had been picked off by one of the unseen Messerschmitt 109s? Either way, it seems very unlikely that he could have got sufficiently close to the Stukas to take hits from their defensive fire. All we know for sure is that Fiske's aircraft caught fire in the air; we do not know how. Was it simply that an in-flight accidental fire, unrelated to any combat action, had done the damage? The truth will probably remain unknown, but the timings seem to show that Fiske was actually on the ground before the Stuka bombs began to fall which was just a few moments after 13.00 hours. A couple of minutes before that, the telephone had rung at the sick bay with the operations room requesting an ambulance to be sent at once onto the airfield for a pilot who had landed and needed assistance. At the double, nursing orderlies Cpl George Jones and AC2 Cyril Faulkner (*right*) ran to their Albion ambulance and with 'Bill', their trusty civilian driver, made off

around the eastern perimeter and then along the southern boundary. There, all hell broke loose. Faulkner takes up the story:

"Suddenly, and without any warning at all, the airfield came under a dive-bombing attack and one of the bombs fell just twenty-five yards away from us. A bit shaken, we pulled up for a few moments but then decided to carry on anyway to the Hurricane that was up against the western boundary. When we got there the pilot was still in the cockpit. It was Billy Fiske. For the life of me I cannot recall if the aeroplane was on its wheels or its belly, but the airfield was under attack and we got on the wing and managed to lift the pilot out on to the grass. The aeroplane was not burning, but the cockpit was badly damaged by the fire and the pilot was very seriously burned. We managed to get his flying helmet and his jacket off and covered him over.

"I can recall that he was conscious and talking to us, but not terribly coherently, although as we put him in the ambulance he looked back at his Hurricane and muttered 'Goddam thing!' – or something like that. When we returned to the sick bay we found that it had taken a direct hit, although Fg Off Willey, the medical officer (MO), was still there. He examined our injured pilot and said there was nothing he could do for him and told us to get him to hospital in Chichester at once, which we did. He died the next day, and afterwards a personal wreath for Billy Fiske arrived at Tangmere from Prime Minister Winston Churchill."

Courtney Willey, the medical officer for 601 Squadron, also recalled the events of that dramatic day:

"At about 13.00 we got the order to take cover. I was the only MO in the sick bay, and Jones and Faulkner had already gone off in the ambulance to collect an injured pilot. I suppose there were about twelve patients in the sick bay and I managed to get all of them into a bomb-proof shelter we had, but unfortunately we also had the airfield defence officer in. He was an ex-First World War chap and suffering from the DTs, and he was also prone to be quite violent – so I couldn't put him with the others. Instead, I stayed with him back in the sick bay. Suddenly the building got a direct hit from a 500lb bomb and was completely wrecked. The chap with the DTs was OK, but had had most of his clothes blown

Fg Off Courtney Willey, whose portrait was later drawn by the artist Cuthbert Orde.

off. In fact, I think it sobered him up a little bit! I was buried up to my waist in rubble, but after a bit of a struggle I managed to scramble out.

"Just then the ambulance arrived back at the demolished sick bay with Billy Fiske. I got in the back of the ambulance and lifted off the blanket and found he was charred black from the waist down. He was conscious and talking, but I gave him a shot of morphine although I realised we had to get him to hospital. In any case, the sick bay was no longer there! Unfortunately, because of the bombing, all of the roads on the airfield were blocked and covered in debris so we couldn't get him away for at least twenty minutes or so. I can remember a woman, a civilian not a WAAF, was sitting in the ambulance with him but I don't know who she was or where she came from. Later, I heard that he had sadly died in hospital. From a medical point of view, I was not entirely surprised."

For their actions that day both Jones and Faulkner were awarded the Military Medal, a Military Cross going to Willey for staying at his post and rendering first aid despite having been buried in rubble and suffering from shock and slight injuries. Here, then, is the story of yet more heroism in the face of a terrifying Stuka attack. According to one account of the event, Fiske was plucked from his Hurricane by "unknown rescuers". That is not the case.

The testimonies of both Faulkner and Willey are significant in that they place Fiske already on the ground before the attack started, whereas all previously published accounts have him landing during and after the raid, which certainly does not appear to be the case. Similarly, accounts of Fiske landing his "blazing aeroplane" and then taxying into a bomb crater and the aircraft exploding are patently untrue.

Further evidence on the timing question may be gleaned from Fiske's flying log book that had been filled in after his death by the squadron intelligence officer. The duration of his final flight is given as thirty-five minutes. If this is accurate then we also know from 601's operations record book that he took off at 12.25 and this puts him back on the ground at 13.00 exactly, just before the attack started. (Interestingly, Fiske's landing time is marked '?' in the operations record book.) The final word on timings should surely go to Cyril Faulkner, the only person still living who was there. He remarked that he and Jones were awarded the MM only because they effected the rescue *during* the attack, and he rightly points out that it would have been impossible for Fiske to have landed and for Jones and himself to have got in the ambulance, driven all the way to the western boundary and then rescued Fiske, all within the duration of the raid. In addition, the sick bay where they worked and where the ambulance was kept had been destroyed by almost the first bomb to fall.

As stated, Archie Hope subsequently recalled his part in the events of the day, though, unfortunately, that involvement is not confirmed by the squadron's official record. He further recalled that he rushed to the scene where Fiske had landed and assisted Jones and Faulkner in removing Fiske's parachute, as the two medics could not undo the harness. Whilst Faulkner did not recall this, he conceded that it may well have happened However, if it did then it also means that Hope landed back at Tangmere while the raid was under way. This seems most unlikely and, in any case, the rest of the squadron that Hope was apparently leading are all shown to have landed back between ten and twenty minutes after the air raid. By this time, Fiske was either in the ambulance or outside the sick bay or even enroute to the hospital. Hope's account of assisting at the rescue scene, and also the operations record book entries, would, if accurate, suggest that Hope stayed on the ground during this action. However, he certainly flew later that afternoon when he spectacularly shot down a Bf 110 into the ground of Shopwyke house, just half a mile west of the airfield. It could well be that Hope had muddled his recollections of intercepting the Tangmere raiders with the events of the later Stuka attacks on 18 August.

Mystery also surrounds the identity of the woman that Willey recalls sitting with Fiske in the ambulance, but since Billy's wife, Rose, lived very close to the airfield it is entirely likely that someone had called her there when it was known he was injured. Additionally, it was not uncommon for the officers' wives who lived locally to meet in the officer's mess at lunch times. Either way, Fiske's wife was certainly at his bedside in St Richard's Hospital, Chichester, as he succumbed to his mortal wounds. In an adjacent ward was Billy Fiske's good friend on the squadron, 'Mouse' Cleaver, who had been shot down and blinded just the previous day. He recalled later:

"On 17 August Rosie Fiske was brought to my room. My head was completely bandaged and I could see nothing. She came to my bedside and took my hand, and I could feel drops of some kind hitting my hand. She told me Billy was dead. I then realised that what I was feeling dropping onto my hand were her tears."

Shock and disbelief gripped the remnants of 601 Squadron when they heard of Billy's demise, for although the personal prognosis of MO Willey had not been good the pilots had clearly not expected his death. According to the death certificate, issued to 601 Squadron's adjutant, Fg Off T.G. Waterlow, the cause was 'Due to War Operations'. More specifically, though, he died of medical shock arising from his severe burns, and Willey also recalled that he had suffered extensively from the inhalation of smoke and hot fumes. Nonetheless, the disbelief on the squadron was

Plt Off Fiske was laid to rest with full military honours.

compounded by the fact that Archie Hope had visited Billy in hospital on the evening of the August 16 and found him …"sitting up in bed and as perky as hell!"

Fiske was laid to rest in the churchyard of Sts. Mary & Blaise, Boxgrove Priory, just to the north of RAF Tangmere, at 14.30 on Wednesday 20 August, 1940. The funeral, with an RAF band in the cortege, was attended by most of the pilots from the squadron who, with Billy's widow, followed the coffin draped with the union flag and stars and stripes into the ancient church. Listed prominently among the chief mourners was Gp Capt William Elliot; the same officer who had done so much to smooth Billy's passage into the RAF. Appropriately, and just as the coffin was being lowered into the Sussex clay, a section of Hurricanes returned overhead to nearby RAF Westhampnett and Prime Minister Winston Churchill was getting to his feet in the House of Commons to deliver his famous speech, which included the immortal lines:

"The gratitude of every home in our island, in our Empire, and indeed throughout the world, except in the abodes of the guilty, goes out to the British airmen who, undaunted by odds, unwearied in their constant challenge and mortal danger, are turning the tide of war by their devotion. Never in the field of human conflict was so much owed by so many to so few."

That same day, the following obituary notice was posted in *The Times* by Lt-Col J.T.C. Moore-Brabazon, MP, one of Billy's pals from their St Moritz days:

"A very gallant gentleman – 'Billy' Fiske – has given his life for us. As a racing motorist, as a bobsleigh rider, as a flyer he was well known, but as a 'Cresta' rider he was supreme. Taking some years to become first class, his fame eventually was legendary. No record he did not break, no race he did not win, he was the supreme artist of the run; never did he have a fall – he was in a class by himself. An American citizen, blessed with this world's goods, of a family beloved by all who knew them, with a personal charm that made all worship him, he elected to join the Royal Air Force and fight our battles. We thank America for sending us the perfect sportsman. Many of us would have given our lives for 'Billy', instead he has given his for us. The memory of him will live long in the Alps, where he had his greatest success; in the hearts of his friends it will endure forever."

Billy Fiske would have been proud to be numbered amongst Churchill's 'few' but he was not the only American to serve the RAF in 1940 or to die in the Battle of Britain, although sometimes he is incorrectly portrayed as such. At least nine American citizens flew and fought during the Battle, and, of these, three had died during the official Battle of Britain period. It is true though, that Fiske was the first American RAF pilot to die *during* that Battle, and true to say that he has undoubtedly become the most famous. It is perhaps not true, however, to say that he was the first American fighter pilot to die in RAF service during World War Two. That distinction possibly belongs to Flt Lt J.W.E. 'Jimmy' Davis, who was a 79 Squadron Hurricane pilot shot down and killed over the Channel on 27 June, 1940.

Both, of course, were gallant fighter pilots but Billy Fiske alone captured the hearts and the imagination of two nations. On 4 July, 1941, in the Crypt of St Paul's Cathedral, a plaque in his memory was unveiled by Sir Archibald Sinclair, Minister for Air, in the presence of the American Ambassador to London, Mr J.G. Winant. It was, indeed, a rare honour. Placed alongside the bust of George Washington it bore the inscription: 'An American citizen who died that England might live'. Unfortunately, it incorrectly records his date of death as being 18 August, 1940, although he had certainly died just the day after being injured.

Aside from the plaque in St Paul's Cathedral, the green turf at Tangmere on the spot where Billy's Hurricane slid to a halt is now covered by acres of greenhouses and there is no trace or hint of what once happened here. Just up the road at Boxgrove Priory his gravestone had been in a poor and rapidly deteriorating condition. A private headstone as opposed to the more usual Commonwealth War Graves Commission marker, it was replaced by an exact copy paid for by public subscription. It was re-dedicated in a ceremony that took place there on 23 September, 2002.

As for Billy's Hurricane on that particular day (P3358), the author Tom Molson in his history of 601 Squadron, *The Flying Sword*, states that "within days" it was repaired and back in service. Other published sources say it was repaired as a kind of memorial to Fiske. Neither account is true; P3358 was immediately declared Category 3 (damaged beyond repair) and struck off charge.

CHAPTER 11 The Hardest Day

ALTHOUGH SATURDAY 17 AUGUST WAS largely sunny and fine there were no significant air attacks against the British Isles, and if the Luftwaffe units were resting after what had been an effort at full-stretch, they were also preparing for a maximum assault to be launched the next day. So widespread and concentrated were those air actions to become that it turned out to be the heaviest fought day of the entire Battle of Britain. With good reason Sunday 18 August would later become known as 'The Hardest Day', and amongst the units preparing for action were the Stukas of StG3 and StG77.

As with previous Stuka raids mounted against British mainland targets, the incoming formations would split on approaching the English coast and each head for their pre-assigned targets. Such tactics inevitably made it difficult for RAF fighter squadrons to cover and intercept with absolute efficiency the multiple tracks of the raiders after the force had broken up. Controllers could only second-guess the intended targets and the likely track of the formations, but on 18 August there were five full fighter squadrons up to intercept the incoming mass of raiders and, this time, they did manage a considerable degree of success. However, the force that they faced was formidable in both size and capability. In total, 109 Junkers 87s were deployed along with 157 Me 109s. Of the latter, however, some fifty-five of the protective Me 109s of JG2 were flying on a *Frei Jagd* ranging out ahead from the main formations and seeking and sweeping for troublesome defenders.

This time, no long-range Messerschmitt 110 fighters were engaged on the operation; close escort was purely down to the Me 109 units and, as ever, they had an extremely challenging job shepherding and protecting their charges. Interestingly, we have comments from both a Messerschmitt 109 pilot and a Junkers 87 pilot engaged in operations that day. Both of them question the adequacy of the fighter escort provided for the Stuka force, although once again some elements of the attacking dive-bomber units got through unscathed, dropped

Hptm Herbert Meisel led I./StG77 in the attack against RAF Thorney Island but was killed in the raid. His body was later washed ashore in France.

Major Helmut Bode of III./StG77 led the mass attack by 109 Junkers 87s against British targets on 18 August.

their bombs and withdrew unharmed – either totally, or relatively so. For others, it was different.

The operational orders from Flieger Korps VIII for 18 August 1940 detailed the following units and their respective targets:

I./StG77 with twenty-eight Junkers 87 to airfield at Thorney Island
II./StG77 with twenty-eight Junkers 87 to airfield at Ford
III./StG77 with thirty-one Junkers 87 to radar station at Poling
(All above operating from Caen)
I./StG3 with twenty-two Junkers 87 to airfield at Gosport
(Operating from Angers)

Perhaps for the first time the entirety of Stuka Geschwader 77 (all three Gruppen) were committed in the attacks that day, and one of the pilots involved was Hptm Otto Schmidt. With his I Gruppe he was headed for Thorney Island and in 1971 wrote up the story of dramatic events over the Sussex coastline:

"For shorter range as a jumping-off point we had moved up to Tonneville, near Cherbourg, for this mission. Our Gruppe was to make a bombing attack with all three Staffeln on Thorney Island airfield. Two other Gruppen from our Geschwader were going to other targets.

"The briefing emphasised it was to be a straightforward attack but if more imagination had been applied it would surely have been realised that we were to stir up a hornet's nest. But we were quite confident, and had no qualms that our Me 109 escort might be insufficient. This, as it turned out, was our biggest mistake and for which we were to suffer. In fact, it was to be fatal for many of us.

"Take-off was about lunchtime, but we were not unduly excited by it. Since the start of the war I had flown sixty-five sorties, including against Dunkirk and Channel targets, and I had always returned unscathed from such missions. We had enough experience and confidence in our machines to think our attack would be more than safe.

"In flight, we remained in close formation and were led by the commander who gave hand signals and our three groups gained height to about 12,000ft and at a speed of about 200mph. It was a beautiful summer's day and although our fighter escort hadn't yet shown up we were sure they were in the vicinity. It was all so calm and peaceful. As the coast popped up in front of us, the two other groups peeled off. We could make out Thorney Island and we intended to go down one after the other on the target. The leading aircraft looked like a string of pearls as they started to go in. Then, by chance, I glanced outwards and saw the first wedge of British fighters screaming towards us. Initial evasive action brought my own flight to safety, but the speed of the British fighters left me speechless and the last flight in our formation took the brunt of their attack.

"One Ju87 went into the sea like a flaming torch, I remember. All of this time, there were no sounds or words on the radio. In any case, we were too preoccupied to take any notice of wireless signals. There was no time to think about what was happening. The main thing was to remember the correct moment to start the attack. And now it was my turn. First, I made the wing-waggle (indicating that I was just about to dive) then I was going down with my nose pointed on the target. Now, my vision was only downwards but I couldn't help sparing a thought for my radio operator and his predicament. All he could do was gaze up into the sky, not knowing when the bombs left the aircraft or if his pilot was efficient. Or even if he was still alive! As for myself, I was completely concentrating on the target.

Hptm Otto Schmidt of I./StG77 in a photograph taken later in the war. Although his Junkers 87 was hit and badly damaged on 18 August he struggled back to France but his radio operator died in hospital from his wounds on 2 October 1940.

Uffz Heinz Selhorn, one of the radio operators with I./StG77, sits reading astride a bomb shortly before taking off for RAF Thorney Island on 18 August. Selhorn later said of the raid: "There were burning Stukas all over the place. I fired and fired, and saw the muzzle flashes from the attacking fighters. We radio operators felt as though we were human armour plating to protect the pilot sitting behind us!"

"By this time, I saw the two channels down each side of Thorney Island which gave me a fix on the airfield where I could see the hangars close to one another. Certainly, below me, were the twenty-four multi-engine machines we had seen on our recce photographs. The hangar complex grew in my sight, and without any correction I dropped lower and lower. Then, at last, there was just one hangar trapped in my cross wire. I pressed my bomb-release button, and my job was done. All I had to do now was to get the aircraft onto an even keel and make for home. Making a wide turn, I went to re-join the formation.

"Normally, we would re-form into flights without much trouble and giving no thought to the fact that all of us must be attacked by fighters at some time.

"I noticed the scattered wreckage of an aircraft in the mirror-calm Channel and then, behind me, looming ever larger, was a Spitfire trying to get into a firing position. I had to act fast to get out of his way, and turning would not have saved me. So I side-slipped, which was a tricky manoeuvre for a Junkers 87. She came out of the slip, and the fighter was foiled. Now, I looked round at my wireless operator and he was hanging forward in his straps and his machine gun was pointing aimlessly into the sky. I didn't realise that either he or the aircraft had been hit. In the meantime, the Spitfire had turned again and was coming in for another attack. It was quite obvious that he had selected me for his personal target. In that short breathing space, however, I had time to gather my senses and when he came in again I knew what to do. He must have seen my helpless gunner and he made for my tail, but I slipped him again and he went screaming past. Then, something else happened.

"One of my comrades in low-level flight suddenly plunged into the sea and disappeared, while yet another Ju87 was shot down. I remember that he bounced on the surface of the water, and then he vanished. The situation became frightening and another Spitfire joined in the attack on me, but when it followed my side-slip it touched the water with its wingtip and met its end. By this time, I felt that I had had it. I was like a hare on the run, and there was nothing I could do. However, the engine droned on and was untouched and the aircraft responded to the controls. Then, I felt a strike on the aircraft. It shuddered along its length and I lost so much height that I touched the sea with my undercarriage. Yet I never knew what caused it.

"I suppose I escaped destruction because of my desperate evasive action but it was a truly terrifying experience. Cold shivers run down my spine when I think about it and I get nightmares of aircraft going into the water and splashes made in the sea by the attacking fighter's guns.

"By this time, all my ammunition had gone and I started to worry about fuel and whether the aircraft would get me home. For the first time, I noticed blood on my arm and realised I had been hit without knowing. Then, I was back over Caen and with relief I put my Ju87 on the ground – and that was my next surprise! My landing was rough and fast, and it was only then that I realised my undercarriage had been shot away.

"The ground crew took my radio operator out of the cockpit from where he had sheltered me from many bullet wounds and, at the same time, they found more than eighty hits in the aircraft. From my own Staffel, only one other aircraft escaped; an inexperienced pilot so unnerved by what happened that he was grounded and never flew again. My poor radio operator died a few weeks later.

"It seemed to us that the attack could have been better planned; that we were sacrificed for no good reason and that fighter escorts we should have had failed in their tasks and were insufficient in numbers."

Another pilot who flew this mission was Oblt Kurt Scheffel who highlighted the concerns of Stuka crews undertaking these long-distance two-way flights across the Channel, and whilst the German air-sea rescue service was well advanced and efficient the prospect of a ditching for Junkers 87 crews was worrying:

"We only had life jackets, and we tied air beds around our bodies for these missions during the Battle of Britain. These were underneath the parachute harness and tied around our waists with string. They had to be blown up by mouth once we were in the water. Only one aircraft in each Kette had a dinghy, and this was stowed in the radio operator's position. The dinghy had to have its inflation bottle opened slowly, and then thrown out by dropping it up-wind of the man in the water."

For many of the I./StG77 crews that day, however, there would be no need for life jackets, air beds or dinghies and Scheffel himself must have wondered if he would make it back to France. Hit over Thorney Island just before he went into the attack dive, Scheffel was peppered by glass, Perspex and metal splinters with a one-inch shard of metal embedding itself in his right thumb. Behind him, his gunner lolled lifelessly in his harness and as he neared the bottom of his dive and pressed the bomb release the jagged metal splinter sent its stinging pain through his hand. Now, pulling out of the dive, he had to run the gauntlet of RAF fighters and a crossing of the English Channel in an already damaged aircraft.

Although the attack went in on Thorney Island with considerably destructive results (two hangars badly smashed, a fuel dump hit, three aircraft destroyed and two damaged) it was the

Another of the pilots who took part in the attack on Thorney Island was Oblt Kurt Scheffel of Stab I./StG77. On 18 August Scheffel got back to France in his badly shot-about Stuka, wounded, and with his radio operator killed.

Bullet strikes in the landing gear and wheel spat of Kurt Scheffel's Junkers 87 Stuka after returning from the Thorney Island attack.

single formation of Stukas engaged against south-coast targets that day that took the most punishment. Initially, it was the Hurricanes of 43 and 601 Squadron which got amongst the Ju87s and very quickly accounted for several of these I Gruppe aircraft; one sent flaming into the ground at North Barn, Chidham, killing both crew, one smashing to earth at Spring Gardens, West Ashling, with one POW and one killed, another

At Chidham, in West Sussex, the smashed-up wreckage of a I./StG77 Stuka lies in mangled heaps at North Barn. Both of the crew were killed, although no trace of either man was ever reported as found. The firemen, soldiers and ARP wardens who swarm over the crash site are unaware that the full bomb load is buried just beneath their feet. It was not until the 1970s and 1990s that the bombs were finally accounted for and made safe.

plunging into the mud of Chichester Harbour at Fishbourne and the last one diving vertically to earth at Whitehouse Farm, Chichester. (The latter aircraft was famously photographed in its death-dive in an image which would become one of the most enduring and iconic pictures of the Battle of Britain, see page 192.)

Of the RAF pilots in the 'wedge' of fighters that Schmidt described as attacking his Stukas, one was Sgt 'Jim' Hallowes of 43 Squadron:

"We took off at 14.10 and climbed to 15,000ft and a few minutes later sighted a large formation of Ju87s at about 10,000ft with a fighter escort above of Me 109s circling at about 18,000ft – the latter appeared to head towards Portsmouth and the balloon barrage whilst the Ju87s went into line astern for Thorney Island.

"I followed Blue Leader in line astern but lost sight of him as we engaged the enemy. I caught up with one formation of five Ju87s in line astern, opened fire at about 300 yards and two people baled out of the number five machine and a further two from the number four machine, both aircraft going into a dive about three to four miles east of Thorney Island.

"I then carried out a quarter attack on a third Ju87 without any apparent result. Observing another Ju87 at about 200ft that had released its bombs on Thorney Island, I came up into a position astern and gave it three short bursts. I was closing too fast and had to break away to the right, coming in again for a beam attack on the same machine which broke in two just in front of the tail fin and fell into The Solent halfway between the mainland and The Isle of Wight."

It total, Hallowes was credited with three Ju87s destroyed that day (in Hurricane P3386) and a Messerschmitt 109 as damaged. The latter aircraft had shot-off the tail of a Hurricane that was, in turn, shooting at another Junkers 87.

Pilots of 601 Squadron were again in the fray, and one of those had been Flt Sgt 'Bill' Pond who was clear about events that memorable day:

"We were directed to an area north of Selsey Bill and almost before we got there we saw a long line of Ju87s stepped up in line astern. Our method of attack was to go into line astern and then every man for himself. I approached this lot and remember a couple of 109s in a Rotte formation on a reciprocal formation and climbing up. They were far enough away on my left for me to feel that I could get in a quick attack and I approached one by turning to my right, starting with a beam attack becoming a quarter attack. I gradually tightened the deflection, having put on too little at first. I got closer and closer and could see the fellow in the back firing back at me. He was a very brave man. I was quite surprised to get hit – after all, he only had one gun. Then someone jumped from the '87 and shortly afterwards the whole of my windscreen went black and oil began to seep into the cockpit. Then I got a bit worried. I remembered the 109s I had seen earlier and as I could do nothing useful I resolved to beat a hasty

Sgt Herbert 'Jim' Hallowes of the Tangmere-based 43 Squadron was one of the Hurricane pilots who made multiple claims for Stukas destroyed on 18 August 1940.

retreat, rolled over and peeled off towards Tangmere. It was a pretty heavy landing, and people who watched said they had never seen anyone get out of an aeroplane so quickly – even with a parachute on, which is quite difficult. Only the day before, 'Billy' Fiske had died from burns following a similar crash landing when his Hurricane had burst into flames. I think he just hadn't got out quickly enough, and I had resolved not to do the same thing."

On the ground at Thorney Island, only five civilians were injured when a shelter there had a near miss and, remarkably, there were no fatalities. Once again, the Stukas had hit a target that was not crucial in the defensive chain that formed RAF Fighter Command and, despite the damage, the airfield was not put out of action. Moreover, the cost to the raiding force had been considerable. It was different along the coast at Ford, though. Although spared the previously scheduled attack on 13 August that had been called off due to bad weather, the airfield's period of remission was now up. Here, the attackers were the twenty-eight Stukas of II./StG77 and we look at that attack from the perspective of some of those on the ground. One of those was PC Ray Herrington:

"The Sunday 18 August raid is still very vivid in my mind. The sirens sounded about 1 pm and as I was working the 'Down' beat my action point was the 'phone box in Littlehampton arcade. The strict instructions were that you remain within hearing distance of the ringing tone should you be required. Why this place was chosen I will never know! I was completely surrounded by plate glass – the whole of the roof, the large shops and café windows throughout the entire length of the arcade and for good measure the shops at either end also had large plate glass windows! It was a lovely sunny day, hot, and with practically no cloud. For a long time it was all very quiet, nothing happening and just a few people about as most had gone to the shelters. As it was quiet and the bell on that particular 'phone box was fairly loud – some you couldn't hear more than ten yards away – I had gone to the High Street end because no way was I going to be under a plate glass roof during an air raid alert waiting for a 'phone call that was not likely to come anyway.

"The owner of the café in the arcade had no customers because of the siren, and came out and we stood chatting more or less in the middle of the road. I have no idea of the time other than it must have been just after 2pm because I was having to remain on my beat on duty as I was there when the siren sounded and my relief would have been kept on stand-by at the police station – and I was getting very hungry!! We heard planes coming and saw, as far as I can recall, about twenty coming in from the sea and again following the siren. They were in a V formation and flying fairly high. Not being very well up in aircraft recognition at that time we said "Some 'Spits coming back". We should have realised our fighters did not fly in that formation, and in a matter of seconds we knew how wrong we were.

"They went into a single line, swung over on to their backs and came screaming down. As I looked (the café owner had disappeared!) up the High Street towards Ford the planes seemed to be diving down off the end of the road – but of course they were a good way down to the naval air station. They dived very low, and each one was dropping four small and one large bomb. The noise was terrific. With each bomb blast the shop windows were doing vertical ripples but none actually broke. A huge pall of black smoke rose high in the air over the airfield and billowed off to the north-east. Suddenly, some fighter aircraft appeared as the dive bombers were pulling out and trying to climb away back over the sea. They were quite low, and bullets from the fighters were flying all over the place, hitting the roof and smashing tiles which were falling on to the pavements in places and a whole line came right down the centre of the High Street chipping up the terrace.

"By this time I was too scared to move. About half an hour after the bombing had stopped a small saloon car came down the High Street from the direction of Ford sounding its horn and going quite fast. Roped to the roof was a sheet of corrugated iron, and strapped to that was a very badly wounded man covered in blood. They were rushing him to hospital. He had been one of the Royal Marine Police on duty at the main South Gate. He seemed fairly well in due course and I often had a chat with him but he was never able to work again. There were many casualties – some civilian. There was, so far as we could tell, very little fired at the aircraft from the ground. At the height of the raid the commanding officer [sic[11]] of Ford Naval Air Station apparently in frustration ran out from the admin block and was firing his .45 revolver at a diving plane. The dive bomber had fixed machine guns which they fired in their dive in order to aim their bombs on to the target and the CO was killed in a hail of those bullets."

Another policeman, PC Jack Hamblin, was the first non-serviceman to reach Ford airfield after the attack and what he saw was utterly shocking. The matter-of-fact report rather belies the true nature of what he must have found there:

11 Actually, this officer was Lt Cdr Michael de Courcy and when his dismembered body was later found outside the ward-room his right hand was still gripping his service revolver.

"I beg to report having acted as Incident Officer at the R.N.A.S., FORD, as a result of an enemy dive-bombing attack which occurred at approximately 14.30 on Sunday, 18th August 1940.

"This incident occurred during an Air Raid Warning at Arundel. The enemy planes could be seen at a great height above Ford and they appeared to form into 'line-ahead formation' and then dive, one after the other on to the aerodrome. Probably about twenty planes took part in this raid, which only lasted for a few minutes and after which two columns of black smoke were seen to rise.

"Arriving on the scene I saw that the canteen and various other buildings had been demolished, and that one or two of the hangars were also damaged. An oil tank was blazing and there were one or two other fires but these were being put well under control by Littlehampton, Arundel and Bognor Fire Brigades assisted by the A.F.S. Foam apparatus was employed to control the blazing oil.

Police Constable Jack Hamblin was one of the first outsiders to reach Ford aerodrome after the attack. He was met with an almost incomprehensible scene of carnage and destruction.

"Ambulances from the surrounding district augmented by First Aid Parties, Casualty cars and doctors were dealing efficiently with the dead and injured. These were conveyed to various hospitals and mortuaries.

"Various unit of the Army were deployed guarding roads leading to the aerodrome and ammunition which had been removed. A Field Service Telephone unit were engaged in

Billowing black smoke rises above the naval air station at Ford on 18 August 1940; another funeral pyre ignited by the Stukas.

Sub Lt Christopher Draper DSC was armaments officer at Ford during the summer of 1940 and used this car as his personal run-around to inspect the aerodrome defences. After the Stuka attack of 18 August the little car became one of the casualties of the raid.

restoring communications as the telephone wires were down and the system out of order. Guards had been placed round one or two exploded bombs.

"It was reported to me that an unknown civilian girl had been killed at the entrance to the aerodrome, apparently as she was about to visit a naval rating. Her body was taken to Goodwood and enquiries revealed her to be Kathleen Murphy of 'Orlan', Kilkelly, County Mayo, Ireland. She was identified by A/Mech J.Spooner. It has since been ascertained that about twenty-six officers and men attached to R.N.A.S. Ford were killed and a number injured."

The scene was one of utter carnage and devastation and the Stukas had done their grim work effectively. However, and yet again, a target had been selected that was not vital in terms of destroying the RAF and eliminating its air superiorty. Ford was not an RAF fighter base. Instead, it was, in fact, a Fleet Air Arm base, HMS Peregrine. In remarkable commonality with many of the other sites attacked by Stukas, though, there were also exceptional acts of bravery and courage on the ground during the raid. (See Appendices for detailed reports of the raid, bravery commendations, aircraft losses and casualties etc.) However, and although less badly mauled than I Gruppe, the II Gruppe Stukas didn't get away entirely unscathed.

At around 14.00 it was almost a repeat performance of the events of 16 August for 602 Squadron at RAF Westhampnett. At 'Released' state, the squadron were again scrambled unexpectedly – and again to counter an incoming Stuka raid. Led this time by Flt Lt Dunlop Urie, the squadron got into the air just in time and Urie takes up the story:

"When we ran to our aircraft I found that the fitters were changing the wheels on my Spitfire but a new aircraft had been delivered that morning and was close by. I grabbed my parachute and helmet and ran for the new one. Its guns had not yet been lined up with the gunsight but it was important that I got airborne to lead the squadron. There was no time to detail someone else.

"When we were up we were ordered to patrol Tangmere at 2,000ft with the controllers no doubt thinking that Tangmere was in for a return visit. We had been doing this for about two minutes when we spotted Ju87s dive-bombing Ford. With a 'Tally-ho!' we made for them. There were two groups of about twenty-four aircraft and the first group were actually dive-bombing when we saw them and the second group about to dive. We got to them just as they were completing their dive and the leading aircraft were climbing. The lowest were at about 500ft.

"Ever since the days when the Ju87 was used to bomb fleeing civilians in Belgium, Holland and France I had hated the Stuka[12]. I remember deciding that I would shoot at as many as I could, that it didn't matter if I shot them down so much as sending them home so badly damaged and wounded that they wouldn't come again.

"I shot at five aircraft before I ran out of ammunition. I certainly damaged them all, but more than that I cannot say as I couldn't stop to look. My last rounds were used on the leader of the second group and I pulled away to go back for more ammunition. As I did so, the controller called me up and asked me if we were engaged. There was a machine on my tail which I assumed was my No 2. It wasn't! There were four very loud bangs and I was blasted out of my seat by the cannon of a Me 109. As I struggled to get back into my seat he attacked me again, and I felt my legs go numb. He then broke off as I did a gradual turn to port as I daren't have tried any sudden manoeuvres as I was afraid my controls must be badly damaged and I was at about 500ft and too

Top: Flt Lt Dunlop Urie of 602 Squadron received numerous splinters in his feet and is pictured here, his feet bandaged, back at RAF Westhampnett.

Above: Holes the size of dinner plates were punched in the fuselage of Urie's Spitfire, X4110, with the cannon shells then exploding inside the fuselage and peppering the entire aircraft with shrapnel. A brand new aeroplane with only twenty-five minutes flying time; it was written off and never flew again.

low to jump if they broke, so I returned rather gingerly to Westhampnett. My radio was destroyed, and it transpired I had no flaps or brakes and both tyres had been shot through. My guardian angel was watching over me, however, as I made a good landing and stayed upright.

"My legs and parachute were full of shrapnel and the Spitfire was written off as four 20mm cannon rounds had exploded in the fuselage and broken her back. My life had been

---

12 The use of the Junkers 87 as a terror weapon against fleeing civilians is one of the popular 'Stuka myths'. In fact, there was no military reason or purpose for such actions and it is certainly the case that refugees were never deliberately targeted in this way. In any event, such actions would have detracted from the urgent tactical requirement to employ the Stuka force against pinpoint military objectives. Many of these targets involved roads, bridges and junctions etc and it was an unfortunate consequence of those missions that civilians were often caught up in such attacks thus leading to the supposition that it was the refugee masses who were being intentionally targeted. Very often, too, the civilians were intermingled with military columns which were legitimate military targets.

saved by the seat armour, but the Spitfire was written off after a service life of just twenty minutes. The war was over for X4110. And so was my personal war against the Stuka!"

For another pilot of 602 Squadron, Sgt Basil Whall (*right*), one of the Stukas wobbled into his gunsight and he took careful aim, spattering the dive bomber with a hail of bullets and sending it down to crash land onto the golf course at Ham Manor, Angmering. Michael Wilcox, then an impressionable teenager, recalled:

"The noise of the raid was interminable and the house rocked with explosions as we ran to shelter under the staircase with saucepans on our heads! The Bofors gun on the golf course opened up briefly, and then fell silent. There seemed to be little opposition to the Stukas which came again and again – so low that we felt some would fail to clear our rooftop. Always an ear-splitting screaming noise, and the continuous rattling of machine-gun fire. I don't recall how long it lasted, but I remember father running home to grab his Smith & Wesson revolver and ramming a 1914 tin hat over my ears and shouting that he was off to capture the crew of a Stuka – or else to shoot them!"

The Stuka at Ham Manor: before and after. This must have been one of the most comprehensive souvenir hunting sprees conducted against downed Luftwaffe aircraft in the British Isles!

When Frederick Wilcox got there, with Michael following up the rear, it was clear that the crew were in no state to be difficult. Both were wounded, and the gunner was still in his seat groaning and blood-soaked. In fact, the pilot Ofw Schweinhardt was seriously wounded but survived, although his gunner, Obfw Willi Geiger, died later that same day from his wounds. Remarkably, save for one or two bullet holes, the Junkers 87 was intact – so much so that it was later decided to effect minor repairs and then for the RAF to fly it out for evaluation purposes. So much for their ambitious plans! Unguarded for just a while, the aircraft was totally stripped by locals who comprehensively took the Stuka apart leaving just a hulk.

Almost certainly the second large group of Stukas that Dunlop Urie had seen going down were about to attack the nearby radar station at Poling, housing both a chain home and chain home low station, and these were the aircraft of the III./StG77. On the ground at Poling, all hell was about to break out. Again, we rely on an account from one who was there, WAAF Corporal Hearn-Avis:

Corporal Hearn-Avis, an operator at the Poling radar station, was awarded the Military Medal for staying at her post during the Stuka attack of 18 August 1940.

"Our own station at Poling picked up a mass of aircraft over France which began to build even bigger.

"I had in front of me a big map which was squared off, and although I was not actually plotting I could tell more or less where they were. The siren went, and the Sgt in charge of our radar equipment rang through and just said "Duck!" When you heard that you just had to take cover, but I told him I couldn't leave the 'phone because of all the information coming through. By this time I could actually hear the bombers and when Truleigh Hill said 'Poling, do you realise what we have just given you is right on top of your station?' the bombing had already started. There was this awful scream of diving 'planes and bombs dropping so I could hardly hear what they were saying. Stanmore asked: 'Are you all right, Poling?'….and then the line went dead."

When it was all over, Cpl Hearn-Avis found the walls cracked, broken glass everywhere and a bomb-proof door buckled double but still, somehow, hanging on its hinges. There had been no casualties, but the CH site was out of action and despite Hearn-Avis' almost matter-of-fact description she was decorated for her bravery that day with the award of the Military Medal: "During an enemy air attack, bombs were dropped on buildings of the unit doing very considerable damage", ran the wording of her citation published in *The London Gazette* on 16 January, 1941. "Several heavy bombs fell alongside a block where Corporal Hearn-Avis was working alone controlling telephones… doing her work as far as the terrific noise would permit. This airwoman displayed courage and devotion to duty of the highest order."

AC1 Edward Martin was also at Poling. He recalled:

"One group of Stukas hit our transmitter side and the others the receiver side. One of the receiver towers was hit and toppled to the ground. Only one of these towers was wired up

The main gate to the Poling radar station, badly hit during the Stuka attacks of 18 August.

for use, but as luck would have it it was that tower that was hit! The tower was hit about half way down and chopped in two. Later, we went and picked up a mobile reserve unit and set it up in the woods behind Angmering where we operated for some months before Poling was repaired."

Again, one of the Poling raiders from III./StG77 was caught and shot down by Sgt Basil Whall of 602 Squadron, who sent the bomber into the sea off Littlehampton killing both Uffz Moll and Uffz Schwemmer. By now, the scattered raiders from all three Gruppen of StG77 were heading pell-mell across the English Channel in disarray, many of the survivors in varying states of distress. Also streaking homewards were the Stukas of I./StG3 which had just paid a return visit to Gosport (Grange) airfield after their previous attack there on 16 August. The reason for the return visit is not clear, but it is likely that the post-strike photo reconnaissance from that raid had shown far less damage amongst the buildings and infrastructure than had been intended. Certainly, it was the case that the damage inflicted at Grange was markedly less than at other sites attacked that day. But now the Stukas of I./StG3 were back and an official report of the attack set out the stark details:

"14.00 hours. Twenty-one Junkers dive bombers approached the airfield in three groups of seven. They were in no definite formation and the attack was made from a south-westerly direction at about 4,000 to 5,000ft. On approaching the station they broke in a wider formation flying in line astern and seemed to carry out a quick survey of the buildings before diving. They then carried out very steep diving attacks out of the sun, the angle being seventy to eighty degrees. They each attacked a separate place and followed each other with only a small gap between each machine. After diving they pulled out at 200 to 500ft, turned left inside the aerodrome boundary and disappeared toward the south. Most of the bombs were dropped in the dive at about 800ft, the salvos consisting of one large and four small bombs.

"The actual attack lasted four to five minutes. No notice was taken of AA fire. There were no casualties. Several buildings were destroyed. Two hangars were damaged. Several aircraft were damaged or written off from the Torpedo Development Flight and Station Flight. The bomb salvos fell across Grange Moat, the transport section, main stores and military road, torpedo workshops, No 4 Hangar and FAA MU, No 3 Hangar and parachute section, operations room, petrol dump and Fort Rowner between 1 and 3 warhead stores. The parachute section, band room, machine-gun test butts, articulated trailer shed, petrol trailer shed, MT shed, Station HQ and torpedo workshops were all damaged beyond repair."

Clearly, the damage caused had been considerable. And yet, once again, the Stuka force had been sent against a target that was wholly unworthy of such attention. For the crews of I./StG3, though, the only up-side of all of this was that, yet again, they flew to target, bombed, and returned home without being engaged by a single RAF fighter through the dedicated efforts of the Me 109 pilots of Major Edouard Neumann's I./JG27. However, the fighter escorts that day had all been hard pressed to adequately protect all of the diverse Stuka units as they dealt with their assigned targets. Over The Solent, Hptm Karl-Wolfgang Redlich of I./JG27 had a hard fight leading the top cover for the Gosport raiders as they engaged with the Spitfires of 234 Squadron, losing three Me 109s with two pilots killed and one POW. Speaking of the operations on 18 August 1940, 'Edu' Neumann was clear in his views:

"Attacking four targets over such a wide front presented the escorting fighter pilots with an almost impossible task. Stukas were difficult to escort, anyway, because they flew low and slow – and this was at the extreme limit of our useful operational range in the Me 109. It was only by a miracle, and some sacrifice by us fighter pilots, that the Stuka losses that day were not appreciably higher."

Aside from the good fortune of Hptm Walter Sigel's I./StG1, it had of course been a very different experience for other Junkers 87 crews that day. Overall, the Stuka force committed on 18 August 1940 had endured a loss rate of 13%. A loss rate that could not even be set against any large scale or significant damage to high value targets. Only Poling had really been worth attacking. For now, though, the work of the Stuka force against British mainland targets was done. They would not return again in force, although there would yet be some sporadic activity before, finally, the Stuka vanished from British skies forever.

CHAPTER 12 Recovering the Last Stuka

ONE OF THE LOSSES SUSTAINED during the attack against RAF Thorney Island had been a Junkers 87 of 2./St G77 flown by Oblt Johannes Wilhelm and his gunner, Uffz Anton Wörner. Like Otto Schmidt, he had been caught during the run-in to target and had not even had time to deliver his bomb load before the aircraft was hit and crippled at about 12,000ft. On the approach, Wilhelm already had the target in sight through the window in the bottom of the cockpit and briefly glimpsed three or four RAF fighters flashing past beneath. Behind, he heard Worner's MG15 rattle its defiant defensive fire as an attack from the Tangmere-based Hurricanes of either 43 or 601 Squadrons closed in. Ahead, he watched as another Stuka from the leading Staffel was suddenly engulfed in flames and fell away, earthwards.

At once, a hail of .303 bullets smashed into the engine compartment of Wilhelm's Ju87 with at least one bullet piercing the oil cooler as a gush of black oil spurted back over the front canopy blotting out all vision. Suddenly, there was a loud bang in the engine and a small gout of flame and puff of smoke. The motor was still turning, but Wilhelm knew they were doomed and he could dimly see that the oil pressure had dropped alarmingly, the engine temperature was off the clock and the Jumo 211 engine was showing signs of obvious distress. The situation was hopeless, and Wilhelm called "Aus!" to his gunner, slid back his canopy and rolled the Stuka onto its back. As he did so, he instantly received a face full of hot engine oil but he waited a few seconds until he guessed Wörner had gone, and then he jumped himself.

As he cleared the cockpit canopy the slipstream threw another massive aerosol mist of oil over his tumbling body, but the relief as the parachute canopy cracked open above him was immeasurable. He couldn't see much because the oil was in his eyes, and he had no idea where his gunner was. Down below he thought he had seen his Stuka plunge into a harbour but, as he descended, he was faintly aware through his oil-blinded eyes that he was being circled by a RAF fighter. He expected a burst of gunfire, but it never came. Then, he was down himself. Almost immediately he was surrounded by soldiers, Home Guard, civilians and policemen.

As Wilhelm had thought, his Junkers 87 had indeed gone into a harbour. In fact, it had gone into Fishbourne Creek, a tributary of Chichester Harbour, on the mud flats just above the low water mark. On impact, the mud had literally swallowed up the dive bomber and left virtually no trace of it showing above the surface. So total was its destruction and disappearance that there was virtually nothing for RAF Intelligence to report on. Even the local souvenir-hunting schoolboys were deterred from venturing to this crash site – so inaccessible was it, and so deep the black mud, that even they were kept away! In fact, within a few tides any visible traces had all but gone although for many years a single undercarriage leg protruded above the mud, its seaweed encrusted shape a familiar mark in the harbour and an obstruction that became known to local boatmen and fishermen. All else of the Stuka had vanished. It was not until the late 1970s that anyone bothered to look for it again.

During November 1976 it was the Wealden Aviation Archaeological Group who ventured out into the harbour at low tide to search for the lost and unique Stuka. With the tide out it was possible to walk along the centre of the shallow channel running from Mill Lane southwards towards the main harbour; the harbour-trekking team scanning the mud banks as they went. Eventually, in the area believed to have been the impact point, a small piece of unidentified material was observed protruding above the smooth mud – although traversing across the thick gooey morass to this unidentified object was challenging. The black slime stuck to boots and oozed over

Some of the team of enthusiasts from the Wealden Aviation Archaeological Group who spent weekend after weekend at the crash site of Wilhelm's Stuka, digging the wreckage of the dive bomber from the glutinous mud.

wellington tops as the intrepid wreck searchers struggled towards the item that beckoned them. Eventually, in mud about eighteen inches deep, the team reached the item and discovered that it was, in fact, a section of airframe still painted dark green and with a distinct yellow anodised interior treatment. Without doubt, this was metal from the Junkers aircraft factory. Prodding and probing around the object revealed a mass of buried wreckage and as the team worked petrol and oil bubbled to the surface. This was certainly the Junkers 87 Stuka that had been left there by Johannes Wilhelm, although getting it out was going to be an interesting challenge to say the very least.

By the spring of the following year, and with the co-operation of Chichester Harbour Conservancy Board and the landowner, a full recovery was undertaken between tides over a period from 23 April to 7 May 1977. Despite its tricky location, a crawler tractor was taken out to the site to pull out items that had been excavated in the thick mud, and with extreme difficulty, by a team of dedicated aviation archaeologists. The mud stuck and pulled at the team, and slid into the holes being dug which, in turn, also filled with water. The time between tides was limited, and so a frenetic chain gang of bucket and spade-wielding enthusiasts worked quickly between each low and high water – eventually finding themselves waist deep in mud and water that also hid razor sharp pieces of airframe. Incredibly, the finds that emerged were tantamount to an embarrassment of riches. After all, the Junkers 87 was a relatively rare aeroplane in terms of numbers actually shot down over the British Isles and without a doubt this crash site held the substantial remains of the entire aeroplane.

However, the initial recovery work over April and May 1977 had to an extent been limited in its success. Although the tail unit, complete with its bullet-holed swastika, and a quantity of miscellaneous fuselage items had been pulled out it was clear that a great deal more lay buried very much deeper – the engine and propeller assembly included. The question was; how could they be recovered? A mechanical digger was out of the question and the only possibility was a renewed attempt by hand. This time a bigger party was organised with shovels, baling pumps and makeshift shoring and shuttering.

Over the early summer of 1979 a considerable excavation was achieved, down through the mud and into the clay and shingle harbour floor where much of the aeroplane was clearly embedded. Of course, with each tide the hole was flooded with mud and water and so it was almost back to square one with each return visit although, eventually, the engine and props were revealed and cables and buoys attached. Now came the next part of the plan which involved baling the hole for almost one last time and sliding a prefabricated raft of 50-gallon oil drums down on top of the engine and propeller and securing the cables to the raft. All that remained was to sit in a dinghy alongside and wait for the incoming tide to do its job – which it surely did. Slowly, and then with a rush, the raft bobbed up with the rising water after sitting, rather worryingly, completely inert under the incoming tide for a few minutes. Now, at last, the engine and prop were out although it needed a few more tides before it was possible to juggle both raft and wreckage ashore. However, the task was not finished yet and one last visit to the crater was carried out to check for other engine parts and a missing propeller blade. It was at this point that a somewhat dramatic discovery was made.

Beneath the remaining broken engine parts lay two large triangular steel plates…and then a third appeared. Straightaway the team recognised them for what they were. Bomb fins! Indeed, feeling around in the mud in the bottom of the crater there was no doubt about it. One very large bomb was sitting there, almost vertically down in the mud and clay. However, and given that the team would only later discover from their research that the Stuka had been caught on its run in to target, the presence of the bomb was perhaps not surprising and although it had lain hidden for nigh on forty years it could certainly not be ignored. Here was a live 250kg bomb within a few hundred yards of dwellings and public highways.

Reported to the Royal Navy bomb and mine disposal unit at HMS Vernon, a team led by Lt Brian Jervis dug the bomb free of its muddy pit in an operation assisted by the RAF Explosive Ordnance Unit from RAF Wittering. Finally, on Monday 25 June, the bomb was taken out by landing craft to a position off West Wittering where it was lowered onto the sea bed and demolition divers attached a timed charge to the bomb casing. Thirty-nine years after the bomb had been destined for nearby RAF Thorney Island it exploded on the sea bed, sending up a column of water almost two hundred feet into the air. It was a sobering demonstration of the destructive potential these weapons still have long after the war.

As for the artefacts recovered over a period spanning almost two years, the list is certainly an impressive and intriguing one. Apart from the engine, propeller and tail fin the team found the control column, flare pistol, first aid kit, gunners' tools, radio, instruments, gas mask in its service case, ammunition saddle drums for an MG15, data plates and both oxygen masks and oxygen

Lt 'Jumbo' Jervis RN supervises the lifting of the bomb ready for demolition in an explosion on the sea bed.

Former Sgt Pilot Hallowes was one of the possible victors over Wilhelm's Stuka and attended many of the recovery operations at the crash site. Here, he examines the bullet-holed tail fin of the Junkers 87 that had been salvaged from the harbour.

regulators. Two cockpit clocks by Junghans, one from the front and the other from the rear cockpit, were discovered – both of them stopped at the time of impact. Perhaps the most significant find was the control column, complete from top to bottom, along with the map box containing flight maps. Still legible was the pencilled-in course, and a German magazine dated 4 August 1940 was found stuffed into the bottom of the box. When raised from the mud the centre section of the cockpit canopy revealed a Luftwaffe NCO's and officer's belt, both of them buckled up and looped around one of the canopy struts. Dangling from each belt was a leather holster, with a Walther Model 9 in the officer's holster and a Luger P08 in the NCO's. Incredibly, and despite the wreck's location, all the recovered items were in superb condition.

The name of the pilot who shot down Johannes Wilhelm's Stuka is difficult to establish with any certainty, since a number of pilots from 43 and 601 Squadron claimed Ju87s as destroyed that day and there was clearly confused over-claiming and multiple claims for individual Stukas. One of the pilots who claimed was Sgt Jim Hallowes (later wing commander) and he attended many of the recovery operations at the crash site during the 1970s. He had shot at the rearmost of five Stukas that were in line astern "…about four miles east of Thorney Island" and was surprised to see the crew bale out almost immediately. Hallowes has generally been credited with this victory, although the numbers of pilots making claims does create some considerable difficulty when trying to establish who shot down what. Another 43 Squadron pilot who also hit a Stuka at the same time and also saw the crew bale out was Plt Off Cliff Gray. However, Gray was immediately compelled to break off the action when his windscreen was sprayed liberally with oil from his quarry. That spray of oil might, perhaps, add weight to Gray's claim for this particular Stuka since the possibility that this was the same liberal gush of oil that had soaked Wilhelm cannot be ignored.

Wilhelm and Wörner landed quite close to Fishbourne Creek, although Wörner's parachute failed properly to deploy and he fell too quickly although he was saved serious injury, or worse, by landing in the mud. Marjorie Norris recalled the event during the 1970s and wrote saying"… I saw the pilot [sic] hit the mud. Had it not been for such deep mud I would have gone to his aid." In fact, Wörner suffered concussion and severe bruising to his legs, but in 1976 he was reticent about talking of those events, saying: "I cannot understand what good it will do and

Oblt Johannes Wilhelm as POW at Chichester railway station whilst enroute to the London 'Cage' and interrogation.

what importance it all is. If you consider this as an interest then I can find no taste in these old stories. I believe that in this age of new Europe we should leave such old memories to lie quietly and look to the future." Less unwilling to share his memories had been Johannes Wilhelm who enthusiastically wrote of his experiences and even entered into correspondence with Wg Cdr Hallowes. However, Johannes was still sore about one newspaper account that he had read in 1940.

When taken under armed escort by train from Chichester to London, Wilhelm was photographed at Chichester railway station and a series of photographs appeared the next day in the daily newspapers. One of those photographs shows Wilhelm sitting on a platform bench accepting a cigarette from a British soldier and this, according to Wilhelm, later appeared in *The Daily Mirror* of 21 August 1940 with a caption something along the lines of: 'British Soldier presents cigarette to a Nazi baby killer.'

Quite apart from evoking widely differing memories and emotions amongst those who had been involved in the incident during 1940, the recovery of artefacts from Junkers 87 Stuka B-1 Werke Nummer 5518 was unique amongst recoveries of Battle of Britain aircraft wrecks. Its recovery during the 1970s is now almost as much an historical event as was the crash itself; a time span of little over thirty-five years separated the crash from the recovery of the aircraft, and a time span of thirty-five years separates that recovery from this written account of the project.

CHAPTER 13

Stuka Swansong

BY THE TIME THE MUD of Fishbourne Creek had finally settled over the last visible pieces of Johannes Wilhelm's Junkers 87, it wasn't exactly the last that had been seen of the Stuka in Britain. Albeit that Wolfram von Richthofen's VIII Fliegerkorps Ju87 units had been withdrawn from his command towards the end of August 1940 and transferred up to Fliegerkorps II in the Pas de Calais, there were sound operational reasons for doing so. And these reasons were not in any way connected to the Stuka attrition rate and 'unacceptable losses' as has so often been suggested. As the Air Ministry in its 1948 summary of the Battle of Britain concluded: "This move…was in effect a new disposal of forces in preparation for the invasion itself. The dive bombers were now placed in a tactical position for army support in the coming invasion operation in a similar manner to the other continental campaigns."

By the time the Stuka force had settled in around the Pas de Calais, the continuation of the campaign against RAF airfields was already drawing down and the Luftwaffe bomber force was preparing for its round-the-clock offensive against London and other cities in the Blitz. Once that campaign was underway on 7 September 1940 there was no longer a current role for the Stuka in attacks against mainland Britain. Using the Junkers 87 to dive-bomb targets in London, for instance, would surely be futile. This was not what the weapon was designed for and it was not how the bombing of dockland and industrial targets would be conducted. Leastways, not for the present! Instead, and for now, the Stuka units rested, trained and replaced losses as they waited for the expected invasion. When it came, they would deal with any Royal Navy ships that threatened the operation and they had already ably shown what they were capable of in that respect. Once ashore, it was reckoned, the German army would be supported by the dive bombers as the troops advanced across south-east England with the Stuka crews being tasked to take out defensive positions, artillery, troop concentrations, vehicles and armour.

This was the role in which they had excelled in Poland and France, and with attacks followed up on the ground by Panzers and infantry, the quick seizure of key military objectives was anticipated. In all probability, at least some RAF airfields would be taken early on and thus provide useful forward operating bases for the Stuka units and their fighter escorts. Such were the plans. In the event, of course, Operation Sealion was called off by Hitler on 17 September and at that point the Stuka force that was being held at readiness in the Pas de Calais was temporarily redundant.

Already, German eyes were cast eastwards and with plans formulating for the invasion of the Soviet Union in Operation Barbarossa the intention was that the USSR would be dealt with first. Then, with the anticipated defeat in the east achieved by the autumn of 1941, attention could

On 7 September 1940 the Luftwaffe changed tactics and started the day and night Blitz against London and other British cities. Tower Bridge is outlined against the blazing docks and East End. With attacks against airfields no longer the primary objective, there was no further work for the Stuka force operating against Britain although, briefly, the Junkers 87 would be used in experimental night attacks against the capital.

again be focused on dealing with Britain and employing much strengthened forces. Meanwhile, the day and night Blitz evolved into an almost purely night Blitz, the Luftwaffe bomber force being greatly protected from risk of interception by the cover of darkness and undeveloped state of Britain's night-fighter force as well as a not wholly successful anti-aircraft defence. On a more strategic front, the solution for dealing with Britain lay in starving her of food supplies through combined air and sea attacks on her shipping. To this end, Göring issued a further directive as to the conduct of the air war against the British Isles. Amongst the ten points he set out was included this particular order: "Attacks, [to be carried out] with fighter escort, on convoys in the Channel and on assemblies of shipping in the Thames."

The Junkers 87 force ranged against Britain was back in some kind of gainful employment, but before any attacks against Channel and Thames shipping would resume a tentative operation of a different kind was conducted by Stukas on Tuesday 29 October. Helmut Mahlke, who had been operational since 1 September 1939, and who had taken part in the opening shots of the Blitzkrieg on 10 May and had survived the Battles of France and Britain, was now flying against England again:

"On 29 October we sent up the whole of III./StG1 against Folkestone, but the idea was that this was simply to draw RAF fighters into action for our fighters to engage and we then withdrew before we got to the coast, hoping that we had acted as a decoy. I'm glad we got away before the fighters came up. Acting as live bait was not my idea of fun!"

Two days later, though, and it would be for real.

Again, it was Mahlke's III./StG1 who were detailed for action. Just like the sorties flown during the early summer, and in accord with Göring's recent instructions to re-commence action against coastal convoys and Thames shipping, it was an attack on vessels in the estuary of the Thames at around 14.30 that was the focus of the Gruppe's attention. With around twenty Stukas, Mahlke led an action that he later described as "inconclusive" although, in fact, his dive bombers had sunk the coaster SS *Letchworth* near the Oaze Light Vessel. The ship, and others in the vicinity, had come under attack by the twenty-odd Stukas and *Letchworth* took a direct hit in the engine room which sank the 1,317 ton ship immediately. Newcastle registered, she had on board a cargo of coal from the north-east collieries. Seventeen survivors were picked out of the water, but the chief engineer was missing and presumably went down with his ship. The SS *Lear*, just ahead, had a lucky escape as bombs fell all around her.

Not so lucky was the Oaze Light Vessel (officially, Trinity House Light Vessel 60) and being close to the group of shipping that Mahlke's men had attacked, L.V. 60 was singled out for attention. This may well have been simply because the Stuka crews mistook her for one of the ships in convoy, or it may well have been a deliberate attack. Either way, she was stationary and thus a sitting duck. Certainly, the light vessel performed an important function at this the assembly point for south-coast convoys and was on station to control safe passage at an entrance to a defensively mined area. There has often been controversy about the sinking of light ships, but the reality was that they guided and controlled British coastal shipping, merchant and naval alike, and thus were surely legitimate targets. This, of course, was of no consolation to her six crew members; all of them lost their lives in the attack that sent her to the bottom. Joining her was the Royal Navy minesweeper HMT *Tilbury Ness*, also a victim of the same dive-bomber attack.

Alerted by the CH radar stations at Dover and Dunkirk (near Canterbury), RAF Fighter Command had managed to get the Spitfires of 74 and 92 Squadron up in good time to intercept the incoming raid, although the Stukas were ably escorted by the Me 109s of JG26 – amongst their number the notable Luftwaffe aces Adolf Galland and Gerhard Schöpfel, with both pilots adding to their scores that day; Galland claiming a 74 Squadron Spitfire and Schöpfel shooting down a 92 Squadron aircraft. The latter may well have been the Spitfire flown by an Australian pilot, Fg Off Maurice Kinder. Wounded, and having lost a good deal of blood, Kinder managed to get his Spitfire down beside the Canterbury to Ramsgate road where he promptly lost consciousness. Found by soldiers from his home country, the Australian squaddies thought the blood-soaked pilot to be dead and promptly set about taking his helmet, gloves and buttons as souvenirs! After the robbing of the bodies of Linse and Messerschmidt in August, there was clearly no differentiation to be shown between friend and foe when it came to taking souvenirs. The soldiers, however, were considerably startled when Kinder came to and began to swear at them with some gusto. Later, he completed his obligatory combat report for the sortie and entered a claim for two Ju87s destroyed.

In fact, III./StG1 lost only one Stuka that day and this was W.Nr 5227 (6G+KS) flown by Gefr Werner Karach with his radio operator Gefr Max Aulehner. Karach was missing, presumed dead, whilst his luckier crew-man was thrown clear and rescued, unhurt, by a MTB. This aircraft, it is suggested, was actually shot down by AA fire although in the confusion of battle it is entirely likely that Kinder may have been the victor. In recent years, the dredging of the Thames channel near The Oaze for the Thames Gateway project has resulted in the recovery of a Junkers Jumo 211 engine, and this may well have originated from Stuka 6G+KS. Reports of another dive-bombing attack that day are also suggested, with the loss of another naval trawler, HMT *Torbay II*, reported in The Downs area of the English Channel near Dover as being attributed to

The engagement on 7 November was later the dramatic subject of a painting by renowned aviation artist Mark Postlethwaite.

'dive-bombing'. Also covering the Stukas on this operation was the *entire* Geschwader of JG53, and whilst this vast mass of Me 109s reported no tangible results their very presence must have aided in the Stukas' ability to get on with their job and in preventing or discouraging RAF fighters to get to the dive bombers more successfully.

Partly due to the weather being unsuitable for Stuka operations, and partly due to the lack of suitable shipping targets, there was a lull of almost a full week until the dive bombers returned to the Channel once more on 7 November. This time, it was the turn of aircraft of I./StG3 to attack another convoy assembling in the Thames Estuary off Southend with the formation of fifteen or so Stukas escorted by large phalanxes of Me 109s as was now usual. The Hurricanes of 249 Squadron had been scrambled from North Weald, but the controller had sent them to a much higher altitude before realising that the raiders were considerably lower. Seeing aircraft below, the squadron went down into a screaming dive reaching speeds of around 400mph as

they did so. As they burst through the bottom of hazy cloud they found themselves hurtling through the gaggle of Stukas, surprising both Luftwaffe and RAF pilots alike. As Plt Off Tom 'Ginger' Neil (*right*) recalled: "The first thing I saw was a big fat Stuka surging towards me at an unseemly rate. Backwards!"

So fast had been Neil's encounter with the Stuka, that as he approached it from astern and at high speed it had seemed for all the world as if the aircraft was flying backwards towards him. Flashing past, the three airmen exchanged momentary surprised glances with each other before both aircraft were lost in the whirling melee of a dogfight that had suddenly developed. Down below, the naval escort vessel HMS *Egret* was blazing away with seemingly every gun that she had, resulting in one Stuka being claimed by her AA fire. In the short sharp dogfight that followed, Neil claimed two Me 109s and a Junkers 87 as destroyed. However, the two Stukas that were claimed as destroyed in this action were apparently rather optimistic claims since only one aircraft was hit and damaged, this being a 1 Staffel machine flown by Lt Eberhard Morgenroth. This pilot managed to struggle home with a serious wound to his heel, his radio operator unharmed. On the German 'claim' side, one merchant vessel, the SS *Astrologer*, was hit. Although damaged the *Astrologer* wasn't sunk, but because of her condition there was no other option than to beach the vessel nearby. She was eventually wrecked in a storm that managed to finish off the Stuka's work on 15 November.

The day after Tom Neil's rather alarming encounter with the Stuka, the dive bombers were again back over the Thames Estuary. This time, the raiding force comprised two formations of around forty dive bombers with machines from (St)/LG1, I./StG3 and III./StG1, all of them accompanied by the usual fighter 'umbrella'. The latter Stuka unit, of course, saw Helmut Mahlke back in action again and he claimed a 6,000 ton ship as hit. In fact, the only merchant vessels that were damaged were the SS *Fireglow* and the SS *Catford*, but neither of them were sunk. Additionally, neither vessel was anywhere near to 6,000 tons although the escort destroyer HMS *Winchester* was hit and damaged in the attack and it may have been this ship that Mahlke claimed to have struck. On this occasion, the Hurricanes of 17 Squadron were able to get amongst the raiders in timely fashion in order to wreak their havoc and in the ensuing battle the squadron made a massive claim of fifteen Stukas destroyed, six probably destroyed and two damaged. These claims, however, were very far from reality with the true figure being three Stukas shot down. One was damaged in the fuel system during the engagement, but managed to limp back for a forced-landing near Dunkirk.

Meanwhile the Hurricanes of 46 and 249 Squadron had taken on the escorting fighters from JG51 and thereby allowed 17 Squadron to go about its Stuka-killing business relatively unhindered by the Me 109s. Given the fact that so few ships were hit and none of them sunk, it was almost certainly the case that the pilots of 17 Squadron had managed sufficiently to disrupt the Stukas in their intent to render such bombing as was carried out to be either ineffective or inaccurate. Even if they didn't shoot down as many as they had thought, 17 Squadron had given good service in its protection of the convoy. As Helmut Mahlke put it:

"On that occasion, the RAF fighters really were a very big problem for us. They had got amongst us and were buzzing around like angry wasps. Well, I suppose we were stirring up their nest! It really was difficult to select a target and concentrate on the task we had to do. However, my unit came home that day without loss."

Again, the entire Geschwader of JG53's Me 109s were also engaged on this Stuka escort and the low loss rate amongst the Ju87s must have been more about the effectiveness of the huge protective shield of fighters than it was about the RAF fighter pilots' inability to shoot the dive bombers down.

Three days later, Mahlke again led his Stukas back to the now familiar Thames Estuary. It was here, of course, that all of the eastbound (CE) and westbound (CW) Channel convoys assembled or dispersed and very often there would be ships assembling and riding at anchor for days, just offshore at Southend. Consequently, the Stuka boys knew that this would be a good hunting ground and hence their repeated visits. On 11 November, ships were already assembling early for the next CW run which would depart, weather permitting, on the 17th. Whilst there was clearly good sense in sailing these ships in convoy for better protection they were potentially vulnerable as they assembled, in plain view, and exactly where Luftwaffe reconnaissance aircraft knew where to look for them. Thus it was that, on the morning of the 11th, a snooping recce aircraft saw the assembling ships and Mahlke's III./StG1 were tasked with yet another shipping strike. The Stukas were now very much back in the fight.

By late morning, Mahlke's entire Gruppe was headed for the estuary. This time, a *Frei Jagd* of Me 109s had swept ahead – engaging the Hurricanes of 253 and 605 Squadron – along with a fighter bomber strike on London. The German hope, generally, was that squadrons that had engaged the free-hunting '109s would be back on the ground re-fuelling and re-arming and thus be unable to counter raids that were scheduled to come in whilst those squadrons were on the ground. RAF fighter controllers were, of course, aware of these dangers and careful husbandry generally ensured that there were more than enough fighters ready to go up to meet what followed. Such was certainly the case as the Stuka formation droned towards North Foreland and the River Thames that morning. However, when the 11 Group controller put up 17, 64, 257, and 603 Squadrons he must have seen that the size of the force warranted a hefty response. In fact, there was a vast armada of protective cover this day; JG3, JG51, JG53 and JG54 all contributing to the escort.

Once again, 17 Squadron managed to plunge into the Stuka formation, no doubt confident of the outcome after the success of their similar engagement with Ju87s just a few days prior. Perhaps *over* confident was Plt Off Dennis Wissler who dived down through the Stukas and was presumably hit by their defensive cross-fire. He was never seen again. For once, though, the over claiming was a little less extreme with two Ju87s of III Gruppe being lost; one from 7 Staffel and the other from 9 Staffel against four claimed as destroyed. On the negative side for the Stukas, they had achieved no success against the merchant shipping they had come to sink – but still this supposedly 'withdrawn from battle' asset of the Junkers 87 Stuka would be back for more. However, the operation flown on 14 November would prove to be the last Stuka mission flown in any force against the British Isles. Once more, Helmut Mahlke led it:

"The last mission of this era was bound to be a fiasco from the very start and although our escort fighters met us and flew with us across the English Channel, things soon started to go very wrong. First, we had been sent out to attack shipping that had been reported in the Dover Strait area; a convoy, in fact. When we got there, there were no ships to be seen. [Note: Convoy CE 16 was passing through the Channel at that time and due to arrive off Southend later that day. However, visibility was poor and down to about three to four miles and this was probably the reason why Mahlke's Stukas could not find the ships; Author.] However, and although that was annoying, we did have a secondary target. This was to be the Dover radar station. So, as we flew down the coast towards Dover, and as we had seen no ships, we had to prepare for the attack on the big pylons. Then, getting close to Dover, our fighter escort left us because the Me 109 pilots did not want to get caught in the Dover flak barrage and they stood off some distance from us. This wasn't helpful, and we were soon in a really disastrously exposed and dangerous position."

This was certainly Mahlke's situation. Emerging from the murky visibility, he could see the approaching specks that were growing ever bigger as they raced towards his formation of forty-odd Stukas; RAF fighters. Meanwhile, his protective escorts had exited stage-left and were now loitering off in the distance – both out of reach of the anti-aircraft guns and unable to come to the immediate aid of the Stukas, or, and perhaps more importantly, to provide the close cover protection that was essential. Worse for Mahlke, if his distant escorts had not seen the incoming fighter threat, there was absolutely nothing he could do to alert the Me 109s. "We could talk to each other, Stuka to Stuka", explained Mahlke "…but we were completely unable to communicate by radio with our escorts. Our radio frequencies were set up differently."

The incoming specks, now rapidly closing on III./StG1, were the Spitfires of 66 and 74 Squadron who were quickly amongst the Stukas. Although the escorting Messerschmitts did eventually get through to the RAF fighters, it was far too late to avoid the mayhem that a couple of dozen Spitfires were causing in the dive-bombing formation. At once, the Stuka pilots became intent on avoiding attack (or even collision) and although the masts of the CH radar station were now in sight there could be no hope of setting the formation up into position for attack and it quickly became every man for himself – British and German! Some of the Stukas, though, did manage to attack Dover Harbour and although the results were far from dramatic HM Drifter *Shipmates* was sunk and the vessels *Lord Howe, Yorkshire Lass* and *Cirrus* were all hit and a number of port installations damaged. Other bombs were also dropped on a coastal gun battery, but this may have been more by accident than design.

From the combat reports of those Spitfire pilots involved it is clear that most of the pilots fired at at least one Stuka, and sometimes more. In the general confusion it is clear that many of these pilots fired at a Stuka and then saw it wobble out of formation, perhaps smoking, before they passed on to another one to shoot at. It is also clear that several pilots shot at the same two Stukas that *did* eventually go down, but the multiple claims for Junkers 87s definitely destroyed proved to be yet another classic case of over-scoring in engagements such as these and in this single battle 66 Squadron claimed two destroyed with three unconfirmed and three damaged whilst 74 Squadron claimed an astonishing fourteen destroyed, two unconfirmed and three damaged. In fact, there were only two Stukas lost in that action but in confirmation of the engagement's ferocity, Mahlke's recall in 1974 was that: "….all of my unit bar one aircraft went home with hits that day. I think the most hits we counted on one aircraft was eighty-two. The pilot who got home unscathed was one of my Staffelkapitäns, Oblt Schairer. He got away because he successfully out-manoeuvred very many attacks from the Spitfires."

Schairer may well have been the pilot twisting and turning away from the guns of 66 Squadron's Flt Sgt Matthew Cameron, who reported of his attack on one Stuka: "During this attack the aircraft did a very good barrel roll which I followed, but I had now expended all of my ammunition."

Aircraft were literally being flung about the sky in every direction, twisting and turning with guns blazing. And it was not just the guns of the aircraft that were blazing, either. From the ground, anti-aircraft guns were putting up an intense barrage such that Flt Sgt Cameron further noted: "The AA guns were an awful nuisance and were firing all the time the fight was in progress."

It would seem that the escorting Me 109s had good cause to be nervous about the Dover AA guns, and that concern was also reflected in the combat report of another 66 Squadron pilot, Plt Off 'Dizzy' Allen:

"I attacked the '87s from every conceivable angle, not always firing but endeavouring to split them up from their sections by frightening them – to say nothing of myself! During one of these alarming attacks I noticed one of my targets, a Ju87, smoke and break away. When the '87s began their attack [sic] on Dover I ceased my harassing attacks and followed him down. When at the bottom every light AA battery in Dover appeared to open fire on my

Pilots of 66 Squadron in the former Gravesend Flying Club clubhouse that had been commandeered by the squadron. The squadron were scrambled to deal with the Stuka raid in the Dover Strait area on 14 November 1940 ('Dizzy' Allen seated fourth from right).

Anti-aircraft batteries caused problems for both the attacking Stukas and defending RAF fighters on 14 November and resulted in the Me 109 fighter cover standing off some distance from the Dover barrage and thus too far from their charges to be readily on hand. From the RAF fighter pilots, there were complaints that the AA fire seriously impeded their ability to deal with the Stukas.

target. I was within 500 yards of it and most of the fire appeared to burst in my immediate vicinity which probably caused the pilot of the Ju87 less anxiety than it caused me."

Allen then goes on to describe how he later watched as flame appeared in the port wing of 'his' Stuka and then spread rapidly before it "....crashed into the sea with considerable violence in the region of the Goodwin Sands".

Ever the wag, 'Dizzy' Allen also wrote to the author in 1981 of this event:

"I imagine that I was about the only target that AA Command hit during the whole of the war. They hit me on 14 November 1940 when a gaggle of Stukas bombed Dover, but apart from puncturing my leg they didn't break any important pipes and things."

Less lucky was Plt Off William Armstrong of 74 Squadron. Details of his action that day were given in the operations record book:

"Plt Off Armstrong closed to attack on a Ju87 who immediately jettisoned his bombs. Rear gunner opened fire without effect. Closed to 200 yards and opened fire with a four-second burst which silenced the rear gunner. A further three-second burst was made at 100 yards and pieces were seen to break away from enemy aircraft. Aircraft then flicked over suddenly and fell vertically towards the sea. He then attacked a second Ju87 opening fire at 200 yards closing right in and observed his fire going into the aircraft which also dived towards the sea. He could not follow it down because of a heavy AA barrage from the coast."

Climbing to re-join the squadron, there was suddenly a loud explosion in his engine and flames poured from the exhaust manifolds. Almost certainly he had been hit by AA fire. Forced to bale out, Armstrong landed safely but his Spitfire (P7386) buried itself deep into the ground on impact at Bellers Bush Farm, Sandwich.

Singly, or else in straggling groups, Mahlke's battered Stukas made it back across the Channel, low on the water, and as fast as they could go. Later, he reflected on that rather disastrous and chaotic mission:

"I think this event was good evidence of the quality of the Junkers 87 as well as the poor quality of senior leadership. The officer who commanded this whole mission knew much about fighter tactics, but less or very little about Stukas. I think it was the first time such an operation had been ordered and planned by a fighter leader, but it was a complete failure. The officer concerned was removed from his post the next day."

One of the two Junkers 87s that had been sent crashing into the Channel had been a 9th Staffel machine flown by Oblt Otto Blumers and his radio operator Gefr Willy Koch. Fished out of the Channel, Blumers was taken POW and the RAF intelligence report on his interrogation gives us a contemporary perspective:

"In the afternoon six aircraft from his Staffel took off and flew north-westwards to join about fourteen other Ju87s and a strong fighter escort. They flew across the Channel to the North Foreland, and then along the coast to Dover at a height of about 10,000ft.
    "When approaching Dover, and before having made any attack, the formation was

Although the photo of this massed formation of thirty Ju87s of III./StG77 was taken in the Crimea during 1941 it is, nevertheless, typical of the large formations deployed against British targets in 1940.

intercepted by about twenty Spitfires who were flying straight towards them. The Spitfires did not attack immediately, but circled round and delivered their attacks from the rear. The second burst of machine-gun fire set his aircraft on fire and he baled out and landed in the water, being picked up by MTB and taken into Dover. The wireless operator, whom he left to his fate, is presumed to have been killed in the crash."

It was a somewhat ignominious end to massed Stuka operations against the British Isles, but it was one that had been hastened by deteriorating weather and shortening daylight hours rather than any factors arising out of operations like the one on 14 November. For the time being the Stukas stood ready and waiting for targets of opportunity that might arise from the Channel passage of CE and CW convoys. On 29 November, 1940, a reconnaissance Messerschmitt 110 of Stab./StG1 (Stukageschwader 1's staff flight) was out in the Dover Strait at around 10.00 hours, no doubt looking for Convoy CE 18 which had sailed from Southend earlier that morning and which would make an excellent target for StG1's Stukas. The III Gruppe, reported Mahlke, had made good its losses and repaired all damage so as to declare itself combat ready just a few days after the mauling of 14 November. Unfortunately for the crew of the Me 110, though, they ran slap-bang into eleven Spitfires of 603 Squadron up from RAF Hornchurch.

Ordered to patrol Ramsgate, the squadron had climbed rapidly over Kent but one of their number, Plt Off William Rafter, had inexplicably dived out of formation enroute and was killed when his Spitfire crashed at Kingswood, Kent. East of Ramsgate, and finding the solitary Me 110, the Spitfire pilots lined up for something of a turkey shoot. Against such unequal odds, the Me 110 was overwhelmed and the RAF pilots had their revenge for the loss of Rafter when they sent the Messerschmitt slamming into the sea in a wall of white spray. Oblt Pytlik and Oblt Fryer had stood no chance[13]. Both of them were killed before any information as to the position and course of CE 18 could be got to the waiting Stukas. As Mahlke recalled: "We waited and waited, but it soon became clear that it was hopeless. And so our planned operation was stood down." And yet, despite everything, it wasn't quite the event that brought down the final curtain on Stuka operations against Britain.

As the Stukas had struggled back home during that late afternoon of 14 November, crews at Luftwaffe bomber bases across France and Belgium were busying themselves for a mission that night which would become one of the most notorious raids of the Blitz; the attack on Coventry. Whilst that operation, per se, has no particular relevance to the Stuka story it points up the fact that the night Blitz was now the Luftwaffe's primary concern in terms of attacks against Britain. For now, the Stukas had no real work to do on the Channel front and they didn't appear over Britain again during 1940.

By January 1941 the night Blitz was continuing with almost unabated vigour and on the night of Wednesday 15/16 January the Stuka, incredibly, was instructed to join the night attacks on London.

That night, two aircraft of StG1 were tasked with a dive-bombing attack on London and another targeted against the port of Dover. It was an extraordinary measure. The aircraft, heavily laden with a single 1,000kg bomb (a much heavier single bomb than had ever been carried by the Stuka during the summer and autumn operations) and with their pale blue undersides re-painted matt black, dive-bombed the capital at around 00.23 operating at an altitude of 4,500 metres and diving to release at 2,000 metres. These altitudes, or certainly the release altitudes, were much higher than the normal daylight operational heights although probably for good reason. Diving in complete darkness and against a blacked-out city was a hazardous occupation by any standards and the margin of safety for the pull-out was necessarily much greater. The crews, though, were doubtless aided by sprinklings of snow that had settled across London under a full moon. If night dive-bombing operations were to be conducted by the Stuka, these were perhaps the optimum conditions for doing so. One of the bombs that night had been directed at Deptford and the other on Kidbrooke, with hits reported on large blocks of buildings at both locations. At Dover, the bomb-release height for the Stuka was a much lower 800 metres but the crew were unable to see any results due to being far too busy avoiding the harbour's barrage balloon defences.

The Stuka night-bombing 'experiment' was repeated again on the nights of 17/18 January and 19/20 January. On the first occasion, three Stukas were sent out with one bombing

13 The body of Pytlik was washed ashore at Shakespeare Cliff, Dover, on 21 January 1941. No trace was ever found of Fryer.

Woolwich, one West Ham and another targeting Croydon Airport. At Woolwich, the large explosion would surely have been heard at The Royal Herbert Hospital where there was a dedicated ward for injured Luftwaffe POWs. Amongst their number were a few Stuka men who could not have imagined that the nocturnal bombing that rattled their windows had been carried

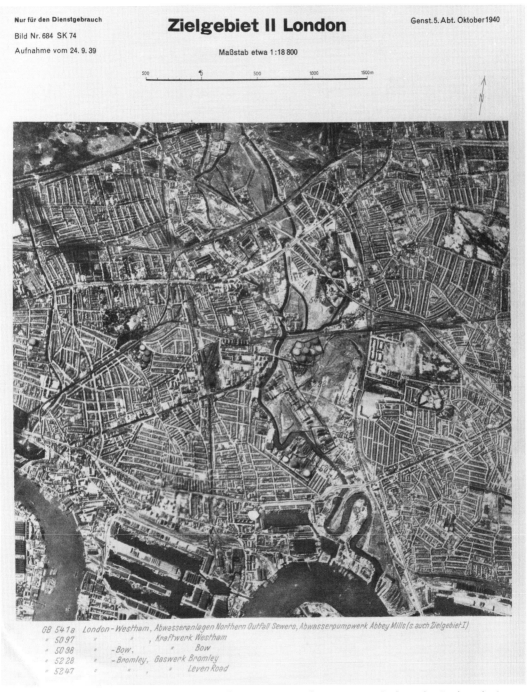

Incredibly, a few experimental night attacks against London were carried out by Stukas during the winter of 1940/1941 with West Ham being one of the targets. This is a Luftwaffe target photograph of the area.

out by a Junkers 87! On the second occasion, Greenwich and central London were in the dive bombers' sights. Again, 1,000kg bombs were delivered during all of these raids although the results are unclear. Certainly, it had been a departure from 'normal' Stuka operations.

By February 1941 Stuka operations against targets in the British Isles or its coastal waters were drawing to a close and it was almost symptomatic of the decline in these Ju87 operations that these last sorties were flown by singletons or very small groups. The first of the February attacks was carried out on the 5th and the second on the night of 11/12th. The operation flown on 5 February was an unescorted single sortie by a Kette of three aircraft of 2./StG1 that was engaged by four Spitfires of 92 Squadron, airborne from RAF Manston on convoy patrol. Although the 92 Squadron pilots assumed there was just a single attacker involved there were in fact three.

Plt Off R. Fokes, Plt Off C.H. Saunders, Sgt H. Bowen-Morris and Sgt C.A. Ream had taken off at 08.45 for patrol and were near Ramsgate at about 09.45 when Red 2 (Saunders) spotted an explosion on one of the ships below. At first, the pilots thought the vessel must have struck a mine but as they went down to have a look they met a Ju87 approaching them at 5,000ft. Fokes attacked him head-on, as did Saunders, but the Stuka twisted and turned as it tried to get away and the pursuit turned into a dogfight as each of the Spitfire pilots followed the hapless dive bomber, each of them jockeying to get into firing position as the five aircraft snaked around the sky. Eventually, the four pilots drove the pilot over land and Fokes managed to get a beam shot into the aircraft just as he turned, causing the Stuka to blow up and crash. Coincidentally, this was right over 92 Squadron's base at Manston where the CO, Sqn Ldr 'Johnny' Kent, was on hand to witness a squadron 'kill' shared by four of his pilots:

"Having been on the first patrol of the morning, I had been back to the Mess for breakfast and was just returning to dispersal when I heard gunfire. I stopped the car and got out to stare in amazement at the sight of one lone Stuka weaving madly in an attempt to avoid the attention of four Spitfires. All five were coming towards me and it occurred to me that I was in the line of fire so I hid behind a vehicle that was handy. Then I saw a notice on it reading *100 Octane* – it was one of the refuelling bowsers. So I darted back to my car! Just as I made it the Stuka reached the edge of the airfield almost directly above me at about a hundred feet. Here he was headed off by one of the Spitfires and I could clearly see both gunner and pilot in their cockpits with the De Wilde ammunition bursting around them. The Spitfire overshot and pulled away and the German made another desperate attempt to land and turned violently to port but at this instant Plt Off Fokes, in my aeroplane, flashed past me and gave a short burst with the cannons. I can still hear the 'thump-thump-thump' of them followed by the terrific 'whoosh' as the Stuka blew up and crashed just outside the boundary of the airfield."

The aircraft had been W.Nr 5225, J9+BK, flown by Lt Ernst Schimmelpfennig with his radio operator Ogefr Hans Kaden, both men being killed as the Stuka exploded into the ground at Cheeseman's Farm, Minster. The other two Stukas escaped unharmed and unseen by the four pilots of 92 Squadron.

The ship that the pilots had seen blow up was HMT *Tourmaline* engaged on CE convoy escort duty and her loss would be the last suffered by a British vessel in British waters to Stukas. Allan Waller, then a temporary midshipman, was on board *Tourmaline* when she was hit:

"Dawn broke. It was still fine and clear and the Kent coast was clearly visible in the area of the South Foreland and Deal. Three Spitfires arrived to give air cover and there was some

On 5 February 1941 this Junkers 87 of 2./StG1 became the last Stuka to fall on British soil when it was shot down by Spitfire pilots of 92 Squadron near RAF Manston. Here, the victorious pilots inspect their 'kill'.

HMT *Tourmaline*, an anti-submarine trawler.

broken cloud with a base of probably 3,000ft.

"I was at my action stations with the point-fives and we had all been at action stations almost continuously since sailing the previous afternoon. By ten o'clock we were off the North Foreland. Not far to go! Then, there was the unmistakeable scream of a Stuka dive bomber diving out of the cloud about half a mile ahead of us, the bombs were dropped but missed their target, a merchant ship. The aircraft levelled off and flew quite close to us down the port side and we gave it a short burst probably shooting off part of its tail fin. The three Spitfires fell upon it, shooting it down on the coast. Above us was an almost completely round break in the cloud with the blue sky above it. I thought this was a likely place for a Stuka to dive through and had the guns trained towards it. I was right. About a minute later a Stuka dived through and right aft over *Tourmaline*. We lined it up on the cartwheel sights absolutely according to the drillbook. Fire was opened, and after a short burst both barrels jammed. Bad ammunition! I saw the bombs leave the Stuka and remember saying 'They've missed!' I was wrong. *Tourmaline* was hit a few feet aft of the funnel, almost on the centreline. As the boats were not badly damaged, the blast must have gone directly upwards.

"There was a dark grey choking cloud. I couldn't see and my right ankle hurt. I was on the deck below the gun zareba and groped and found the rung of a ladder. I climbed up and the gun appeared to be off its mounting. Part of the metal side had gone, and there was no sign of my two companions. Smoke and steam were roaring out the top of the engine casing and 'Number One' was casting off the Carley Float on the port side. I am not clear what happened in the next few minutes but have a vague recollection of going along the deck passing a bunker hatch from which smoke and steam were pouring. I found myself on deck in the waist, amidships and ahead of the bridge structure.

"The captain shouted 'Abandon ship!' I could see a red and white life buoy against the ship's side and started to crawl towards it when the captain shouted: 'Put the midshipman in the boat!' My next recollection was being in the bottom of the boat with the steward at the helm and two or three members of crew pulling at the oars. They told me they were looking for my gun crew who had been blown over the side. They were found already being picked up by the *Mastadonte*. Meanwhile, game to the last, *Tourmaline* had gone down upright and on an even keel allowing all the surviving members of crew[14] to get away quite easily. She had taken about ten minutes to sink."

The very first Royal Navy ship to be sunk in British waters by Stuka, HMS *Foylebank*, had seen the award of a Victoria Cross to Seaman Jack Mantle and when the *Tourmaline* was sunk it saw further bravery and fortitude in the face of Stuka attack. And only a matter of a few days before her sinking, *Tourmaline* had been involved in an encounter with an E-Boat off Hopton on Sea on 23 January 1941 which saw an award of the DSC to Lt Henry Carse, a DSM to Ldg Sm Stanley Taylor and Sm Frederick Swinton and a Mention in Despatches to Temp Midshipman Allan Waller and Sm David Wilson. It almost seemed as if the *Tourmaline* incident and the shooting down of Schimmelpfennig's Stuka was somehow symbolic of the perceived 'defeat' of the Junkers 87 over Britain by RAF Fighter Command in 1940, coming as it did on the very edge of a Fighter Command airfield and, coincidentally, with the sinking of the last vessel by Stuka in British waters.

14 Chief Engineman Roseveare and a stoker were killed outright in the engine room. Stoker Holroyd was very badly scalded. Waller and his gun crew were all injured and two of them also suffered from exposure through being thrown into the icy cold English Channel.

There were, however, just a few more ineffectual Stuka night operations and one more Stuka loss. The latter again involved StG1 which sent a group of 5 Staffel aircraft against the naval base at Chatham during the full moon of the night of 10/11 February during which the Royal Navy were able to avenge the loss of *Tourmaline*.

That night, HM Drifter *Eager* was going about her patrol duties in the Thames Estuary when she came under attack by a Stuka at around 04.00, the aircraft dropping bombs from around 400 to 500ft which fell into the sea off her port quarter. At once, *Eager* engaged the raider with her two Lewis guns, a Holman Projector and two rifles with "many hits being scored". To the surprise of the crew, the Stuka blew up in mid-air with considerable violence and fell into the sea fifty yards from the vessel and it is recorded that Skipper G.A. Good, RNR, was in the process of salvaging debris from the first Stuka when they were attacked by a second. This aircraft also dropped further bombs on the *Eager*'s port quarter, and although she was also engaged by the same weaponry and hits were observed, the Stuka flew off eastwards. During this second

Stukas of III./StG77, so recently deployed in the Battle of Britain, now stand ready for operations eastward from a Balkan airfield.

Dummy Ju87s on airfields recently vacated by the aircraft make it appear that it was 'business as usual'.

attack L Cpl E. Bowles (recorded as being from 12th Command) was seriously wounded and later taken ashore at Clacton. Later, in a signal to Flag Officer Harwich, it was recommended that Seaman William Loftus be considered for decoration or award for "....good shooting and coolness in holding his fire until the enemy 'plane was in a vulnerable position, this being undoubtedly responsible for the destruction of the Junkers." Yet again, then, we find another example of coolness and bravery in the face of attack by a Stuka and it was apparently the marksmanship of Loftus that resulted in the loss of the Junkers 87 that had carried Fw K. von Cramm and Uff P. Trager to their deaths. The next night, another StG1 aircraft of 9 Staffel (J9+LL) was lost in the Thames Estuary to unknown causes resulting in the deaths of Fw F. Lewandowski and Uffz L. Rener.

Before the spring of 1941, the Stukas were being largely withdrawn from France and Belgium in readiness for new objectives in the Mediterranean and eastwards against the Soviet Union. In attempts to cover the re-location of the Stuka force towards new fronts, dummy Stukas constructed from wood and canvas were placed at the airfields now being vacated by the Junkers 87s. They looked convincing enough from the air, and perhaps the absolute last gasp of Stuka

operations helped in some small way to bolster that illusion when a few isolated Stuka night-bombing raids were carried out in mid-September and early October 1941 against Dover, Margate and Ramsgate. By the end of that autumn, however, both Hellfire Corner and the British Isles at large had seen the very last of the Junkers 87 Stuka.

Although the use of the Stuka against the British mainland had come to an end, the scourge of the Junkers 87 dive bomber would continue to beset British forces in North Africa and the Mediterranean and the aircraft would also continue to operate, albeit in upgraded versions, until the very end of the war. During that time its fame and reputation would never diminish, nor would the exploits of those who flew it lessen. Indeed, one of the most highly decorated pilots of the war was Major Hans-Ulrich Rudel (*right*) who famously survived 2,530 combat flights, an all-time record. During that period, and operating solely on the Eastern Front, he was credited with knocking out 500 Soviet tanks. Captured by the Allies at the war's end he was brought, briefly, to RAF Tangmere as POW during the June of 1945 to be interviewed at the RAF Fighter Leaders' School. As he looked about him at the battered station, Rudel would have seen the still evident scars of war that had been caused by the visiting Stukas on 16 August 1940. He was almost certainly unaware as to exactly how such extensive bomb damage had been caused. It was surely a moment of supreme irony.

CHAPTER 14
In Retrospect: The Stuka's Role in The Battle of Britain

T HE STUKA OFFENSIVE AGAINST THE British Isles during 1940 had not really taken a particularly heavy loss rate up until 16 August, and, as we have seen, some attacks had got through entirely unhindered or without sustaining a single loss. In the attacks on shipping in the Channel up until 8 August 1940, the Stuka had also shown its worth and taken a heavy toll on the ships singled out for attention. The attacks on 16 August, and then again two days later, resulted in a rather different outcome for the Stuka force with losses that were certainly significant. The 18 August raid, for example, saw a total of 109 Stukas committed against south coast targets and was the largest co-ordinated attack ever mounted by the Junkers 87 dive bomber. The preceding chapters tell the story of that attack – a raid in which the Stuka force lost 21% of its aircraft destroyed or damaged. In the raid against Thorney Island, for example, ten of the Stukas were shot down, one returned damaged beyond repair and four others had returned with serious damage. Amongst those shot down and killed had been the Gruppe commander, and the three other Gruppen had lost six aircraft and had two others damaged between them. It had been the first real setback for the Stuka force since they were thrown into battle over Poland during September 1939. Without a doubt the losses were too heavy to be accepted just as a matter of course.

Whilst it is certainly the case that after 18 August, 1940, there were no significant Stuka operations against the British Isles during the Battle of Britain, the question needs to be asked; were they actually withdrawn from service because of 'unacceptable losses' as has been suggested across subsequent decades? In considering the cessation of Junkers 87 operations against Britain during the summer of 1940, it is necessary to look at the bigger picture of what had been happening in the focus of Luftwaffe air attacks against the country. First, though, it may be apposite to look at how the official narrative of the Battle of Britain, produced by the Air Historical Branch in the immediate post-war period, had perceived the part played in the battle by the Junkers 87. The heading of that particular commentary was nothing if not direct in its judgement:

"The Failure of the Junkers 87
There is certainly no doubt that the Germans were convinced by the operations during the first half of August that Ju87s could not be used where they would meet fighter opposition. After 18 August they were withdrawn from the battle, the intention being to use them against Channel shipping when an invasion expedition was launched. This accounts for the concentration of dive bombers in the Pas de Calais during the first days of September and their complete inactivity during that and the following months."

Junkers 87 aircraft of Stuka Geschwader 77 hidden under trees during the Battle of Britain, France 1940.

In its assessment of why the Junkers 87 force had been concentrated in the Pas de Calais, the Air Historical Branch historians had certainly got it right. But their perception as to why the Germans had failed to use the Stuka in attacks against Britain after 18 August may have been a little skewed. The dismissal, here, of the Ju87 as a 'failure', and the suggestion that its withdrawal was purely based upon that premise, is doubtless the origin of the long held belief that the decision was purely attrition based. It is necessary to look a little deeper into the background of that draw-down of usage, and also to understand the evolving German strategy in air attacks against Britain.

The sustained Stuka assault against shipping targets in the English Channel that had gained momentum in early July leading up to 8 August 1940 had also shown the value of the dive bombers, and it had also taken a very heavy toll on the ships singled out for attention. These shipping attacks had tailed off by the end of the first week in August in pursuit of the fresh German objective to "…eliminate the Royal Air Force both as a fighting force and in its ground organisation". These aims had been set out clearly in Adolf Hitler's Directive No.17 issued on 1 August 1940; namely, attacks against flying units and their ground installations. It was primarily in pursuance of that aim that the Stuka force was directed away from shipping in the Channel and towards land-based RAF targets.

Certainly, the shock to the Stuka force in 1940 occasioned by the mid-August losses must have caused a re-evaluation of how they were employed and of their vulnerability against defending fighters, but it cannot really be said that their lack of use over Britain post 18 August was the result of unacceptable losses. In fact, if we look at the total number of Junkers 87 losses during the Battle of Britain up to and including 18 August we see that just fifty-two were actually destroyed during that period and if we take the unit to have suffered the greatest losses (StG77)

The Stuka was an aircraft that could often take exceptionally heavy punishment and still get back. This is an example of damage to one such Junkers 87 that still brought its crew safely home.

it is interesting to note that all aircraft, and their crews, had been fully replaced to that unit within a week. Additionally, if the losses had been so catastrophically unacceptable one might have expected at least some units to have been stood down or, at least, subsumed into other formations. None were. Instead, their sudden disappearance from the war-torn skies of southern England probably had more to do with a further shift in emphasis of the German war aims and the impending invasion of Britain, Operation Sealion, than with anything else.

For the most part, the Stuka force had been committed against airfields and RAF targets situated directly along the south coast and with the exception of the Detling attack had not ventured very far inland, with those airfields situated further away from the coast being assigned as targets to the conventional bomber force. Although the Stuka force had the range it was former Oblt Johannes Wilhelm of StG77 who explained to the author something of the Luftwaffe reasoning behind Ju87 target allocation, some of the geographic considerations thereof and his view as to the supposed withdrawal from operations of the Ju87 due to excessive losses.

"Our dive bombers required the close escort of Me 109 fighters, and flying as we were across the widest part of the Channel the operational endurance of the Me 109 was pretty much at its limit once we reached the English coast. This range problem of the Me 109

Bombs on Dover; smoke and violent explosions during one of the Stuka attacks on the port in 1940. The last such daylight attack on the port by Stukas took place on 14 November 1940.

escorts had been exacerbated by their need to constantly weave and zig-zag across our formations in order to stay with our slower aircraft, and this had further increased their fuel consumption. So, they were at the extreme range of their usefulness once we had reached the Sussex coast or the Isle of Wight. We could not have had effective fighter cover further inland and the Me 110, which *did* have the range, was as good as useless for escorting the Stukas as it pretty much needed its own fighter cover! In any case, because of our relative low speed and perceived vulnerability, I think there was a resistance by our staff officers to take our formations too far inland over enemy territory when the balance of air superiority still rested with the RAF. Best to go in hard on the coast and run away quickly; we only had to go into the hornet's nest briefly over the target area and get out again. We didn't have a long gauntlet to run on the way in, and mostly the British fighters left us alone once we got further away from the coast.

"It was certainly the case that by the end of the day that I was actually shot down (18 August 1940) the Stuka units operating from our part of France on the Cherbourg peninsula had fairly well exhausted all of the RAF targets that our high command had identified in our own particular operational sector [ie West Sussex and Solent area; Author] – and we had already been told that we were to be imminently moved east up into the Pas de Calais, anyway. The reason was obvious. We would be operating against Royal Navy ships in the Dover Strait area and against British defences on the ground as the invasion unfolded while our troops moved inland. I never heard from other POWs who later came into the prison camps that the Stukas had been pulled out of the battle as a direct result of the losses, and I don't think they ever were. Some of those who later joined me as guests of His Majesty were old Stuka colleagues who had later been captured over Malta, the Mediterranean or

North Africa and I don't remember that they ever mentioned any withdrawal on the Channel front in 1940 because of losses."

Here, then, is an informed insight into the real reasons behind the draw down of Stuka operations after 18 August 1940. A similar view about the actual impact of Stuka losses was shared during a 1983 conference at the US Army War College attended by Major Paul-Werner Hozzel of I./StG1. At this event, Professor John Stolfi of the US Navy Post-Graduate School, Monterey, California, in conversation with Hozzel put forward the view that whilst Stuka losses over Britain in 1940 were severe it was necessary to look at it statistically and "spread the thing out in time". In other words, he suggested, one should look at the Stuka losses in context with other German bomber types; for example, the Heinkel 111. Stolfi suggested that whilst there were no single attacks during which the He 111 suffered comparable grievous losses they ultimately lost just as many aircraft throughout the Battle of Britain. If not more. The same could be said of other bomber types. It was a proposition with which Hozzel did not disagree.

Although the allocation of targets to the Stuka force had often been flawed in terms of some of them being wrongly identified as of 'high value', the target list in the coastal belt had been steadily eroded as Johannes Wilhelm had intimated and whilst the conventional bomber forces continued with their actions against other RAF airfields even that strategy was about to shift. When the entire Stuka force was re-positioning itself in the Pas de Calais during late August, the Luftwaffe was about to embark upon the Blitz and the day and night attacks against London, major cities and industrial centres; an assault which commenced on 7 September 1940. Meanwhile, and far from being non-operational, the Stuka force stood primed and ready – but it was a force that would have been of little value against targets such as London, in any case. The Stuka was most certainly not the tool for that particular job, and thus the Junkers 87 units stood by waiting for the invasion and for the most part honed their skills by practicing against targets just off the French coast. There was, though, another factor in the draw down of Stuka operations by Fliegerkorps VIII and the transfer of the entire Stuka force to Luftflotte 2 in the Pas de Calais.

Clearly, and notwithstanding the successes on 4 July when RAF fighters failed to interfere with Stuka operations in the Channel, it was apparent to the Luftwaffe that the Junkers 87 was extremely vulnerable to fighter attack and needed close escort. This in itself was a problem in respect of the operations mounted from the area of the Cherbourg peninsula and across one of the widest parts of the English Channel against British land targets. And the problem, specifically, was the operational range of the Messerschmitt 109. As noted by Oblt Wilhelm, by the time the escort had crossed the Channel with their much slower charges, zig-zagging above them to both protect the Stukas and to stay with the much slower aircraft, their operational endurance once over the south coast was extremely limited. In fact, the Me 109s could really only fly with the Stukas to the target and then pretty much withdraw at once.

Certainly, if they were engaged by British fighters ahead of the target, or over it, the Me 109s would very quickly have to break off the engagement and run for home because of the limitations on their fuel. Additionally, the duration of a Stuka attack could be many minutes while individual Ju87s went down in their dives to deliver their bomb loads. This added period of time simply compounded the problem of the Me 109s not being able to loiter over the target area throughout the entire period an attack was in progress. Indeed Me 109s *could* be sent on ahead, or else other units of Me 109s sent out to cover the Stukas' withdrawal, but this did not fulfil the requirement for close and effective fighter escort over the target. Endurance, however, was not a problem for the much longer-range Me 110s although their unsuitability as a fighter matched against the RAF's Spitfires and Hurricanes had already become apparent.

The best the Me 110s could often hope to do was to draw off the defending RAF fighters, but the British pilots were well aware of the Me 110's limitations and, also, they were very much aware that the Stukas were their real target. Thus, it had become difficult if not nigh-on impossible to mount a wholly effective fighter escort screen for Junkers 87 operations against targets in West Sussex, Hampshire, The Isle of Wight and Dorset. To a very large extent, this had resulted in the losses experienced across 13, 16 and 18 August 1940. On the other hand, if Stuka formations could be taken to targets within easy range for the Me 109s, and with a sufficiently large and effective fighter escort, the outcome could well have been different.

When the Stuka force was relocated to the Pas de Calais it had already shown itself to be a potent weapon against shipping, and this would have thus presented the Royal Navy with a most dangerous challenge as its capital ships and destroyers were committed to wreaking their own havoc amongst the German invasion fleet. Against ships and fixed land-based targets, within easy range of adequate fighter cover, the Stuka would have theoretically been

Generalfeldmarschall Wolfram von Richthofen, commander in chief of VIII Fliegerkorps, under whose command fell the majority of Stuka units at the commencement of the Battle of Britain; some 280 Junkers 87 aircraft in total.

back in its element and operating in the specific role for which the weapon had been designed. However, by mid-September, Hitler had postponed Operation Sealion and the role of the Junkers 87 Stuka dive bomber against Britain was effectively over. In the air war over the British Isles the Stuka force was now redundant, but they would soon have work anew.

As we have seen, there had been a sporadic return to operations against shipping in the Channel over the winter of 1940/1941, and even a short-lived and rather pointless involvement in one or two night-bombing raids against British targets. But, to all intents and purposes, the Stuka's war against these islands had come to a natural conclusion and the Junkers 87 units were urgently prepared for operations in the east, against the Soviet Union, and in the Mediterranean and North African campaigns. Once again, the deadly nature of attack by Stuka became self-evident and notwithstanding its shortcomings, and often heavy losses, the dive-bomber force remained a potent weapon even in the face of determined fighter opposition.

As a precision weapon, the Junkers 87 was the only aircraft on either side during the first two years of the war that could deliver accurate bombing attacks against pinpoint targets, and therein lay the basis of the aircraft's fearsome reputation. Despite this, however, the Ju87 did have its weaknesses and these were very quickly identified and exploited by the RAF's fighter pilots. These weaknesses were also understood by the Luftwaffe, too, and the escorting fighters adapted their tactics accordingly in order to best protect their charges. At least, insofar as they were able to.

That said, protection by the Me 109 escorts could not adequately compensate for the main weakness of the Ju 87; the point when it pulled out of its dive. When they were in the dive, however, the Stuka was almost invulnerable to attack as Plt Off Frank Carey of 43 Squadron found out: "In the dive they were very difficult to hit[15], because in a fighter one's speed built up so rapidly that one went screaming past it. But it couldn't dive forever!"

Ideally, of course, the Stuka formations needed to be hit before they started their bomb-delivering dives but the Me 109 close escort could be a force to be reckoned with (or to at least be cautious about) on the run-in to target. On 18 August, for example, there were over 150 escorting Messerschmitts; more than one per Stuka! In their fighter-protection role to the Stuka, the Me 109s flew in a mass formation as top cover to the dive bombers on their approach to target, but the fighter formation then split with one half remaining with the Stukas at altitude whilst the others dived to around 3,000ft to protect the Ju87s when they pulled out of their dives. Thus, in theory, the higher formation could cover the Stukas' backs as they dived, ready to descend on any pursuing defenders and when the bombers had pulled out of their dives at around 1,000ft (often much less than that) the lower formation of Me 109s were already in position again to protect them from above.

On 18 August, though, the defenders managed to catch and shoot down at least four of the bombers before they commenced their dives. This was just at the point when the high level escort was at its weakest, simply because half their number had already split off to provide the low-level cover. It also seems likely that a good number of the single-engine fighter escorts had already turned for home, low on fuel, as discussed previously. Thus, they were either no longer present to interfere with the RAF fighters or else had insufficient fuel to remain long enough over England in order to do so.

Pulling out of their dives, the Stukas' tactic was to leave the target area in loose gaggles flying at cruising speed. If one of their number came under fighter attack the pilot simply opened his throttle and accelerated past the dive bombers in front, thus drawing his pursuer into the guns of the Stukas he had just overtaken. That, at least, was the theory. Meanwhile, of course, the covering fighters above might well be on the attacking fighters' tails, too. These, then, were some of the Stuka's weaknesses. But what of its strengths?

In terms of the land targets hit by Stukas during the Battle of Britain, the specific accuracy of the aircraft was clearly apparent and scarcely a bomb landed outside the immediate area surrounding each target. In many instances, targeted buildings had taken multiple direct hits and at Ford the airfield was put out of use for several weeks. Those at Thorney Island and Gosport had remained operational but with much reduced efficiency and the chain home radar station at Poling was out of action for some days. It had been a similar picture at RAF Tangmere, just two days previously, where there had been grievous damage, destruction of aircraft and loss of life. If any were needed, this was proof that a small load of bombs delivered accurately could have a far more devastating military effect than many times greater that weight of bombs dropped conventionally and with less precision. It was also a potent demonstration of the Stuka's awesome ability.

Worth recording, perhaps, that on completion of his training the Stuka pilot was expected to put at least half his bombs within a radius of twenty-five metres from the centre of the practice target. Little wonder that the targets hit by the Junkers 87 during the air campaign against Britain had fared so badly. On the other hand, it is also the case that many of the targets selected for the Stuka treatment represented an almost entirely wasted effort.

15 The diving speed of the Junkers 87 was 450kph, or 280mph.

In previous chapters we looked at the near futility of the attacks on Detling, Lympne and Gosport but these attacks were symptomatic of the Luftwaffe's repeated failure properly to understand the use or significance of specific airfields or other installations. Into the latter category, of course, fell the RAF chain home and chain home low radar sites and whilst these were singled out for attack they were rarely the target for Stukas. In fact, it fell to the Me 110s of ErpGr210 to dive-bomb the radar sites at Pevensey, Rye and Dunkirk (near Canterbury) and in each case significant damage was caused. Although the tall lattice towers were nigh-on impossible to topple, and none ever were, it was also the case that their open lattice work construction from which the aerial arrays were supported presented a very small area vulnerable to blast or bomb-splinter damage. Nevertheless, the attacks by the Me 110s on 12 August had shown the sites to be vulnerable to damage to vital infrastructure, including electricity supply etc. It is, however, entirely possible that the Germans failed to realise properly that any of these sites had ever been put off the air. With the towers and buildings remaining visibly intact after the bombing raids against them, the Luftwaffe may well have concluded that effort expended in further attacks would have been wasted. Nothing could have been further from the truth.

In fact, the attack by Stukas against the Poling radar site had shown that these sites could certainly be knocked out of action by the Ju87. Had there been repeat Stuka attacks against Poling and, say, the principal stations of Ventnor, Pevensey, Rye and Dunkirk then the outcome for the RAF could have been utterly disastrous. In effect, the RAF could have been 'blinded' in terms of its early warning capability and would have become wholly reliant on the Observer Corps. By the time even the observers on the extremities of the coast had sighted and reported incoming formations it would have allowed insufficient time to scramble RAF squadrons and get them to the requisite altitude and position to intercept the raiders. Without a doubt, and had the Luftwaffe spent its Stuka effort on these radar sites instead of on the abandoned Lympne, irrelevant Detling and insignificant Gosport, the outcome could have been different for the RAF. And for the Luftwaffe the losses sustained by the Stuka force in taking out these radar sites might well have been a sacrifice worth making.

In conclusion, it can be seen that there was no withdrawal of the Stuka force due to unacceptable losses and that their lack of use after 18 August 1940 was primarily due to other, misplaced, operational and strategic considerations. Between early July and mid-August 1940 the Junkers 87 Stuka had managed to achieve not inconsiderable results, especially considering that it was a tactical aircraft and had been employed to try to bring about a strategic objective. The Stuka had driven the Royal Navy's destroyer flotilla of Dover Command from its home port; the Stukas having effectively sunk or neutralised the destroyers that might have interfered with the invasion fleet. They had disrupted and wreaked considerable havoc amongst the east and westbound Channel convoys and they had forced the complete re-routing of Outbound Atlantic convoys from the Channel after the devastation caused by Ju87 attacks on Convoy OA178. Additionally, they had caused major damage to seven RAF airfields (albeit not all of them in Fighter Command) and had hit and disabled for a period three vital radar stations. All in all, the role of the Stuka during the Battle of Britain was not a completely unmitigated disaster. It was, perhaps, less the case that the Stuka was the 'failure' that the Air Historical Branch had declared and more the case that any 'failure' lay with how the Stuka was employed against Britain in 1940 as well as clear inadequacies in Luftwaffe intelligence assessments and the flawed target selection that was consequential upon those inadequacies.

APPENDIX I

Junkers 87 Versions in use during the Battle of Britain: Technical Specifications

The second version of the Ju87 to go into production, the 'Berta', would become the main production version of the aircraft during the early part of World War II. Fitted with a Jumo 211A engine developing 1,200hp for take-off, the 'Berta' was a considerable improvement over the Ju 87-A 'Anton': the cockpit was streamlined, 'spats' replaced the mainwheel 'trousers' and there were two 7.92mm machine guns firing forwards. The additional engine power enabled the 'Berta' to carry a two-man crew and a 1,100 pound bomb load, and the new version was fitted with additional bomb racks under the wings outboard of the dive brakes to carry four x 50kg bombs.

In October 1938 five early-production Ju 87Bs were sent to the 'Kondor Legion' in Spain and operated with considerable success during the closing months of the Civil War in that country.

During 1937 and 1938 a total of 395 Ju 87As and Bs were built, including prototypes and pre-production aircraft. During 1938 production of the dive bomber was transferred to the Weser plant at Berlin-

This head-on view of the Junkers 87 illustrates the classic and distinctive inverted gull-wing configuration.

Templehof, and the first aircraft came off the new production line that autumn. During 1939 production a total of 557 'Bertas' came off the line at Templehof and on the outbreak of war on 1 September 1939 these aircraft equipped nine dive bomber Gruppen.

During the closing months of 1939 the B-2 succeeded the B-1 on the production line. The new version featured a number of minor changes, including ejector exhaust stubs, hydraulically powered cooling gills for the engine and a new propeller with broader blades, and when flown as a single-seater could carry a maximum bomb load of 2,200 pounds (1,000kg).

In parallel with the B-2, the Ju 87R intended for extended range operations was also built in moderately large numbers. The version was fitted with an additional 33 Imp gal (150lit) fuel tank in each outer wing panel, and could carry 66 Imp gal (300lit) drop tank on the bomb rack under each wing. The extra tankage enabled the version to carry up to 190 Imp gal (900lit) of additional fuel, giving it a maximum range of 875 miles (1,400km) or more than twice that of the Ju 87B.

SPECIFICATIONS

Junkers Ju 87B-1

Dimensions

Length: 36 ft 1 in (11m)

Height: 13 ft 2 in (4m)

Wing span: 45 ft 3¼ in (13.8m)

Gross wing area: 343 sq ft (31.9 sq m)

Weights

Empty: 5,104lb (2,315kg)

Normal operational take off:
9,560lb (4,335kg)

Power

1 x Junkers Jumo 211 Da liquid cooled 12 cylinder inverted 'V' piston engine developing 1,200hp for take off

Performance (without bomb load)

Maximum speed: 238mph (381km/h) at 13,130ft (4,000m)

The Junkers 87R (R for Reichtweite or 'range') was equipped with two underwing long-range fuel tanks of 300 litre capacity.

Maximum cruising speed: 209mph (336km/h) at 12,145ft (3,700m)

Maximum Range: 490 miles (785km)

Service ceiling: 26,240ft (8,000m)

Junkers 87B-2

Dimensions (as per Ju 87B-1)

Weights

Empty: 7,086lb (3,205kg)

Powerplant: 1 x Junkers Jumo D.

Bomb Loadings

During August 1940 RAF Intelligence reported on the arrangements for loading of bombs on the Junkers 87 aircraft:

> "The bomb loads have two arrangements, either one x 500kg or one x 250kg with four x 50kg bombs. For ease of tabulating, these are referred to as 'A' and 'B' loads respectively. This does not, of course, mean that only two arrangements are possible; the Ju87 can, for instance, also carry a 1,000kg bomb."

The report went on to note that, on occasions, when a 'B' load was employed it was not always the case that four x 50kg bombs had been carried. Sometimes, this was restricted to two (or even three) 50kg bombs and it was thought this was possibly due to shortages of 50kg bombs on the unit when usage outstripped re-supply.

Junkers 87
Units and Commanders
from 1 July 1940

Unit	Commander	Base	Strength
Stab StG1	Major Walter Hagen	Angers	2
I./StG1	Major Paul-Werner Hozzel	Angers	27
II./StG1*	Hptm Anton Keil	Pas de Calais	32
III./StG1	Hptm Helmut Mahlke	Angers	26
Stab StG2	Major Oskar Dinort	St. Malo	3
I./StG2	Hptm Hubertus Hitschhold	St. Malo	29
II./StG2	Hptm Walter Enneccerus	Lannion	33
III./StG2	Hptm Heinrich Brücker	St. Trond	31
Stab StG3	Oberst Georg Edert	Caen	2
I./ StG3	Hptm Walter Sigel	Caen	14
Stab StG77	Major Clemens Graf von Schönborn-Wiesentheid	Caen	3
I./ StG77	Hptm F-K Frhr Von Dalwigk zu Lichtenfels	Caen	33
II./ StG77	Hptm Waldemar Plewig	Caen	25
III./ StG77	Hptm Helmut Bode	Caen	37
IV.(Stuka)/LG1	Hptm Bernd von Brauchitsch	Tramecourt	45

*II./StG1 was formed on 6 July 1940 by the re-designation of what had been III./StG51

RAF Fighter Command Claims for Ju87s July – December 1940

The following table sets out claims made by pilots of RAF Fighter Command for Junkers 87 Stuka aircraft operating against targets in the English Channel and over mainland Britain. Given the total of known losses sustained by the Luftwaffe of 101 Stukas (see Appendix IV) it will be seen that there was a huge element of over-claiming by the RAF with 171 'confirmed' and 63 'unconfirmed'. However, over-claiming is a typical element of all aerial combat and fighter actions against the Stuka may well have given rise to a greater incidence of over claiming than usual due to the large numbers of RAF fighter pilots who typically attacked single Ju 87 targets. In many cases, pilots genuinely believed that they were the sole victor, and may sometimes have been unaware of other attackers engaging the same target.

9th July 1940

609 Sqn Spit	Fg Off	D.M. Crook	D	Off Portland	21.30~
	Plt Off	M.J. Appleby	S		
	Fg Off	P. Drummond-Hay	S		
	Fg Off	D.M. Crook	U	Off Portland	21.30~
	Plt Off	M.J. Appleby	S		
	Fg Off	P. Drummond-Hay	S		
	Fg Off	D.M. Crook	U	Off Portland	21.30~
	Plt Off	M.J. Appleby	S		
	Fg Off	P. Drummond-Hay	S		

11th July 1940

601 Sqn Hurr	Fg Off	G.N.S. Cleaver	D	Portland Area	11.35
	Fg Off	C.J. Riddle	U	Portland Area	11.35
	Sgt	L.N. Guy	U	Portland Area	11.35
	Flt Sgt	A.H.D. Pond	U	Portland Area	11.35
	Flt Lt	Sir A. Hope	U	Portland Area	11.35
	Flt Lt	Sir A. Hope	U	Portland Area	11.35
	Sgt	L.N. Guy	Dam	Portland Area	11.35
609 Sqn Spit	Fg Off	B.W. Little	U	SSE Portland Bill	08.05

13th July 1940

56 Sqn Hurr	Fg Off	R.E.P. Brooker	D	Dover Strait	17.00~
	Sgt	J.R. Cowsill	D	Dover Strait	17.00~
	Sgt	G. Smythe	U	Dover Strait	17.00~

13th July 1940

	Flt Lt	J.H. Coghlan	U	Dover Strait	17.00~
	Sqn Ldr	G.A.L. Manton	U	Dover Strait	17.00~
	Sgt	P. Hillwood	U	Dover Strait	17.00~
	Sgt	R.D. Baker	U	Dover Strait	17.00~

14th July 1940

615 Sqn Hurr	Flt Lt	J.R.H. Gayner	D	Dover Strait	15.45
	Fg Off	P. Collard	D	Dover Strait	15.45
	Plt Off	P.H. Hugo	U	Dover Strait	15.45

19th July 1940

87 Sqn Hurr	Sgt	L.A. Thorogood	Dam	W Portland	19.00

20th July 1940

32 Sqn Hurr	Plt Off	J.B.W. Humpherson	D	Dover Area	18.00
	Sqn Ldr	J. Worrall	Dam	Dover Area	18.00
	Sqn Ldr	J. Worrall	Dam	Dover Area	18.00
	Sqn Ldr	J. Worrall	Dam	Dover Area	18.00
615 Sqn Hurr	Fg Off	H.S. Giddings	Dam	Off Boulogne	18.20

25th July 1940

56 Sqn Hurr	Plt Off	A.G. Page	D	Dover Area	18.25~
	Plt Off	F.B. Sutton	D	Dover Area	18.25~
	Plt Off	M.H. Mounsdon	U	Dover Area	18.25~
64 Sqn Spit	Sqn Ldr	A.R.D. MacDonnell	D	Off Dover	14.56
152 Sqn Spit	Plt Off	R.D. Hogg	D	Portland Area	11.15
	Fg Off	E.C. Deanesly	S		
	Sgt	Walton	S		

27th July 1940

238 Sqn Hurr	Plt Off	C.T. Davis	D	Weymouth Bay	09.50

29th July 1940

41 Sqn Spit	Sqn Ldr	H.R.L. Hood	D	Dover Area	07.40
	Flt Lt	J.T. Webster	Dam	Dover Area	07.40
64 Sqn Spit	Plt Off	J.J. O'Meara	D	Dover Area	07.25
	Plt Off	J.J. O'Meara	D	Dover Area	07.25
	Sqn Ldr	A.R.D. MacDonnell	D	Dover Area	07.25
	Plt Off	J.J. O'Meara	Dam	Dover Area	07.25
501 Sqn Hurr	Plt Off	J.A.A. Gibson	D	Dover Area	07.45
	Plt Off	J.W. Bland	D	Dover Area	07.45
	Plt Off	B.L. Duckenfield	D	Dover Area	07.45
	Flt Lt	G.E.B. Stoney	S		
	Plt Off	J.A.A. Gibson	U	Dover Area	07.45
	Sgt	D.N.E. McKay	U	Dover Area	07.45
	Flt Lt	G.E.B. Stoney	Dam	Dover Area	07.45
	Plt Off	R.C. Dafforn	Dam	Dover Area	07.45
	Plt Off	K.N.T. Lee	Dam	Dover Area	07.45
	Flt Sgt	P.F. Morfill	Dam	Dover Area	07.45
	Flt Sgt	P.F. Morfill	Dam	Dover Area	07.45
	Sgt	E.F. Howarth	Dam	Dover Area	07.45

8th August 1940

43 Sqn Hurr	Flt Lt	T.F. Dalton-Morgan	D	S Isle of Wight	16.20
	Plt Off	H.C. Upton	D	7m off Ventnor	16.20
	Plt Off	H.C. Upton	D	7m off Ventnor	16.20
	Flt Lt	T.F. Dalton-Morgan	U	S Isle of Wight	16.20
	Plt Off	C.A. Woods-Scawen	U	St Catherines Pt	16.20
	Plt Off	C.A. Woods-Scawen	U	St Catherines Pt	16.20
	Plt Off	C.A. Woods-Scawen	U	St Catherines Pt	16.20
	Plt Off	H.C. Upton	U	7m off Ventnor	16.20
	Sgt	C.A.L. Hurry	U	S Isle of Wight	16.25
	Sgt	C.A.L. Hurry	U	S Isle of Wight	16.25
	Sgt	C.A.L. Hurry	Dam	S Isle of Wight	16.25
	Sgt	C.A.L. Hurry	Dam	S Isle of Wight	16.25
	Sgt	C.A.L. Hurry	Dam	S Isle of Wight	16.25
145 Sqn Hurr	Fg Off	G.R. Branch	U	5m SSW Needles	09.00
	Plt Off	A.N.C. Weir	U	Off Isle of Wight	09.00
	Fg Off	G.R. Branch	D	3m S Isle of Wight	09.00
	Sqn Ldr	J.R.A. Peel	U	St Catherines Pt	09.00
	Flt Lt	R.G. Dutton	U	S St Catherines Pt	09.10
	Flt Lt	R.G. Dutton	U	S St Catherines Pt	09.10
	Fg Off	G.R. Branch	Dam	3m S Isle of Wight	09.00
	Plt Off	J.E. Storrar	Dam	5-6m SSW Needles	09.00
	Flt Lt	R.G. Dutton	U	S St Catherines Pt	15.10
	Plt Off	J.E. Storrar	D	S Isle of Wight	15.12
	Flt Lt	A.D.McN.Boyd	D	S Isle of Wight	15.15
	Plt Off	P.W. Dunning-White	D	S Isle of Wight	15.15
	Plt Off	P.L. Parrott	D	St Catherines Pt	15.15
	Fg Off	G.R. Branch	U	S St Catherines Pt	15.25
	Plt Off	D.N. Forde	D	S Isle of Wight	15.10
	Sqn Ldr	J.R.A. Peel	D	S St Catherines Pt	15.10
609 Sqn Spit	Flt Lt	J.H.G. McArthur	D	Off Isle of Wight	12.40~
	Flt Lt	J.H.G. McArthur	D	Off Isle of Wight	12.40~

12th August 1940

501 Sqn Hurr	Sgt	J.H. Lacey	D	Off North Foreland	11.30
	Plt Off	J.A.A. Gibson	D	E N Foreland	11.30
	Plt Off	K.N.T. Lee	D	10m N N Foreland	11.30
	Plt Off	R.C. Dafforn	D	10m N N Foreland	11.30
	Sgt	P.C.P. Farnes	D	8m N N Foreland	11.30
	Plt Off	P. Zenker	U	5m N Westgate	11.30
	Sgt	J.H. Lacey	U	Off North Foreland	11.30
	Plt Off	J.A.A. Gibson	Dam	E North Foreland	11.30
		Unknown Pilot	Dam	Ramsgate Area	11.30~
		Unknown Pilot	Dam	Ramsgate Area	11.30~
	Plt Off	J.A.A. Gibson	D	Ramsgate Area	11.30

13th August 1940

87 Sqn Hurr	Plt Off	W.D. David	D	Portland	17.45

13th August 1940

152 Sqn Spit	Flt Lt	D.P.A. Boitel-Gill	D	Portland Area	15.30~
609 Sqn Spit	Plt Off	C.N. Overton	D	Portland Area	15.55
	Plt Off	C.N. Overton	D	Portland Area	15.55
	Plt Off	R.F.G. Miller	D	5m W Dorchester	16.00
	Plt Off	M.E. Staples	D	Portland Area	16.00
	Flt Lt	F.J. Howell	D	5m W Warmwell	16.00
	Fg Off	H.McD. Goodwin	D	5m W Warmwell	16.00
	Fg Off	H.McD. Goodwin	D	5m W Warmwell	16.00
	Sgt	A.N. Feary	D	Lyme Bay	16.15
	Fg Off	J.C. Dundas	D	Lyme Bay	16.00
	Plt Off	R.F.G. Miller	U	5m W Dorchester	16.00
	Flt Off	P. Ostaczewski	U	Portland Area	16.00
	Flt Off	P. Ostaczewski	U	Portland Area	16.00
	Plt Off	M.J. Appleby	Dam	Portland	16.00
	Fg Off	J.C. Dundas	Dam	Lyme Bay	16.00
	Plt Off	M.E. Staples	Dam	Warmwell	16.00

14th August 1940

87 Sqn Hurr	Plt Off	H.J. Mitchell	D	5m S Portland	17.30
610 Sqn Spit	Plt Off	S.C. Norris	D	Folkestone-Dover	12.26
	Plt Off	S.C. Norris	D	Folkestone-Dover	12.26
	Sgt	C.A. Parsons	U	S Folkestone	12.25
	Plt Off	B.V. Rees	U	Near Hawkinge	12.30
	Plt Off	S.C. Norris	Dam	Folkestone-Dover	12.36
615 Sqn Hurr	Plt Off	K.T. Lofts	D	Dover Area	12.30~
	Fg Off	A. Eyre	D	Dover Area	12.30~
	Fg Off	A. Eyre	D	Dover Area	12.30~
	Sgt	J.A. Porter	S		
	Sgt	J.A. Porter	D	Dover Area	12.30~
	Plt Off	K.T. Lofts	Dam	Dover Area	12.30~

15th August 1940

54 Sqn Spit	Plt Off	G.D. Gribble	Dam	Dover-Hawkinge	12.00~
	Sgt	N.A. Lawrence	D	Dover-Hawkinge	12.00~
	Sgt	N.A. Lawrence	D	Dover-Hawkinge	12.00~
	Sgt	N.A. Lawrence	D	Dover-Hawkinge	12.00~
	Plt Off	Hopkins	Dam	Dover-Hawkinge	12.00~
87 Sqn Hurr	Fg Off	W.D. David	D	Portland Area	17.45~
	Plt Off	D.T. Jay	D	5m S Portland	17.45
	Plt Off	D.T. Jay	D	5m S Portland	17.45
213 Sqn Hurr	Plt Off	J.E.P. Larichelier	D	Portland Bill	17.45
	Plt Off	W.M. Sizer	D	Portland Area	17.45
	Plt Off	W.M. Sizer	D	Portland Area	17.45
	Flt Lt	J.E.J. Sing	D	5m S Portland Bill	17.45
	Fg Off	J.M. Strickland	D	Portland Bill	17.35
501 Sqn Hurr	Sgt	A. Glowacki	D	Hawkinge Area	11.30~
	Plt Off	J.A.A. Gibson	D	Hawkinge Area	11.30~

15th August 1940

	Fg Off	S. Witorzenc	D	Hawkinge Area	11.30~
	Fg Off	S. Witorzenc	D	Hawkinge Area	11.30~
	Flt Lt	G.E.B. Stoney	D	Hawkinge Area	11.30~
	Flt Lt	G.E.B. Stoney	D	Hawkinge Area	11.30~
	Sgt	P.C.P. Farnes	D	Hawkinge Area	11.30~
	Sgt	P.C.P. Farnes	D	Hawkinge Area	11.30~
	Sgt	D.N.E. McKay	D	Hawkinge Area	11.30~
	Sgt	D.N.E. McKay	D	Hawkinge Area	11.30~
	Flt Lt	G.E.B. Stoney	U	Hawkinge Area	11.30~
	Plt Off	P.C. Dafforn	Dam	S Folkestone	11.30
	Plt Off	P.C. Dafforn	Dam	S Folkestone	11.30
	Plt Off	J.A.A. Gibson	Dam	Hawkinge Area	11.30~

Fg Off Stefan Witorzenc.

16th August 1940

43 Sqn Hurr	Plt Off	F.R. Carey	D	Off Selsey Bill	12.55
	Plt Off	F.R. Carey	D	Off Selsey Bill	12.55
	Sgt	J.H.L. Hallowes	D	Off Selsey	12.55
	Sgt	J.H.L. Hallowes	D	Off Selsey	12.55
	Sgt	J.H.L. Hallowes	D	Off Selsey	12.55
	Sqn Ldr	J.V.C. Badger	D	3m S Selsey	12.55
	Sqn Ldr	J.V.C. Badger	D	3m S Selsey	12.55
	Sqn Ldr	J.V.C. Badger	D	3m S Selsey	12.55
	Sgt	D. Noble	D	Off Selsey	12.55
	Plt Off	D.A.R.L. Du Vivier	D	Off Selsey Bill	12.55
	Plt Off	Van Den Hove	D	Off Selsey	12.55
	Fg Off	H.C. Upton	D	S Selsey	12.55
	Fg Off	H.C. Upton	D	S Selsey	12.55
	Fg Off	H.C. Upton	D	S Selsey	12.55
	Plt Off	C.A. Woods-Scawen	D	Off Selsey	12.55
	Plt Off	C.A. Woods-Scawen	D	Off Selsey	12.55
	Plt Off	C.K. Gray	D	Off Selsey Bill	12.55
	Plt Off	D.G. Gorrie	U	Off Selsey Bill	12.55
	Plt Off	D.G. Gorrie	U	Off Selsey Bill	12.55
	Plt Off	D.G. Gorrie	U	Off Selsey Bill	12.55
	Plt Off	C.K. Gray	U	Off Selsey Bill	12.55
	Plt Off	D.A.R.L. Du Vivier	Dam	Off Selsey Bill	12.55
	Plt Off	F.R. Carey	Dam	Off Selsey Bill	12.55
	Plt Off	F.R. Carey	Dam	Off Selsey Bill	12.55
	Plt Off	R. Lane	Dam	3m off Selsey	12.55
601 Sqn Hurr	Plt Off	H.C. Mayers	D	Tangmere	13.05
	Plt Off	H.C. Mayers	D	Tangmere	13.05
	Fg Off	M.D. Doulton	D	Selsey Bill Area	13.00
	Sgt	L.N. Guy	D	Tangmere Area	13.00~
	Sgt	L.N. Guy	D	Tangmere Area	13.00~
	Fg Off	W.P. Clyde	D	Tangmere	13.00
	Fg Off	G.N.S. Cleaver	D	Tangmere	13.05

16th August 1940

	Fg Off	G.N.S. Cleaver	D	Tangmere	13.05
	Flt Lt	C.R. Davis	D	Tangmere Area	13.00~
	Plt Off	H.C. Mayers	U	Tangmere	13.05~
	Sqn Ldr	Sir A. Hope	U	Tangmere	13.05
	Fg Off	W.P. Clyde	Dam	Tangmere	13.00
		Unknown	S		
	Sqn Ldr	Sir A. Hope	Dam	Tangmere	13.05
	Fg Off	M.D. Doulton	Dam	Selsey Bill Area	13.00
	Fg Off	M.D. Doulton	Dam	Selsey Bill Area	13.00
602 Sqn Spit	Flt Lt	R.F. Boyd	D	S Westhampnett	13.05

18th August 1940

43 Sqn Hurr	Plt Off	R. Lane	D	5m E Chichester	14.20
	Plt Off	H.C. Upton	D	Off Thorney Is	14.20
	Sgt	J.P. Mills	D	Off Thorney Is	14.20
	Sgt	J.H.L. Hallowes	D	ESE Thorney Is	14.20
	Sgt	J.H.L. Hallowes	D	ESE Thorney Is	14.20
	Sgt	J.H.L. Hallowes	D	ESE Thorney Is	14.20
	Plt Off	C.K. Gray	D	Thorney Island	14.20
	Plt Off	H.L. North	D	Thorney Is-Coast	14.20
	Plt Off	H.L. North	U	Thorney Is-Coast	14.20
85 Sqn Hurr	Fg Off	A.V. Gowers	D	E Foulness Island	18.00
152 Sqn Spit	Flt Lt	D.P.A. Boitel-Gill	D	SE I.o.Wight	14.45
	Plt Off	F.H. Holmes	D	E I.o.Wight	14.45
	Sgt	E.E. Shepperd	D	4m E I.o.Wight	14.45
	Plt Off	W. Beaumont	D	4-5m E I.o.Wight	14.30
	Plt Off	W. Beaumont	D	4-5m E I.o.Wight	14.30
	Plt Off	E.S. Mars	D	SE I.o.Wight	14.45
	Sgt	J.K. Barker	D	4m E Ventnor	14.45
	Plt Off	W.S. Wildblood	D	Spithead	14.45
	Plt Off	W.S. Wildblood	D	Spithead	14.45
		Spitfires	S		
		Hurricanes	S		
	Plt Off	W.D. Williams	Dam	4m E I.o.Wight	14.45
257 Sqn Hurr	Plt Off	D.W. Hunt	U	Thames Estuary	17.50
601 Sqn Hurr	Flt Sgt	A.H.D. Pond	D	S Thorney Is	14.15~
	Flt Lt	C.R. Davis	D	Selsey-Thorney Is	14.15
	Flt Lt	C.R. Davis	D	Selsey-Thorney Is	14.15
	Sgt	R.N. Taylor	D	Selsey Bill	14.00
	Fg Off	T. Grier	D	E Selsey	14.15~
	Fg Off	T.Grier	D	Selsey-Thorney Is	14.15~
602 Sqn Spit	Sgt	B.E.P. Whall	D	Ford	14.45~
	Sgt	B.E.P. Whall	D	Ford	14.45~
	Fg Off	P.J. Ferguson	D	Ford	14.45~
	Flt Lt	R.F. Boyd	D	Ford	14.45~
	Plt Off	H.W. Moody	D	Ford	14.45~

Plt Off Harold North.

Plt Off Henry Moody.

18th August 1940

	Sgt	C.G. Babbage	D	Ford	14.45~
	Flt Lt	R.F. Boyd	U	Ford	14.45~
	Fg Off	C.H. MacLean	Dam	Ford	14.45~
	Fg Off	P.J. Ferguson	Dam	Ford	14.45~
	Flt Lt	J.D. Urie	Dam	Ford	14.45~
	Flt Lt	J.D. Urie	Dam	Ford	14.45~
	Flt Lt	J.D. Urie	Dam	Ford	14.45~
	Flt Lt	J.D. Urie	Dam	Ford	14.45~
	Flt Lt	J.D. Urie	Dam	Ford	14.45~
FIU Blenheim	Sgt	Ryalls	Dam	Ford	14.30
FIU Hurricane	Flt Lt	A.G. Miller	Dam	Ford	14.30

6th September 1940

249 Sqn Hurr	Wg Cdr	F.V. Beamish	D	Shellhaven	18.30~
	Wg Cdr	F.V. Beamish	U	Shellhaven	18.30~

1st November 1940

92 Sqn Spit	Plt Off	M.C. Kinder	D	Thames Estuary	15.00~
	Plt Off	M.C. Kinder	U	Thames Estuary	15.00~

7th November 1940

145 Sqn Hurr	Plt Off	Riley	U	Near Tangmere	14.40~

8th November 1940

17 Sqn Hurr	Plt Off	D.C. Leary	D	Thames Estuary	16.40~
	Plt Off	D.C. Leary	D	Thames Estuary	16.40~
	Plt Off	D.C. Leary	D	Thames Estuary	16.40~
	Sgt	N. Cameron	S		
	Plt Off	D.C. Leary	D	Thames Estuary	16.40~
	Sgt	D.A. Sewell	S		
	Sgt	N. Cameron	D	Thames Estuary	16.40~
	Flt Lt	A.W.A. Bayne	D	Thames Estuary	16.40~
	Flt Lt	A.W.A. Bayne	U	Thames Estuary	16.40~
	Sgt	G.A. Steward	D	Thames Estuary	16.40~
	Sgt	G.A. Steward	Dam	Thames Estuary	16.40~
	Sgt	G.A. Steward	Dam	Thames Estuary	16.40~
	Plt Off	M. Chelmecki	D	Thames Estuary	16.40~
	Fg Off	P. Niemec	D	Thames Estuary	16.40~
	Sgt	R.D. Hogg	D	Thames Estuary	16.40~
	Sgt	R.D. Hogg	D	Thames Estuary	16.40~
	Sgt	G. Griffiths	S		
	Sgt	G. Griffiths	D	Thames Estuary	16.40~
	Sgt	G. Griffiths	D	Thames Estuary	16.40~
	Sgt	L.H. Bartlett	D	Thames Estuary	16.40~
	Sgt	L.H. Bartlett	U	Thames Estuary	16.40~
	Sgt	D.A. Sewell	U	Thames Estuary	16.40~
	Sgt	D.A. Sewell	U	Thames Estuary	16.40~
	Wg Cdr	A.D. Farquhar	D	Thames Estuary	16.40~
	Wg Cdr	A.D. Farquhar	D	Thames Estuary	16.40~

11th November 1940

17 Sqn Hurr	Plt Off	J.K. Ross	D	Thames Estuary	12.10~
	Plt Off	J.K. Ross	U	Thames Estuary	12.10~
	Plt Off	G.E. Pitman	D	Thames Estuary	12.10~
	Sgt	L.H. Bartlett	D	Thames Estuary	12.10~
	Sgt	L.H. Bartlett	U	Thames Estuary	12.10~
	Sqn Ldr	A.G. Miller	U	Thames Estuary	12.10~
	Sqn Ldr	A.G. Miller	U	Thames Estuary	12.10~
257 Sqn Hurr	Plt Off	J. Kay	D	Thames Estuary	12.10~
603 Sqn Hurr	Plt Off	P. Olver	U	10m N Margate	12.30~

14th November 1940

66 Sqn Spit	Flt Lt	G.P. Christie	D	Dover Area	14.20~
	Flt Lt	G.P. Christie	U	Dover Area	14.20~
	Plt Off	H.R. Allen	D	Dover Area	14.20~
	Plt Off	H.R. Allen	U	Dover Area	14.20~
	Plt Off	H.R. Allen	Dam	Dover Area	14.20~
	Plt Off	H.R. Allen	Dam	Dover Area	14.20~
	Flt Sgt	M. Cameron	U	Dover Area	14.20~
	Flt Sgt	M. Cameron	Dam	Dover Area	14.20~
74 Sqn Spit	Flt Off	H.M. Stephen	D	Manston-Dover	14.20~
	Flt Off	H.M. Stephen	D	Manston-Dover	14.20~
	Flt Off	H.M.Stephen	D	Manston-Dover	14.20~
	Plt Off	B.V. Draper	D	Manston-Dover	14.20~
	Plt Off	B.V. Draper	D	Manston-Dover	14.20~
	Plt Off	B.V. Draper	D	Manston-Dover	14.20~
	Plt Off	B.V. Draper	Dam	Manston-Dover	14.20~
	Sgt	W.M.Skinner	D	Manston-Dover	14.20~
	Sgt	W.M. Skinner	D	Manston-Dover	14.20~
	Flt Lt	J.C. Mungo-Park	D	Manston-Dover	14.20~
	Flt Lt	J.C. Mungo-Park	D	Manston-Dover	14.20~
	Sgt	J.N. Glendinning	D	Deal	14.20~
	Sgt	J.N. Glendinning	D	Deal	14.20~
	Fg Off	W.D.K. Franklin	D	Dover	14.20~
	Sgt	L.E. Freese	D	Dover	14.20~
	Sgt	L.E. Freese	Dam	Dover	14.20~
	Plt Off	W. Armstrong	U	Deal	14.20~
	Plt Off	W. Armstrong	Dam	Deal	14.20~
	Fg Off	R.L. Spurdle	U	Dover	14.20~

Sgt John Glendinning.

Destroyed =171   Unconfirmed =63   Shared =16   Damaged =56

Quite apart from the over-inflated claims submitted by pilots of RAF Fighter Command, a number of anti-aircraft units also filed claims for destroyed Junkers 87 Stukas. Here, a scoreboard for the West Sussex based 391/48 (Hants) Searchlight Battery, Royal Artillery, records claims made by its Lewis gunners for four Stukas on 16 August and two on 18 August. None of these claims can be substantiated and are almost certainly aircraft already downed by RAF fighters that were then fired on in their last moments by the searchlight crews. However, figures such as these illustrate the scale of over-claiming against Luftwaffe aircraft operating against Britain during 1940.

APPENDIX IV

Junkers 87 Operational Losses July – December 1940

The following tables represent an accurate listing of all Junkers 87 Stuka aircraft lost during air operations against Britain between July and December 1940.

Notes:

FF = Flugzeugführer   (Pilot)

BF = Bordfunker   (Wireless Operator)*

BS = Bordschutze   (Air Gunner)*

Essentially, both of these crew categories performed the same function and flew as the 'back-seater' in the Junkers 87, operating as wireless operator/air gunner. The difference between these classifications as either a Bordfunker (BF) or Bordschutze (BS) in Luftwaffe records was simply down to the formal crew qualification held by the individual concerned.

JULY 1940

3 July 1940

II./StG77 Junkers Ju87B-1. Crash-landed at Picauville, cause not stated. Crew unhurt. Aircraft 60% damaged but repairable.

II./StG77 Junkers Ju87B-1. Crash-landed at Picauville, cause not stated. Crew unhurt. Aircraft 45% damaged but repairable.

4 July 1940

7./StG51 Junkers Ju87B-1. Badly damaged by AA fire during attack on shipping south of Portland and engine exploded during return flight 8.50 a.m. FF Lt Wilhelm Schwarze baled out but parachute failed and missing, BF Uffz Julius Dörflinger missing. Aircraft 100% write-off.

7./StG51 Junkers Ju87B-1. Engine badly damaged by AA fire during attack on shipping south of Portland and ditched off Cotentin Peninsula on return flight 8.50 a.m. Crew both unhurt. Aircraft under 60% damaged but repairable.

(This unit was being re-designated as 4./StG1 at about this time)

5 July 1940

Stab StG1 Junkers Ju87B-1. Damaged in forced-landing at Bapaume following engine failure. Crew both unhurt. Aircraft 40% damaged but repairable.

9 July 1940

Stab I./StG77 Junkers Ju87B-1. Shot down by Green Section of No.609 Squadron (F/O D.M. Crook, P/O M.J. Appleby, and F/O P. Drummond-Hay) following attack on shipping and crashed in sea 20 km south of Portland 5.05 p.m. FF Hptmn Friedrich Fr von Dalwigk zu Lichtenfels (*Gruppenkommandeur*) and BF Fw Karl Götz both missing. Aircraft 100% write-off.

11 July 1940

9./StG2 Junkers Ju87B-1. Shot down by Hurricanes of No.601 Squadron during attack on convoy and crashed in the Channel 15 km south-east of Portland Bill 11.35 a.m. Probably that claimed by F/O G.N.S. Cleaver. FF Uffz Wolfgang Grosche and BF Uffz Horst Fietz both missing. Aircraft 100% write-off.

6./StG77 Junkers Ju87B. Wrecked when undercarriage collapsed in heavy landing at Flers. Crew both unhurt. Aircraft 100% write-off.

12 July 1940

III./StG1 Junkers Ju87B-1. Forced-landed near Théville due to ruptured oil feed pipe. Crew both unhurt. Aircraft 60% damaged – write-off.

9./StG77 Junkers Ju87B-2 (519). Starboard undercarriage leg collapsed and wing damaged in heavy forced-landing outside Dreux emergency landing ground following engine failure during delivery flight from Lippstadt to Argentan. FF Uffz Wilhelm Moll unhurt. Aircraft F1+GP 35% damaged but repairable.

(Unit recently re-designated from II.(St)/KG76)

13 July 1940

10.(St)/LG1 Junkers Ju87B-1. Returned damaged following attack on convoy south of Dover 6.30 p.m. FF Oberlt Arnulf Blasig unhurt, BF Fw Robert Heidfeld badly wounded – admitted to hospital in Ardres. Aircraft L1+GU 30% damaged but repairable.

II./StG1 Junkers Ju87B. Crash-landed on beach at Cap Gris Nez badly damaged in attack by Hurricanes of No.56 Squadron over the Channel off Calais 4.15 p.m. Possibly that claimed by Sgt J.R. Cowsill. Crew both unhurt. Aircraft under 60% damaged but repairable.

II./StG1 Junkers Ju87B. Forced-landed at Norent Fontes damaged in attack by Hurricanes of No.56 Squadron during engagement over the Channel off Calais 4.20 p.m. Possibly that engaged by F/O R.E.P. Brooker. Crew both unhurt. Aircraft 30% damaged but repairable.

14 July 1940

11.(St)/LG1 Junkers Ju87B-1. Shot down in flames over the Channel by Yellow Section of No.615 Squadron (F/O J.R.H. Gaynor, F/O P. Collard and P/O P.H. Hugo) during attack on convoy south-east of Dover 3.50 p.m. FF Uffz Sebastian Huber killed, BF Uffz Heinz Hecke missing. Aircraft 100% write-off.

The body of Sebastian Huber was washed ashore on the Dutch coast on 18 August, 1940.

11.(St)/LG1 Junkers Ju87B-1. Shot down by Yellow Section of No.615 Squadron (F/O J.R.H. Gaynor, F/O P. Collard and P/O P.H. Hugo) during attack on convoy and crashed in sea south-east of Dover Harbour 3.50 p.m. FF Oberlt Kurt Sonnberg killed, HS Uffz Fritz Donath missing. Aircraft 100% write-off.

The body of Kurt Sonnberg was recovered by the German air-sea rescue service from Boulogne.

20 July 1940

II./StG1 Junkers Ju87B-1. Forced-landed at Norrent-Fontes damaged by Hurricanes of Nos.32 and 615 Squadrons during attack on convoy 'Bosom' off Dover 6.15 p.m. Crew both unhurt. Aircraft 30% damaged but repairable.

II./StG1 Junkers Ju87B-1. Returned damaged by Hurricanes of Nos.32 and 615 Squadrons during attack on convoy off Dover 6.20 p.m. and over-turned forced-landing at Cap Gris Nez. Crew both unhurt. Aircraft under 60% damaged but repairable.

II./StG1 Junkers Ju87B. Crash-landed at St Hilaire airfield damaged by Hurricanes of Nos.32 and 615 Squadrons during attack on convoy 'Bosom' off Dover 6.20 p.m. Crew both unhurt. Aircraft 30% damaged but repairable.

4./StG1 Junkers Ju87B-1. Returned damaged by Hurricanes of Nos.32 and 615 Squadrons during attack on convoy 'Bosom' off Dover 6.15 p.m. FF Uffz Johannes Braun slightly wounded – admitted to hospital in Lille, gunner unhurt. Aircraft 30% damaged but repairable.

21 July 1940
I./StG2 Junkers Ju87B-1. Destroyed by fire in refuelling accident at Condé-sur-Ifs airfield. No crew casualties. Aircraft 100% write-off.

22 July 1940
Stab StG77 Junkers Ju 87B-1. Crash-landed at Caen during routine flight. Cause not stated. Crew unhurt. Aircraft 60% damaged – write-off.

24 July 1940
I./StG2 Junkers Ju87B-1. Damaged in crash-landing at Théville airfield during domestic flight, cause not stated. Crew both unhurt. Aircraft 20% damaged but repairable.

The distinctive Scotty dog emblem of I./StG2 during the Battle of Britain.

I./StG77 Junkers Ju87B-1. Collided with landing beacon at Caen aerodrome following domestic flight. Crew both unhurt. Aircraft 15% damaged but repairable.

25 July 1940
11.(St)/LG1 Junkers Ju87B-1. Returned damaged by S/L A.R.D. MacDonnell of No.64 Squadron during attack on convoy off Folkestone 3.00 p.m. Pilot unhurt, BF Uffz Rudolf Klünder wounded. Aircraft 15% damaged but repairable.

6./StG1 Junkers Ju87B-1. Shot down by No.56 Squadron Hurricanes over mid-Channel during attack on convoy between Folkestone and Cap Gris Nez 6.45 p.m. Possibly that claimed by P/O A.G. Page. FF Uffz Viktor Schröder and BF Gefr Herbert Lipsius both killed. Aircraft 100% write-off.

6./StG1 Junkers Ju87B-1. Shot down by No.56 Squadron Hurricanes over mid-Channel during attack on convoy between Folkestone and Cap Gris Nez 6.45 p.m. Possibly that claimed by P/O F.B. Sutton. FF Lt Dieter von Rohden and Gefr Willi Heuberger both killed. Aircraft 100% write-off.

III./StG1 Junkers Ju87B-1. Returned damaged by Spitfires of No.152 Squadron over the Channel north of Cherbourg 11.15 a.m. Crew both unhurt. Aircraft 30% damaged but repairable.

7./StG1 Junkers Ju87B-2. Returned damaged by Spitfires of No.152 Squadron 15 km south-west of Portland Bill 11.15 a.m. FF Oberfw Stiebitz believed unhurt, BF Uffz Walter Meiner slightly wounded – admitted to hospital in Potigny. Aircraft J9+JH 15% damaged but repairable.

8./StG1 Junkers Ju87B-1. Believed shot down by Sgt Walton and P/O R.D. Hogg of No.152 Squadron and crashed in the Channel 45 km north of Cherbourg 11.15 a.m. Pilot believed rescued unhurt, BF Obergefr Josef Stillinger drowned. Aircraft 100% write-off.

27 July 1940
2./StG77 Junkers Ju87B-1. Shot down by P/O C.T. Davis of No.238 Squadron during armed-reconnaissance sortie between Portland and Swanage and crashed in sea, 5 km south-east of Shambles Lightship, 9.50 a.m. FF Uffz Robert Munk and BF Uffz Karl Wagner both missing. Aircraft 100% write-off.

29 July 1940

11.(St)/LG1 Junkers Ju87B-1. Shot down in action with Spitfires of Nos.41 and 64 Squadrons and Hurricanes of No.501 Squadron during attack on convoy off Dover 7.45 a.m. FF Oberlt Erich Kothe killed, BF Uffz Waldemar Preuss missing. Aircraft 100% write-off.

11.(St)/LG1 Junkers Ju87B-1. Shot down in action with Spitfires of Nos.41 and 64 Squadrons and Hurricanes of No.501 Squadron during attack on convoy off Dover 7.45 a.m. FF Lt Josef Fürnweger and BF Uffz Fritz Wierse both missing. Aircraft 100% write-off.

II./StG1 Junkers Ju87B-1. Returned damaged in action with Spitfires of Nos.41 and 64 Squadrons and Hurricanes of No.501 Squadron during attack on convoy off Dover 7.45 a.m. Crew both unhurt. Aircraft 30% damaged but repairable.

4./StG1 Junkers Ju87B-1. Crash-landed at St Inglevert damaged in combat with Spitfires of Nos.41 and 64 Squadrons and Hurricanes of No.501 Squadron 7.45 a.m. Pilot unhurt, BF Uffz Christian Schröder badly wounded – admitted to hospital in St Omer. Aircraft 100% write-off.

5./StG1 Junkers Ju87B-1. Damaged in action with Spitfires of Nos.41 and 64 Squadrons and Hurricanes of No.501 Squadron during attack on convoy off Dover and ditched in the Channel 7.45 a.m. Pilot unhurt, BS Fw Kurt Kuppich slightly injured in landing – both rescued by *Seenotdienst*. Aircraft 100% write-off.

AUGUST 1940

2 August 1940

1./StG2 Junkers Ju87B-1. Stalled from a steep turn and crashed at Ernes airfield, south of Condé-sur-Ifs, during local flight. FF Obergefr Kurt Bellmacher and BF Obergefr Mathias Luckas both killed. Aircraft 100% write-off.

1./StG77 Junkers Ju87B-1. Undercarriage torn off in forced-landing near Bayeux following engine failure on domestic flight. FF Oberlt Jakob (*Staffelkapitän*) and gunner both unhurt. Aircraft 50% damaged but repairable.

4 August 1940

11.(St)/LG1 Junkers Ju87B. Flew into the ground near Tramecourt during practice flight, cause unknown. FF Fw Karl Baindner and BF Gefr Hans Hochegger both killed. Aircraft 80% damaged – write-off.

5 August 1940

I./StG2 Junkers Ju87B-2. Crashed on take-off from Condé-sur-Ifs, cause not stated. Crew unhurt. Aircraft damage state not recorded.

Transportstaffel I Fl.Korps Junkers Ju87B-1. Damaged in crash-landing at Compiègne during local flight. Crew both injured. Aircraft damage state not recorded.

8 August 1940

8./StG1 Junkers Ju87B-1. Returned damaged by fighters during attack on convoy 'Peewit' 20 km south of the Isle of Wight. FF Oberlt Klaus Ostmann badly wounded – admitted to hospital in Valognes, gunner believed unhurt. Aircraft 25% damaged but repairable.

9./StG1 Junkers Ju 87B-1. Returned damaged by fighters during attack on convoy 'Peewit' south-west of the Isle of Wight. FF Uffz Roland Reitter and BF Obergefr Bernhard Renners both slightly wounded – admitted to hospital in Valognes. Aircraft damage state not recorded.

9./StG1 Junkers Ju87B-1. Shot down by fighters during attack on convoy 'Peewit' and crashed in the Channel south-west of the Isle of Wight. FF Fw Herbert Torngrind and BF Gefr Heinrich Bauer both missing. Aircraft 100% write-off.

9./StG1 Junkers Ju87B-1. Shot down by fighters during attack on convoy 'Peewit' and crashed in the Channel south-west of the Isle of Wight. FF Gefr Ernst-Gottlob Walz and BF Gefr Robert Schütz both missing. Aircraft 100% write-off.

I./StG2 Junkers Ju87B-1. Crash-landed at Wuilly-le-Tessin airfield damaged following attack by fighters during attack on convoy 'Peewit' south of the Isle of Wight 12.30 p.m. Crew both unhurt. Aircraft 40% damaged but repairable.

III./StG2 Junkers Ju87B. Returned to base damaged by fighters during attack on convoy 'Peewit' south of the Isle of Wight 12.40 p.m. Believed one of those claimed by F/L J.H.G. McArthur of No.609 Squadron. Crew believed both slightly wounded. Aircraft <60% damaged but repairable.

Stab I./StG3 Junkers Ju87B-1. Shot down by Hurricanes of No.145 Squadron during attack on convoy 'Peewit' and crashed in the Channel 10 km south of the Isle of Wight 3.10 p.m. FF Oberlt Martin Müller (*Gruppenadjutant*) captured unhurt and landed at Gosport, BF Uffz Josef Krampfl killed. Aircraft 100% write-off.

Martin Müller was picked up by the armed trawler HMS Bassett *(T-68) where he shared a cabin with Sqn Ldr Fenton of No.238 Squadron who had also been rescued from the Channel. The body of Josef Krampfl was later washed ashore on the French coast at Veules-les-Roses.*

2./StG3 Junkers Ju87B-1. Forced-landed at Théville damaged by Hurricanes of No.145 Squadron during attack on convoy 'Peewit' 20 km south of the Isle of Wight 3.10 p.m. Pilot unhurt, BF Uffz Josef Bösenecker badly wounded – admitted to hospital in Valognes. Aircraft 10% damaged – repairable.

2./StG3 Junkers Ju87B-1. Shot down by Hurricanes of No.145 Squadron during attack on convoy 'Peewit' 10 km south of the Isle of Wight 3.10 p.m. FF Fw Friedrich Zschweigert killed, BF Fw Herbert Heinrich missing. Aircraft 100% write-off.

2./StG3 Junkers Ju87B-1. Shot down by Hurricanes of No.145 Squadron during attack on convoy 'Peewit' 10 km south of the Isle of Wight 3.10 p.m. FF Uffz Rudolf Kleinhans missing, BF Uffz Karl Quante killed. Aircraft 100% write-off.

3./StG3 Junkers Ju87B-1. Crash-landed at Wuilly-le-Tessin airfield damaged in combat with Hurricanes of No.145 Squadron during attack on convoy 'Peewit' 10 km south of the Isle of Wight 3.10 p.m. Pilot unhurt, BF Fw Valentin Grossmann badly wounded – admitted to hospital in Falaise. Aircraft 45% damaged but repairable.

Stab II./StG77 Junkers Ju87B-1. Shot down by Hurricanes of Nos.43 and 145 Squadrons in combat over convoy 'Peewit' and ditched south of the Isle of Wight 4.20 p.m. FF Hptmn Waldemar Plewig (*Gruppenkommandeur*) captured wounded and landed at Portsmouth, BF Fw Kurt Schauer missing. Aircraft 100% write-off.

II./StG77 Junkers Ju87B-1. Returned to Bougy damaged by Hurricanes of Nos.43 and 145 Squadrons during attack on convoy 'Peewit' in the Channel south of the Isle of Wight 4.20 p.m. Crew both unhurt. Aircraft 25% damaged but repairable.

II./StG77 Junkers Ju87B-1. Forced-landed at Deauville damaged by Hurricanes of Nos.43 and 145 Squadrons during attack on convoy 'Peewit' south of the Isle of Wight 4.20 p.m. Crew both unhurt. Aircraft 80% damaged – write-off.

II./StG77 Junkers Ju87B-1. Crash-landed at Bougy damaged by Hurricanes of Nos.43 and 145 Squadrons during attack on convoy 'Peewit' south of the Isle of Wight 4.20 p.m. Crew both unhurt. Aircraft 70% damaged – write-off.

II./StG77 Junkers Ju87B-2. Forced-landed at Bougy damaged by Hurricanes of Nos.43 and 145 Squadrons during combat over the Channel during attack on convoy 'Peewit' south of the Isle of Wight 4.20 p.m. Crew both unhurt. Aircraft 20% damaged but repairable.

4./StG77 Junkers Ju87B-1. Shot down by Hurricanes of Nos.43 and 145 Squadrons over the Channel during attack on convoy 'Peewit' south of the Isle of Wight 4.20 p.m. FF Hptmn Horst-Henning Schmack and BF Obergefr Rudolf Wuttke both missing. Aircraft 100% write-off.

4./StG77 Junkers Ju87B-1 (5600). Fuel lines damaged in attack by F/O P.L. Parrot of No.145 Squadron during attack on convoy 'Peewit' and forced-landed at St Lawrence, Isle of Wight, 4.30 p.m. FF Uffz Fritz Pittroff captured unhurt, BF Uffz Rudolf Schubert killed. Aircraft S2+LM 100% write-off.

5./StG77 Junkers Ju87B-1. Forced-landed at Cherbourg with injuries received in combat with Hurricanes of Nos.43 and 145 Squadrons over the Channel during attack on convoy 'Peewit' south of the Isle of Wight 4.20 p.m. Pilot believed unhurt, BF Uffz Helmut Umlauft badly wounded. Aircraft 20% damaged but repairable.

11 August 1940
4./StG1 Junkers Ju87B-1. Failed to return from sortie over the Thames Estuary, cause unknown. FF Fw Karl Köhler and BF Sdf Folkerts both missing. Aircraft 100% write-off.

12 August 1940
12.(St)/LG1 Junkers Ju87B-1. Shot down by No.501 Squadron Hurricanes during attack on convoy 15 km east of Ramsgate 11.30 a.m. Possibly that claimed by P/O J.A.A. Gibson. FF Uffz Maurus Spöttl and BF Uffz Herbert Priestaff both missing. Aircraft 100% write-off.

6./StG2 Junkers Ju87R-1. Forced-landed at Lannion aerodrome due to mechanical failure during operational sortie. FF Fw Ehrhard Jähnert and gunner both unhurt. Aircraft T6+LP 40% damaged but repairable.

III./StG77 Junkers Ju87B-1. Crashed on landing at Granville following domestic flight, cause not stated. Crew unhurt. Aircraft 10% damaged – repairable.

13 August 1940
II./StG2 Junkers Ju87R-1. Shot down in the Channel off Portland by RAF fighters 4.00 p.m. Crew both rescued by E-boat. Aircraft 100% write-off.

5./StG2 Junkers Ju87R-1 (5676). Shot down by Spitfires of No.609 Squadron during sortie over Weymouth. Jettisonned bomb load and crashed and burned out opposite entrance to Clover Farm at Rodden, near Portesham, 4.00 p.m. Probably that claimed by F/O H.McD. Goodwin. FF Fw Otto Lindenschmid and BF Gefr Helmut Eisold both killed. Aircraft 100% write-off.

5./StG2 Junkers Ju87R-1. Shot down by Spitfires of No.609 Squadron during sortie over Weymouth and believed crashed in the Channel off Lulworth 4.00 p.m. FF Oberfw Helmut Leesch missing, BF Fw Hans Schulz believed baled out and captured badly wounded – admitted to Portway Hospital, Weymouth. Aircraft 100% write-off.

5./StG2 Junkers Ju87R-1. Shot down by Spitfires of No.609 Squadron during sortie over Weymouth and crashed and burned out near Grimstone Viaduct 4.00 p.m. FF Oberfw Erich Haack and BF Uffz Heinrich Haselmayer both killed. Aircraft 100% write-off.

Both originally buried in a field grave alongside the Dorchester to Maiden Newton road but later re-interred in Brookwood Military Cemetery.

6./StG2 Junkers Ju87R-1. Shot down by Spitfires of No.609 Squadron during sortie over Weymouth and crashed in the Channel 4.00 p.m. FF Fw Erwin Ott and BF Uffz Rudolf Göbel both killed. Aircraft 100% write-off.

The body of Erwin Ott came ashore at Portland on 30 August and was originally buried in the Strangers burial ground in St. John's Churchyard. His gunner, Rudolf Göbel, was washed ashore that same day at St Cast, near St Malo, on the other side of the Channel.

6./StG2 Junkers Ju87R-1. Crashed in the sea off Guernsey after engine caught fire during sortie, cause unknown. FF Uffz Kurt Bufe and BF Gefr Emil Pappert both killed. Aircraft 100% write-off.

5./StG77 Junkers Ju87B (5609). Crash-landed at Brunville, west of Dieppe, during transfer flight from Tonneville 9.00 p.m. Cause not stated. FF Bauer and BS Thiele both unhurt. Aircraft S2+CN damage state not recorded.

III./StG77 Junkers Ju87B. Severely damaged in taxying accident at Argentan. Crew both unhurt. Aircraft 70% damaged – write-off.

III./StG77 Junkers Ju87B. Taxied into flak emplacement at Tonneville aerodrome. Crew both unhurt. Aircraft 50% damaged but repairable.

14 August 1940
10.(St)/LG1 Junkers Ju87B. Shot down in combat with Spitfires of No.610 Squadron and Hurricanes of No.615 Squadron over the Channel off Folkestone during attack on Lympne 12.30 p.m. FF Oberlt Kurt Gramling and BF Uffz Franz Sawatzki both missing. Aircraft 100% write-off.

10.(St)/LG1 Junkers Ju87B. Returned to base damaged in combat with Spitfires of No.610 Squadron and Hurricanes of No.615 Squadron over the Channel off Folkestone during attack on Lympne 12.30 p.m. Pilot unhurt, BF Uffz August Müller burned and slightly wounded in face when ammunition exploded – admitted to hospital in Calais. Aircraft 20% damaged but repairable.

15 August 1940
10.(St)/LG1 Junkers Ju87B-1. Shot down by No.501 Squadron Hurricanes during attack on Hawkinge and crashed in the Channel near South Folkestone Gate lightship 11.20 a.m. FF Hptmn Rolf Münchenhagen baled out and captured badly wounded, BF Fw Herbert Heise killed. Aircraft 100% write-off.

10.(St)/LG1 Junkers Ju87B. Harried by No.501 Squadron Hurricanes during attack on Hawkinge, blundered into HT cables at More Hall, Folkestone, and crashed onto houses in Shorncliffe Crescent 11.20 a.m. BF Uffz Hermann Weber killed, FF Uffz Franz-Heinrich Kraus baled out severely wounded in head and leg, landing outside 81 Harcourt Road – died on admission to Royal Victoria Hospital. Aircraft 100% write-off.

10.(St)/LG1 Junkers Ju87B. Returned damaged by fighters during attack on Hawkinge 11.20 a.m. Pilot unhurt, BF Uffz Wilhelm Klust slightly wounded in leg – admitted to hospital in Guines. Aircraft damage state not recorded.

11.(St)/LG1 Junkers Ju87B. Returned damaged by fighters during attack on Hawkinge 11.20 a.m. Pilot unhurt, BF Fw Wilhelm Aniel badly wounded in stomach – admitted to hospital in Guines. Aircraft damage state not recorded.

1./StG1 Junkers Ju87B. Shot down over the Channel off Portland during sortie to attack Warmwell and crashed in Weymouth Bay 5.45 p.m. FF Fw Horst Steinert and BF Fw Hans Goldschmidt both baled out and captured unhurt. Aircraft A5+EH 100% write-off.

4./StG2 Junkers Ju87B. Shot down by fighters during sortie to attack Yeovil and crashed in the Channel west of Portland 5.45 p.m. FF Lt Ditmar von Rosen killed, BF Uffz Alfred Lewicki missing. Aircraft 100% write-off.

5./StG2 Junkers Ju87B. Returned from sortie to attack Yeovil damaged by fighters over the Channel west of Portland 5.45 p.m. Pilot unhurt, BF Uffz Hans Floitgraf badly burned and wounded – admitted to hospital in Cherbourg. Aircraft damage state not recorded.

6./StG2 Junkers Ju87B. Shot down by fighters during sortie to attack Yeovil and crashed in the Channel west of Portland 5.45 p.m. FF Uffz Peter Biesel and BF Gefr Josef Blümel both missing. Aircraft 100% write-off.

Stukas of I./StG1 and their crews wait for action, summer 1940.

6./StG2 Junkers Ju87B. Shot down by fighters during sortie to attack Yeovil and crashed in the Channel west of Portland 5.45 p.m. Pilot rescued unhurt, BF Uffz Hans-Heinrich Scharfenberg missing. Aircraft 100% write-off.

16 August 1940

I./StG2 Junkers Ju87B-1. Returned damaged by fighters over Selsey Bill following attack on Tangmere 1.00 p.m. Crew both unhurt. Aircraft 50% damaged but repairable.

I./StG2 Junkers Ju87B-1. Returned damaged by fighters over Selsey Bill following attack on Tangmere 1.00 p.m. Crew both unhurt. Aircraft 10% damaged – repairable.

I./StG2 Junkers Ju87B-1. Returned damaged by fighters over Selsey Bill following attack on Tangmere 1.00 p.m. Crew both unhurt. Aircraft 10% damaged – repairable.

1./StG2 Junkers Ju87B-1. Badly damaged by fighters over Selsey Bill following attack on Tangmere and ditched in the Channel 20 km north-west of Caen during return flight 1.15 p.m. Pilot rescued unhurt, BF Uffz Otto Neumann baled out at 120 feet and killed. Aircraft 100% write-off.

3./StG2 Junkers Ju87B-2 (5580). Radiator damaged by S/L J.V.C. Badger of No.43 Squadron causing engine failure following attack on Tangmere and belly-landed through a hedge alongside the B2145 Selsey Road near Church Norton Junction 1.00 p.m. Further attacked by No.602 Squadron Spitfires prior to landing. FF Uffz Paul Bohn and BF Obergefr Johannes Bader both captured unhurt. Aircraft T6+HL 100% write-off.

3./StG2 Junkers Ju87B-1. Badly damaged by Hurricanes of No.43 and No.601 Squadrons following attack on Tangmere airfield, engine failed east of the Isle of Wight, and over-turned on ditching at sea 1.05 p.m. FF Uffz Ernst König and BF Uffz Josef Schmid both rescued by RN launch and captured badly wounded – transferred to air-sea rescue aircraft and admitted to Royal West Sussex Hospital in Chichester. Aircraft 100% write-off.

Due to the severity of his wounds, Josef Schmid was repatriated to Germany in 1943.

Soldiers remove belted ammunition from one of the wing guns of the Stuka shot down at Bowley Farm.

3./StG2 Junkers Ju87B (5618). Shot down by F/L C.R. Davis of No.601 Squadron during sortie to attack Tangmere airfield and forced-landed through trees at Bowley Farm, South Mundham, 1.05 p.m. FF Fw Heinz Rocktäschel captured severely wounded – admitted to Royal West Sussex Hospital in Chichester but died same day, BF Oberfw Willi Witt killed. Aircraft T6+KL 100% write-off.

3./StG2 Junkers Ju87B-1. Shot down in combat with Hurricanes of No.43 and No.601 Squadrons during sortie to attack Tangmere airfield and crashed and burned out at High Piece Field, Honor Farm, north-west of Pagham, 1.00 p.m. FF Uffz Paul Linse and BF Obergefr Rudolf Messerschmidt both killed. Aircraft 100% write-off.

These airmen were originally buried together as 'Unknowns' in St Stephan's churchyard extension at North Mundham, all evidence of identity having been removed from them prior to their recovery. Both are now buried under named headstones at Cannock Chase German Military Cemetery.

Stab III./StG2 Junkers Ju87B-1. Returned damaged following combat with fighters off Selsey Bill 1.00 p.m. FF Hptmn Heinrich Brücker (*Gruppenkommandeur*) and BF Uffz Alfred Zimmer both slightly wounded. Aircraft damage state not recorded.

7./StG2 Junkers Ju87B-1. Shot down by fighters in combat off Selsey Bill 1.00 p.m. FF Lt Fritz-Oskar Kühn and BF Gefr Josef Wenzel both missing. Aircraft 100% write-off.

7./StG2 Junkers Ju87B-1. Shot down in combat with fighters over Selsey Bill and believed crashed in the Channel 1.00 p.m. FF Uffz Hans Liebing and BF Uffz Alfred Wiartalla both missing. Aircraft 100% write-off.

7./StG2 Junkers Ju87B-1. Set alight in attack by fighters during combat off the Isle of Wight and abandoned over Poole Harbour 1.00 p.m. FF Fw Gerhard Gräfenhain baled out and captured badly wounded in both legs, BF Uffz Johannes Voigt missing. Aircraft 100% write-off.

7./StG2 Junkers Ju87B-1. Shot down in combat with fighters over Selsey Bill and believed crashed in the Channel 1.00 p.m. FF Uffz Richard Serwottka and BF Gefr Karl Wagner both missing. Aircraft 100% write-off.

8./StG2 Junkers Ju87B-1. Returned damaged by fighters during combat over Selsey Bill 1.00 p.m. FF Uffz Gerhard Schütz badly wounded, gunner unhurt. Aircraft damage state not recorded.

9./StG2 Junkers Ju87B. Returned badly damaged following combat with fighters over Selsey Bill 1.00 p.m. FF Uffz Willi Knabe badly wounded, BF Obergefr Werner Nobis killed. Aircraft damage state not recorded.

1./StG3 Junkers Ju87B-1. Returned damaged by AA fire over Gosport. FF Oberlt Heinrich Eppen (*Staffelkapitän*) badly wounded – admitted to hospital in Cherbourg, BF Lt Heinz Heyder slightly wounded. Aircraft damage state not recorded.

I./StG77 Junkers Ju87B-1. Forced-landed at Carentan due to engine failure during local flight. Crew both unhurt. Aircraft 10% damaged – repairable.

18 August 1940

Stab I./StG77 Junkers Ju87B-1. Shot down by fighters during sortie to attack Thorney Island and crashed in the Channel 30 km off the English coast 2.30 p.m. FF Hptmn Herbert Meisel (*Gruppenkommandeur*) killed, and BF Obergefr Horst Jakob missing. Aircraft 100% write-off.

The body of Herbert Meisel was later washed ashore on the French coast.

Stab I./StG77 Junkers Ju87B-1. Crash-landed at Carentan damaged by fighters 10 km south-east of Portsmouth following attack on Thorney Island 2.30 p.m. FF Oberlt Karl Henze (*Gruppenadjutant*) slightly wounded – admitted to hospital in Carentan, gunner believed unhurt. Aircraft 60% damaged – write-off.

Stab I./StG77 Junkers Ju87B-2. Returned to Maltot damaged by fighters 10 km south-east of Portsmouth following attack on Thorney Island 2.30 p.m. FF Oberlt Kurt Scheffel (*Gruppe TO*) badly wounded in left shoulder – admitted to hospital in Caen, BF Gefr Otto Binner killed. Aircraft S2+CB 30% damaged but repairable.

1./StG77 Junkers Ju87B-1. Returned damaged by fighters 10 km south-east of Portsmouth following attack on Thorney Island 2.30 p.m. FF Fw Hans Meier and BF Uffz Karl Maier both slightly wounded. Aircraft damage state not recorded.

1./StG77 Junkers Ju87B-1. Shot down by fighters 10 km south-east of Portsmouth following attack on Thorney Island and believed crashed in the Channel 2.30 p.m. FF Uffz Erwin Weniger and BF Uffz Werner Möbes both missing. Aircraft 100% write-off.

Uffz Karl Maier was hit eight times in his body by machine-gun bullets but escaped serious injury. Here, the injured airman poses for the camera after returning to France following the attack on 18 August.

2./StG77 Junkers Ju87B-1. Undercarriage sheered off attempting landing on beach north of Bayeux badly damaged by fighters 10 km south-east of Portsmouth during sortie to attack Thorney Island 2.30 p.m. FF Fw Günther Meyer-Bothling slightly wounded by splinters in head – admitted to hospital in Bayeux, BF Uffz Erhardt Schulz killed. Aircraft 100% write-off.

2./StG77 Junkers Ju87B-1. Shot down by P/O C.K. Gray of No.43 Squadron during sortie to attack Thorney Island and crashed and exploded at Spring Garden, Cutmill, West Ashling, 2.30 p.m. FF Lt Hans Sinn baled out and captured unhurt on landing near Ham Farm, BF Uffz Josef Schmitt attempted to bale out too low and killed. Aircraft 100% write-off.

2./StG77 Junkers Ju87B-1 (5518). Engine caught fire under attack by Sgt H.J.L. Hallowes of No.43 Squadron during sortie to attack Thorney Island and crashed in Fishbourne Creek, between Dell Quay and Hook Farm, 2.30 p.m. FF Oberlt Johannes Wilhelm baled out and captured unhurt landing behind Stockbridge Garage between Birdham Road and Selsey Road, BF Uffz Anton Wörner baled out with damaged parachute and broke both legs on landing in estuary mud – admitted to hospital. Aircraft 100% write-off.

2./StG77 Junkers Ju87B-1. Shot down by fighters 10 km south-east of Portsmouth following attack on Thorney Island and crashed in the Channel 2.30 p.m. FF Oberlt Fritz Sayler (*Staffelkapitän*) and BF Fw Albert Ziera both missing. Aircraft 100% write-off.

2./StG77 Junkers Ju87B-1. Shot down by fighters 10 km south-east of Portsmouth following attack on Thorney Island and crashed in the Channel 2.30 p.m. FF Oberfw Wilhelm Neumeier and BF Uffz Karl-Heinz Schmidtbauer both missing. Aircraft 100% write-off.

The 3./StG77 Junkers 87 Stuka diving to destruction over the rooftops of Chichester, West Sussex, on 18 August with Dann and Kohl on board. It became one of the most famous images of the Battle of Britain.

3./StG77 Junkers Ju87B-1. Shot down by Hurricanes during sortie to attack Thorney Island and impacted at Whitehouse Farm, West Broyle, Chichester, 2.30 p.m. FF Uffz August-Hermann-Adam Dann and BF Uffz Erich Kohl both killed. Aircraft 100% write-off.

Despite confusion in contemporary records the pilot of this aircraft, August Dann, originally identified by name in official casualty reports, subsequently 'lost' his identity and was buried two days later in Christchurch Cemetery, Portsdown, as an 'Unknown German Airman'. Subsequently, the grave of August Dann has been identified and is now marked with a named headstone.

3./StG77 Junkers Ju87B-1. Shot down by fighters during sortie to attack Thorney Island and abandoned over the Channel five miles south-west of Selsey 2.35 p.m. FF Oberfw Günter Riegler and BF Gefr Oskar Langwost rescued by motor-lifeboat *Canadian Pacific* and both captured wounded. Aircraft 100% write-off.

The burning and mangled wreckage of the aircraft flown by Uffz Dann and Uffz Kohl in a pasture at The Broyle, Chichester.

3./StG77 Junkers Ju87B-1. Returned badly damaged by fighters 10 km south-east of Portsmouth during sortie to attack Thorney Island 2.30 p.m. FF Otto Schmidt slightly wounded, BF Uffz Gerhard Bärsch badly wounded – died in hospital October 2. Aircraft 100% write-off.

3./StG77 Junkers Ju87B-1. Shot down by fighters during sortie to attack Thorney Island and believed crashed in the Channel 2.40 p.m. FF Oberlt Dietrich Lehmann and BF Uffz Hans Winiarski both missing. Aircraft 100% write-off.

3./StG77 Junkers Ju87B-1 (5089). Shot down by fighters during sortie to attack Thorney Island and believed that which crashed and burned out at North Barn, Chidham, 2.30 p.m. FF Oberlt Hans-Jakob Schäffer and BF Uffz Ewald Klotmann both missing. Aircraft 100% write-off.

Although official contemporary reports on this incident include mention of the death of both crew, and Schäffer is named in contemporary official reports on the incident, no record of their recovery, identification, or burial has been traced. Shattered Junkers Jumo 211 engine excavated by Kent Battle of Britain Museum in October 1972 along with 250kg bomb later rendered harmless by RE Bomb Disposal Team from Chatham. Aircraft serial number '5089' found on metal tag at the site by air historian Peter Foote in 1984. Further unexploded ordnance in the form of the wing-mounted 50kg bombs were found at the site during 1990s, when a damaged Iron Cross First Class was also picked up at the crash location.

Stab II./StG77 Junkers Ju87B-1. Shot down by fighters during attack on Ford and crashed in the Channel 2.30 p.m. FF Oberlt Heinz Sonntag (*Gruppe TO*) missing, BS Uffz Karl Witton baled out but killed. Aircraft 100% write-off.

II./StG77 Junkers Ju87B-1. Crashed on landing at Barfleur damaged during attack on Ford 2.30 p.m. Crew both unhurt. Aircraft 100% write-off.

5./StG77 Junkers Ju87B-1. Shot down by fighters following attack on Ford and crashed in the Channel 40 km off the coast 2.30 p.m. FF Oberlt Heinz Merensky (*Staffelkapitän*) and BF Oberfw Gerhard Sengpiel both missing. Aircraft 100% write-off.

5./StG77 Junkers Ju87B-1 (5167). Shot down by Sgt B.E.P. Whall of No.602 Squadron during attack on Ford airfield and forced-landed at Ham Manor Golf Course, Angmering, 2.23 p.m. Also engaged by ground-fire from 455 Troop, No.76 Battery, RA, prior to landing. FF Oberfw Kurt Schweinhardt captured badly wounded, BS Oberfw Willi Geiger died of wounds the same day. Aircraft S2+JN 100% write-off.

III./StG77 Junkers Ju87B-1. Forced-landed at Caen damaged by fighters during sortie to attack Poling RDF Station 2.30 p.m. Pilot unhurt, BS Stabsfw August Westphal believed wounded. Aircraft 35% damaged but repairable.

III./StG77 Junkers Ju87B-1. Crashed on landing at Argentan damaged by fighters during sortie to attack Poling RDF Station 2.30 p.m. FF Fw Hans Schulze and BS Obergefr Arno Böcker both killed. Aircraft 100% write-off.

III./StG77 Junkers Ju87B-1. Crashed on landing at Argentan damaged by fighters during sortie to attack Poling RDF Station 2.30 p.m. Crew both unhurt. Aircraft 30% damaged but repairable.

9./StG77 Junkers Ju87B-1. Shot down by Sgt B.E.P. Whall of No.602 Squadron during sortie to attack Poling RDF Station and crashed in flames in the sea 5 km south-west of Littlehampton 2.25 p.m. FF Uffz Wilhelm Moll and BS Uffz Arthur Schwemmer both baled out but killed. Aircraft 100% write-off.

Wilhelm Moll was washed up at the entrance to Newhaven Harbour on 26 August, the body of Arthur Schwemmer coming ashore in France.

25 August 1940
III./StG2 Junkers Ju87B. Crashed on take-off at Ernes airfield due to engine failure. Crew both unhurt. Aircraft 100% write-off.

I./StG77 Junkers Ju87B. Crashed on landing at Maltot following domestic flight, cause not stated. Crew both unhurt. Aircraft 25% damaged but repairable.

28 August 1940
8./StG1 Junkers Ju87B-1 (0479). Collided with Lt Mühlthaler and crashed in the Channel off Deauville. FF Oberlt Wolfgang Kathe killed, gunner believed baled out and rescued unhurt. Aircraft 100% write-off.

8./StG1 Junkers Ju87B-1 (5236). Collided with Oberlt Kathe and crashed in the Channel off Deauville. FF Lt Josef Mühlthaler (*Chef 1.FBK*) and BF Obergefr Georg Zeulner both killed. Aircraft 100% write-off.

30 August 1940
I./StG77 Junkers Ju87B (0355). Crashed on landing at Maltot following domestic flight, cause not stated. Crew both unhurt. Aircraft 20% damaged but repairable.

2 September 1940
11.(St)/LG1 Junkers Ju87B-2 (5773). Forced-landed at Tramescourt following collision during operational sortie. Crew both unhurt. Aircraft L1+AV 20% damaged but repairable.

11.(St)/LG1 Junkers Ju87B-2 (5581). Abandoned by crew following collision over Tramescourt on operational sortie. Crew both baled out unhurt. Aircraft 100% write-off.

3 September 1940
1./StG3 Junkers Ju87B. Crashed at Les Montes d'Eraines air-firing ground, near Falaise, cause unknown. FF Fw Gottlob Ziegler killed. Aircraft 100% write-off.

4 September 1940
Stab StG2 Junkers Ju87B-2 (5574). Wrecked in taxying accident at Condé. No crew casualties. Aircraft 80% damaged – write-off.

5 September 1940
Stabsstaffel StG1 Junkers Ju87B (5447). Crashed at Brias, near St Pol, during domestic flight, cause unknown. FF Fw Johann Blameuser and Uffz Kurt Elsner (1.Wart) both killed. Aircraft A5+HA 100% write-off.

6 September 1940
2./StG77 Junkers Ju87B-1 (5097). Damaged in crash-landing at Maltot airfield, cause not stated. Crew both unhurt. Aircraft S2+LK 15% damaged but repairable.

8./StG77 Junkers Ju87B-2 (5638). Damaged in forced-landing at Argentan airfield following engine failure. Crew both unhurt. Aircraft F1+CN 50% damaged but repairable.

8 September 1940
Stab I./StG77 Junkers Ju87B-2 (5589). Damaged in crash-landing at Maltot following domestic flight. Crew both unhurt. Aircraft S2+CB 10% damaged – repairable.

11 September 1940
2./StG77 Junkers Ju87B-1 (5162). Crashed near Cambes-en-Plaine, 8 km north of Caen, following collision during formation practice. FF Uffz Josef Kramel and BF Gefr Hubert Schmilowsky both killed. Aircraft S2+PK 100% write-off.

2./StG77 Junkers Ju87B-1 (5521). Crashed near Cambes-en-Plaine, 8 km north of Caen, following collision with Uffz Kramel during formation practice. Pilot baled out unhurt, BS Gefr Heinz Söderström killed. Aircraft S2+JK 100% write-off.

3./StG77 Junkers Ju 87B-1 (0472). Damaged in taxying accident at Maltot airfield. Crew both unhurt. Aircraft S2+BL 20% damaged but repairable.

3./StG77 Junkers Ju 87B-2 (5739). Crashed at Courseulles-sur-Mer, 15 km north of Caen, following collision during formation practice. BF Gefr Walter Zedel killed, FF Uffz Georg Schwendtner baled out badly injured – admitted to hospital in Asnelles. Aircraft S2+HL 100% write-off.

3./StG77 Junkers Ju87B-2 (5630). Crashed at Courseulles-sur-Mer, 15 km north of Caen, following collision with Uffz Schwendtner during formation practice. Crew both baled out unhurt. Aircraft S2+FL 100% write-off.

24 September 1940
II./StG2 Junkers Ju87B-1 (5492). Crashed near Bangan due to engine failure on domestic flight. Crew both unhurt. Aircraft 70% damaged – write-off.

25 September 1940
I./StG1 Junkers Ju87R-1 (5461). Crashed on take-off from Angers aerodrome due to engine failure. Crew both unhurt. Aircraft 50% damaged but repairable.

26 September 1940
Stab StG77 Junker Ju87B-1 (5343). Forced-landed at Calais-Marck following engine failure during domestic flight. Crew both unhurt. Aircraft S2+AA 20% damaged but repairable.

30 September 1940
12.(St)/LG1 Junkers Ju87B-1 (0217). Suffered engine failure during local flight and abandoned near Ambricourt. Pilot baled out unhurt, BF Gefr Karl Sievers baled out too low and killed. Aircraft L1+JW 100% write-off.

4 October 1940

6./StG77 Junkers Ju87B-1 (0338). Damaged in taxying accident. Crew both unhurt. Aircraft S2+KP 10% damaged – repairable.

8 October 1940

12.(St)/LG1 Junkers Ju87B-1 (5086). Crashed and burned out following collision with Lt Kühn during local flight over Marles-les-Mines, 5 km south of Lillers. FF Lt Werner Schlegel and BF Gefr Josef Schiehandl both killed. Aircraft L1+MW 100% write-off.

12.(St)/LG1 Junkers Ju87B-1 (0395). Crashed following collision with Lt Schlegel during local flight over Marles-les-Mines. FF Lt Helmut Kühn and BF Obergefr Erwin Dürr both slightly injured – admitted to hospital in Lillers. Aircraft L1+AW 100% write-off.

9 October 1940

3./StG1 Junkers Ju87R-1 (5291). Crash-landed at Evrecy airfield, cause not stated. Crew both unhurt. Aircraft A5+CL 15% damaged but repairable.

10 October 1940

3./StG2 Junkers Ju87B-2 (0513). Collided with Oberlt Brucker in pull-out from the dive during bombing practice over the Forêt-de-Brotonne, south-west of La Mailleraye-sur-Seine. Pilot believed baled out unhurt, BF Gefr Franz Rother killed. Aircraft T6+FL 100% write-off.

3./StG2 Junkers Ju87B-2 (0557). Crashed and burned out following collision over the Forêt-de-Brotonne. FF Oberlt Rolf Brucker and BF Uffz Albert Post both killed. Aircraft T6+JL 100% write-off.

19 October 1940

I./StG3 Junkers Ju87B-1 (0237). Damaged in taxying accident at Bary airfield. Crew both unhurt. Aircraft 10% damaged – repairable.

8./StG77 Junkers Ju87B-2 (5617). Crashed near Occagnes, north of Argentan, following mid-air collision with Gefr Nowack during local flight. FF Gefr Hans-Willi Müller and BF Flgr Siegfried Hörner both killed. Aircraft 100% write-off.

8./StG77 Junkers Ju87B-2 (5628). Collided with Gefr Müller during local flying and crashed near Occagnes. FF Gefr Bruno Nowack and BF Gefr Alois Kaiser both killed. Aircraft 100% write-off.

24 October 1940

12.(St)/LG1 Junkers Ju87B-1 (5200). Damaged on landing at Courtrai following local flight, cause unknown. Crew both unhurt. Aircraft 30% damaged but repairable.

30 October 1940

I./StG1 Junkers Ju87R-1 (5541). Damaged in collision with Do 215 at Brest airfield. Crew both unhurt. Aircraft 20% damaged but repairable.

1 November 1940

StG1 Junkers Ju87B-2 (5712). Crash-landed at Norrent-Fontes airfield due to technical fault. Crew both unhurt. Aircraft 15% damaged but repairable.

5./StG1 Junkers Ju87B-1 (5227). Engine set alight by naval AA fire during attack on convoy north-east of Sheerness and ditched in the Thames Estuary, east of the Nore, 2.30 p.m. FF Gefr Werner Karrach missing, BF Gefr Max Aulehner thrown from aircraft, rescued by MTB, and captured unhurt. Aircraft 6G+KS 100% write-off.

I./StG2 Junkers Ju87B-1 (0292). Crash-landed, circumstances not recorded. FF Fw Schrewe injured, gunner unhurt. Aircraft 20% damaged but repairable.

7./StG77 Junkers Ju87B-2 (5622). Crashed near Bière, north of Argentan, during dive-bombing practice, cause unknown. FF Uffz Arnold Keller and BF Lt Josef Mauerer both killed. Aircraft 100% write-off.

2 November 1940

IV.(St)/LG1 Junkers Ju87B-2 (5567). Forced-landed in Nieuw-Cromstrijenschepolder at Klaaswaal, north of Numansdorp, following engine failure 3.45 p.m. Crew both unhurt. Aircraft undamaged.

7 November 1940

1./StG3 Junkers Ju87B-1. Returned damaged by AA fire during attack on convoy in the Thames Estuary east of Southend 12.30 p.m. FF Lt Eberhard Morgenroth badly wounded left heel – admitted to hospital in Domart, gunner unhurt. Aircraft damage state not recorded.

8 November 1940

12.(St)/LG1 Junkers Ju87B-1 (5231). Shot down by Hurricanes of No.17 Squadron during attack on convoy and crashed in the Thames Estuary 10 km south-east of Clacton 4.30 p.m. FF Lt Herbert Pilgersdörfer and BF Gefr Walter Pollack both missing. Aircraft L1+BW 100% write-off.

1./StG3 Junkers Ju87B-1 (0460). Crash-landed near Dunkirk due to petrol failure during sortie. Crew both unhurt. Aircraft 30% damaged but repairable.

3./StG3 Junkers Ju87B-1 (0315). Shot down by Hurricanes of No.17 Squadron during attack on convoy and crashed in the Thames Estuary off Southend 4.30 p.m. FF Uffz Fritz im Spring and BF Uffz Fritz Krohn both missing. Aircraft S1+ML 100% write-off.

3./StG3 Junkers Ju87B-1 (0239). Shot down by Hurricanes of No.17 Squadron during attack on convoy and crashed in the Thames Estuary off Southend 4.30 p.m. FF Lt Walter Kummer and BF Uffz Ewald Hoffarek both missing. Aircraft S1+EL 100% write-off.

11 November 1940

7./StG1 Junkers Ju87B-1 (0496). Shot down by fighters during attack on convoy in the Thames Estuary off Clacton and crashed in the Channel, 5 miles north of Margate, 11.40 a.m. FF Uffz Gerhard Schütz and BF Obergefr Georg Brück both missing. Aircraft J9+EH 100% write-off.

9./StG1 Junkers Ju87B-1 (5292). Shot down by fighters during attack on convoy in the Thames Estuary off Clacton 11.40 a.m. FF Uffz Dr Heinrich Österreich and BF Obergefr Anton Sabinarz both missing. Aircraft J9+FK 100% write-off.

14 November 1940

IV.(St)/LG1 Junkers Ju87B-1 (0477). Damaged in storm while parked at Tramecourt airfield. No crew casualties. Aircraft 20% damaged but repairable.

I./StG1 Junkers Ju87R-1 (5542). Damaged in storm at Brest airfield. No crew casualties. Aircraft 25% damaged but repairable.

7./StG1 Junkers Ju87B-1 (0333). Returned damaged by Spitfires of Nos.66 and 74 Squadrons off the North Foreland during sortie to attack Dover CH station 2.20 p.m. Crew both unhurt. Aircraft 30% damaged but repairable.

9./StG1 Junkers Ju87B-1 (0436). Shot down in the Channel off the North Foreland by Spitfires of Nos.66 and 74 Squadrons during sortie to attack Dover CH station 2.19 p.m. FF Obergefr Herbert Dietmayer and BF Obergefr Johann Schmidt both missing. Aircraft J9+ZL 100% write-off.

A search by Margate lifeboat, The Lord Southborough, *found nothing.*

9./StG1 Junkers Ju87B-2 (5641). Caught fire under attack by Spitfires of Nos.66 and 74 Squadrons during sortie to attack Dover CH station and abandoned two miles off South Foreland 2.30 p.m. FF Oberlt Otto Blumers baled out unhurt – picked up by MTB and landed at Dover, BF Gefr Willy Koch missing. Aircraft J9+BL 100% write-off.

9./StG1 Junkers Ju87B. Returned damaged by Spitfires of Nos.66 and 74 Squadrons off the North Foreland during sortie to attack Dover CH station 2.19 p.m. Pilot unhurt, BF Uffz Julius Müller badly wounded. Aircraft damage state not recorded.

27 November 1940

1./StG3 Junkers Ju87B-1 (0447). Crashed south-east of Caen during domestic flight, cause unknown. FF Oberlt Günther Scharp killed. Aircraft 100% write-off.

II./StG77 Junkers Ju87B-1 (5223). Crash-landed, cause not stated. Crew both unhurt. Aircraft 100% write-off.

7 December 1940

8./StG1 Junkers Ju87B-1 (5316). Crash-landed at Ostend airfield during sortie, cause not stated. Crew both unhurt. Aircraft 20% damaged but repairable.

11 December 1940

2./StG1 Junkers Ju87R-1 (5433). Lost control and crashed east of Cornimont, 10 km south of Gérardmer, during training flight 2.00 p.m. FF Fw Emil Bischof killed, BF Uffz Martin Boldt badly injured – died December 13. Aircraft 100% write-off.

7./StG1 Junkers Ju87B-1 (0392). Crash-landed at Fruges due to petrol failure during sortie. Crew both unhurt. Aircraft 12% damaged – repairable.

13 December 1940

1./StG77 Junkers Ju87B-1 (0425). Crashed near Caen on domestic flight, cause not stated. FF Uffz Willy Trute killed, BF Gefr Karl Kunz badly injured. Aircraft 100% write-off.

I./StG77 Junkers Ju87B-1 (5277). Force-landed at Caen-Carpiquet during domestic flight due to technical failure. Crew both unhurt. Aircraft 50% damaged but repairable.

15 December 1940

Ergänzungsstaffel StG1 Junkers Ju87B-1 (0438). Crash-landed at Schaffen-Diest airfield due to control failure during domestic flight. Crew both unhurt. Aircraft 50% damaged but repairable.

20 December 1940

3./StG1 Junkers Ju87B-1 (5271). Forced-landed at Lille-Nord due to petrol failure during domestic flight. Crew both unhurt. Aircraft 20% damaged but repairable.

22 December 1940

7./StG77 Junkers Ju87B-2 (0550). Crashed on take-off from Argentan on domestic flight, cause not stated. Crew both unhurt. Aircraft 35% damaged but repairable.

24 December 1940

5./StG1 Junkers Ju87B-1 (5496). Forced-landed at Maastricht during domestic flight, cause not stated. Crew both unhurt. Aircraft 35% damaged but repairable.

Lost = 101; Damaged = 84*

(*all causes, including accidents)

Lost listings table courtesy of Peter Cornwell

APPENDIX V

Stuka Operational Tactics

For an accurate attack it was important that each aircraft was heading as near as possible into the wind during its dive. As he approached the target, the formation leader looked for smoke rising from the ground, or other clues, to give him the wind direction. He would then align his attack taking the wind direction into account.

Prior to entering the dive, each Ju87 pilot carried out the following pre-attack checks:
- Switch on the reflector sight (Revi)
- Trim the aircraft for the dive
- Set the bomb release altitude on the contacting altimeter
- Close the radiator flaps
- Throttle back the engine
- Open the vent blowing air on the inside of the windscreen (this was to prevent the windscreen misting up when the aircraft entered the moist air lower down).

The Ju87 had a window set into the cockpit floor immediately in front of the pilot's seat, and through this the pilot watched the target slide into position beneath him. Immediately before commencing his dive, each pilot rotated the dive brakes to the maximum-drag position. That produced a severe nose-up trim change in the aircraft, and to compensate for it an extra elevator trim tab was lowered automatically.

When the formation leader commenced his attack dive, the remaining aircraft in the formation followed in turn. When attacking targets with a small horizontal extent, for example bridges or small buildings, the Ju87s approached in echelon formation, peeled into the dive and attacked in line astern. Against larger targets, for example harbours or airfield hangars, dive bombers would usually be 'bunted' into the dive in three-aircraft Ketten and all three attacked together.

Once the Ju87 was established in its dive, typically at an angle of 80 degrees, it made an extremely stable aiming platform. The accuracy of the attack depended on the accuracy with which the pilot held a constant angle. To assist with this, a protractor was etched in red into the side of the cockpit canopy so the pilot could read off his dive angle. Experienced pilots could judge their angle within fine limits without resort to this aid, however.

In the dive the speed of the aircraft built up relatively slowly, and it took a dive through 8,000 feet for it to reach maximum velocity of 350mph. When the aircraft reached a point 2,000 feet (600m) above the bomb release altitude set on the contact altimeter, a horn sounded in the cockpit. About 4 seconds later the aircraft reached the previously-set bomb release altitude, typically 2300 feet (700m) above ground level, and the horn ceased. That was the signal for the pilot to release the bombs.

As mentioned above, when the pilot rotated the dive brakes to the high-drag position before entering the dive, a trim tab fitted to the elevator had lowered to cancel out the resultant nose-up pitching moment. The act of releasing the bombs activated a powerful spring, which returned the elevator trim to the neutral position. The severe nose-up pitching moment now returned, and pulled the aircraft out of its dive at a steady 6G.

As the nose of the dive bomber rose above the horizontal, the pilot returned the dive brakes to the low-drag position, opened the throttle, trimmed the aircraft for level or climbing flight as required and turned on to the briefed escape heading.

When attacking ships, Stuka pilots usually dived as steeply as possible (and sometimes at up to almost 90°) towards the stern of the ship. At around 1,500ft the angle was decreased to 45° and the pilot's Revi gunsight was lined up on the target ship's stern as the pilot fired his twin forward 7.92mm MG 17 machine guns, mounted one in each wing. Gradually, the hail of bullets would move along the length of the ship and when the pilot saw his bullets striking the water ahead of the ship's bow, so the bombs were released. In this way, the machine-gun fire was an aid to sighting the bombs and had the additional effect of keeping down the heads of any would-be defenders who might be firing back.

As the Stuka pulled out and drew away from the target, so the rear gunner would take over the machine-gunning to maintain anti-aircraft fire suppression.

The Stuka is much famed for its screaming siren (sometimes appropriately referred to as the 'Trumpets of Jerricho') and although production Junkers 87s were fitted with a wind driven siren on the wheel spats these were actually not used during the Battle of Britain and were either removed or faired over. In the initial stages of the war they were employed as a matter of course, but it later became clear that not only were they causing unnecessary drag but also announced the Stuka's impending arrival since they could not be switched off in flight. The legend of the wailing sirens on the Junkers 87 had long preceded its arrival over Britain, and thus those experiencing Stuka attack here believed they had heard its infamous wail. In fact, what they had heard was the whistle of wind through the extended dive brakes, the screaming whine of the powering Junkers Jumo engine and its propeller as well as the slipstream across the angular airframe. There was, in fact, little need for a siren.

Note: The cruising speed of the Junkers 87 was approximately 250-260kph (160mph) and the dive speed 450kph (280mph).

Report of the Attack Against RNAS Ford

From	...	THE COMMANDING OFFICER, R.N. AIR STATION, FORD,
		NR. ARUNDEL, SUSSEX.
Date	...	1st September, 1940.
To	...	THE REAR ADMIRAL NAVAL AIR STATIONS.

I desire to mention the following officers, men and Wrens for special commendation for their conduct on the occasion of the Air Raid at this Station on Sunday, 18th. August, 1940.

Lieutenant Commander M.H.C. Young,　　　)
Lieutenant Commander M.J.R. de Courcy　　)
Lieutenant Commander M.J.M. Spens　　　　)
2nd Lieutenant E. Owen, R.A.　　　　　　　)

These Officers were killed while making for their action stations after bombing had started. Had they taken cover immediately where they were, they might well have survived.

Lieutenant Commander J.H. McI. Malcolm showed initiative and courage in endeavouring to stop the spread of fire from the petrol tanks, in conditions of considerable heat and danger of explosions from the burning tanks.

Surgeon Lieutenant K.B. Scott, R.N.V.R. showed outstanding initiative, coolness and efficiency following the raid. He was blown into a shelter trench by the blast from exploding bombs. After the attack he set off in his car with supplies of dressings to search for casualties, and subsequently dealt with a considerable number of casualties in a clearing station established in an undamaged hut.

Mr H.L. Kent, Warrant Aircraft Officer, R.N. did very good work in taking charge of fire fighting and salvage operations in the neighbourhood of the burning petrol.

Chief Petty Officer P. Cahalane P/JX.163001 was in a hut cubicle which was blown in on him by a near bomb explosion. Although wounded in the head, he did good work moving casualties to and from the casualty clearing station, until sent away to get his head dressed.

After the attack on Ford very little was left of many of the camp's wooden hut accommodation.

C.P.O Cook A.C. Surling, C/M.2144 at the earliest possible moment took charge in the galley and dining hall, and by his own hard work and good example was able to serve meals to the whole ship's company. On the afternoon of the 19th he was worn out and almost collapsed.

Corporal W. Hullett, 507951 at the time of the raid this N.C.O was working in the oil refinery. This building suffered almost a direct hit. He made good his escape and although he was wounded by a piece of shrapnel in the arm he assisted for a long time as a stretcher bearer.

J.P. Shepherd, A.M. (A) 2. FX.75915 for outstanding initiative and good work in assisting to put out the Storage Hangar when on fire and for his efforts in salving Service material and Stores. This man performed these duties without waiting for orders and when given instructions carried them out in a very commendable manner.

Chief Petty Officer Wren Sims, No.2034 did excellent work after the raid in organising the Wrens, and generally assisting in many directions.

Leading Wren Nina Marsh, No.81* although wounded in the back and elbow she made light of her injuries and gave invaluable assistance in dealing with wounded in the Sick Bay Shelter trench under most trying conditions. She refused to give in until all casualties had been dealt with and evacuated, and was then herself sent to hospital.

Wren Irene Marriott, No.659 coolly directed others to the only possible shelter – the passage. Then she returned to the galley to attempt to put the fires into a state of safety, when she herself was wounded.

Miss M.M. Bond, V.A.D. was in the Sick Bay when the attack commenced and had not the time to get clear. The Sick Bay was severely damaged. She displayed courage and efficiency under most difficult conditions and carried out her duties in a most commendable manner.

Leading Wren J.N. Logan No.2024)
Wren K.R. Shackleton, No.2917)
Wren M.L. Crane)

These three set a fine example to the remainder of the staff. They each did the work of two or more, and, by remaining cheerful and smiling throughout, kept the others in good heart.

Wren E.M. Suter, No.871, a member of the 1st Aid party who deserves special mention for the manner in which she performed her duties following the raid.

Sergeant Hughes, J.O. 69th Med. Regiment, R.A. although himself wounded by one of the first bombs, while bombs were still falling he continued in the open helping wounded men into the shelter trenches. He remained after the raid to take charge of and steady his men until he had eventually to be ordered into hospital.

Sergeant W.J.F. Kelly, R.M.P. This Sergeant saw the enemy aircraft approaching, and gave timely warning to all in reach before himself taking cover. Immediately after the raid he set off searching for casualties, and gave valuable assistance generally.

Mr W.C. MacGregor – Civilian Storekeeper)
Mr F.G. Wakeford – Civilian Labourer)

These men lived outside the Station close to the bombed area and their houses were damaged. Both came in and gave most valuable assistance in fire fighting and salvage work.

Mr T.R. Coupland – Civilian Electrical Fitter. This man was in the centre of the bombed area and must have been considerably shaken, but went quickly to work afterwards on repairing of the electrical plant, and rendered most useful service.

Signed: Captain Officer Commanding RNAS Ford.

*The First Sea Lord approved the recommendation for the British Empire Medal (Civil Division) to Leading Wren Nina Marsh.

List of aircraft destroyed or damaged by enemy action on the ground at RNAS Ford

750 Squadron
Shark II   K8510

                        K8453

                        K8515

                        K8467

                        K8907

752 Squadron
Proctor I   P6078

                        P6030

793 Squadron
Swordfish   K5942

Storage Section
Albacore   L7121

                        L7096

Swordfish   K8883

                        L2719

                        K8372

                        K8352

(Additionally, stored Pegasus III engine (no.115135) written-off and used for parts salvage.)

A number of other aircraft were damaged but repairable on station as under:

Shark – 16   Nimrod – 1   Walrus – 8   Roc – 1   Total – 26

APPENDIX VII

Report of the Air Raid Damage on RAF Poling

18.8.40

Nature of Attack

At about 14.35 during a 'Red' warning, a force of enemy planes believed to number between twenty and thirty made an attack on Poling RAF station in the course of which eighty-seven bombs of various sizes (including heavy, medium, and light types) were dropped. Forty-four fell inside the compound, the remainder within a circle of under ¾ mile diameter; only two of the bombs were unexploded.

The attack appears to have been made from the south, then a sharp circle round the station with bombs falling in all directions. Some direct hits were made on hutments and some private motor cars were set on fire in the station, but the damage considering the weight of bombs dropped, was not so nearly as heavy as would be expected.

As far as can be ascertained, there were only two casualties (one shock and one light injury) in the station, with no civilian.

The population in vicinity is light, but most of the houses in South Poling have suffered damage to tiles, windows, ceiling, etc.

Express information was received from Arundel police at 14.37 with a request that casualty and fire services be sent. This was complied with at once and express report sent to county control at 14.43.

ARP services in Poling consist of two wardens and first aid point. One warden was on duty at RAF station. Chief Warden at once left control to render assistance and being satisfied their own parishes were unaffected, parish head wardens of Lyminster and Warningcamp (adjoining districts) also attended and gave valuable help.

After receipt of 'White' message at 15.02 I also attended with deputy chief warden.

One Junkers 87 machine was forced down about one mile south of the station and the two occupants taken prisoner and conveyed to East Preston institution by C.D ambulance.

As far as can be gathered, all local population took shelter.

Operation of Services

Turn out of services efficient; original information received was vague, but in view of the number of explosions heard in report centre at Worthing, it was decided to send two F.A.P., two ambulances, and two casualty cars stationed at East Preston to the scene. Upon arrival, our fears of heavy casualties were unfounded and the unwanted services returned to their depot by 15.15 (absent only 32 minutes).

Reporting System
With police help, this worked very well, and after arrival of chief warden and others, quite adequate. Interim reports were dispatched at frequent intervals and final report at 18.20.

Working of Service
There was no delay on the part of any service – in order to compile full reports, wardens and officials had to travel considerable distances on foot over fields and rough ground.

F.A. Parties and Ambulances
Already dealt with in operation of services. Leaders showed initiative and good knowledge of duty by returning at once to depot.

Other Services
Officer commanding station asked for assistance of road repair gang which attended from Lancing Manor and helped to clear debris on roads within compound and also effect temporary repair to concrete track at entrance to station. They returned to Lancing at 18.00.

Some people living in houses near the station were evacuated by military and made their own arrangements for temporary accommodation.

No request made for other services except fire; A.F.S. from East Preston attended and dealt promptly with the motor car, etc., inside compound. There was no spread of fire and it was quickly subdued.

The other paragraphs in operation memorandum No. 12 do not apply.

General Remarks
As indicated in situation reports, congestion of traffic caused by private cars of sight-seeing civilians from Worthing and other districts was caused at Poling Corner on A27 Road. If the incident had required other services to attend, I am afraid some delay would have been caused. RAF personnel worked hard on traffic duty at this spot, but the flocking of cars and cycles to scenes of damage is to be deplored. People are naturally curious and air raid damage is new to most, but few of those present today could have thought what a splendid target they made for any lone raider who may have returned with a view to 'mopping up' and machine-gunning workers. I feel very deeply on this point and think it should be the subject of strong comment and action from a higher source than myself.

West Sussex Constabulary

APPENDIX VIII
RAF Intelligence Report into loss of Stuka T6 + KL on 16 August 1940

The following report was compiled by RAF Air Intelligence [A.I.1(k)] based upon documents found in the Junkers 87 Stuka shot down at Honor Farm, Pagham, on 16 August 1940.

Immelmann Geschwader (StG2)

1) Two log books and a note book have been received from the Ju 87 brought down near Chichester on 16.8.40. The aircraft was smashed to pieces and the crew were killed. This has not previously been reported by A.I.1(k).

2) These two men who, during most of the period had flown together, belong to 3./StG2.

3) In the log books the aircraft were always referred to by the werke nummer and not by their lettering right up until the middle of May 1940. However, on this date they changed and the following list of werke nummers and lettering can be compiled:

368	T6 + HL	391	T6 + GL	
441	T6 + BL	5099	T6 + IL	
376	T6 + CL	5102	T6 + JL	
384	T6 + DL	5129	T6 + KL	
385	T6 + EL	5138	T6 + LL	
388	T6 + FL	– - -	T6 + ML	(Junkers 52)

4) At the outbreak of war this unit was based at Kottbus. This unit took part in the Polish campaign, starting at 04.50 hours on 1.9.39.

5) War diary carefully notes the bomb loads carried by the various aircraft on numerous attacks which are probably worked out in accordance with a definite scheme. Unfortunately, the nature of the objective is not always disclosed in the diary.

6) On 10.10.39 they were again at Kottbus, and on 2.11.39 they moved to Wunzendorf where they remained until 4.2.40 when they moved to Köln-Ostheim, transferring to Köln Hohenberg on 8.4.40.

7) During this period they were carrying out almost daily training flights including bomb aiming, numerous formation flying and fighting practices and cross-country navigation.

8) On 5.5.40 they moved to Gotzheim, ready for the pending Dutch campaign. This name is clearly written in several places by both men, but no aerodrome of the name can be found.

9) They started off on 10 May very strenuously, carrying out no less than seven bombing attacks on the first day including one at least against Eben-Emael. On the next day they made four attacks and three on each of the following two days.

10) Finally, the unit moved up to occupied France and have lately been attacking Channel convoys from Condé.

11) This crew, since 10.5.40, have carried out no less than seventy-nine war flights; as an analysis of this will probably prove interesting they are appended.

War Flights of Ju 87 – T6 + KL

Date	Aircraft Marking	Start	Land	Remarks
MAY				
10 (seven flights)	T6 + KL	Gotzheim	Gotzheim	Fort Eben-Emael (entrance) – 500kg and 2x 250kg bombs. Village and fortified positions at Eben Rimpst (troops). Vellingen (troops). Attacked bridge nr Bessingen. Aerodrome St Trond (destroyed 12 a/c) Bridges at Alost
11 (four flights)	T6 + KL	Gotzheim	Gotzheim	Positions west of Eben (twice). Crossroads S.W. of Diest. Station at Fiorlemond and road beyond Louvain (fighters)
12 (three flights)	T6 + KL	Gotzheim	Gotzheim	Aldschot (troops in the town). Station at Louvain (fighters) Namur (railway and road bridge)
13	T6 + KL	Gotzheim	Gotzheim	Attacked fortifications near Sedan
14	T6 + GL	Duisburg	Krefeld	Zuyder See
15 (three flights)	T6 + FL	Gotzheim	Gotzheim	Cortil-Nourmont (troops)
	T6 + FL	Gotzheim	Libin	Cortil-Nourmont (artillery emplacement). Liège (pillboxes)
17	T6 + FL	Libin	Libin	Troops near St. Pierremont
18	T6 + KL	Libin	Libin	Attack on railway station and armoured train at Soissons
19	T6 + EL	Libin	Libin	Attack on fort and town of Amiens

Date	Aircraft Marking	Start	Land	Remarks
20	T6 + KL	Libin	Libin	Attack on troops W. of Cheuny
21	T6 + KL	Beaulieu	Beaulieu	Troops in St. Port-Arras district
22	T6 + KL	Beaulieu	Beaulieu	Village S. of St. Omer
23 (three flights)	T6 + KL	Beaulieu	Beaulieu	Northern exit and outskirts of Arras. Attack on destroyers at Boulogne (Channel)
25	T6 + HL	Beaulieu	Cambrai	Attack on transports (Channel near Calais)
26 (two flights)	T6 + KL	Beaulieu	Beaulieu	Citadel of Calais. Attack on troops in Estaires (Arras)
27	T6 + KL	Beaulieu	Méricourt	Attack on S. exit from Poperinghe (NW of Lille). Wormhoudt and troops on roads
28	T6 + KL	Beaulieu	Beaulieu	Attack on town and surroundings of Poperinghe
29	T6 + KL	Beaulieu	Beaulieu	Ships at Dunkirk and Nieuport
JUNE				
1	T6 + KL	Beaulieu	Beaulieu	Warships and transports in the Channel
2	T6 + KL	Beaulieu	Beaulieu	Warships in Channel and transports
5 (four flights)	T6 + KL	Beaulieu	Laon	Attack on staff in Chateau at Plessier de Roye. Troops and batteries in Neuville. Batteries in Raisme-Bagneux-Bieuxy Juvigny
6	T6 + KL	Laon	Laon	Batteries at Dresbiur. Attacks on armoured cars near Carrequis and Marigny
7 (three flights)	T6 + KL	Laon	Laon	Attack on S. way out of Noyon. Armoured columns and troops at St. Juies and Trilloir
9	T6 + AL	Laon	Laon	Attack on Nanteuil le Haudouin
10	T6 + AL	Laon	Laon	Attack on Chateau Thierry
11	T6 + AL	Laon	Laon	Attack on Nesles near Ch. Thierry
12	T6 + IL	Laon	Laon	Crossroads near Verdelot S. of Ch. Thierry
13	T6 + IL	Laon	Laon	St. Juist
14 (two flights)	T6 + IL	Laon	Ch. Thierry	Exits from Treis. Bridge at St. Paner

Date	Aircraft Marking	Start	Land	Remarks
15 (two flights)	T6 + IL	Ch. Thierry	Ch. Thierry	Bridge and surroundings northern outskirts of Gleu
JULY				
4	T6 + KL	Cherbourg East	Condé-sur-Ifs	Attack on British convoy in Channel (12 ships)
11	T6 + KL	Cherbourg	Condé-sur-Ifs	Attack on British convoy off Portland
17	T6 + LL	Condé-sur-Ifs	Condé-sur-Ifs	Searching for submarines in the Channel
26	T6 + KL	Condé-sur-Ifs	Cherbourg	War Flight
26	T6 + KL	Cherbourg	Cherbourg	Armed reconnaissance in Channel and off Portland
27	T6 + KL	Condé	Condé	Long distance recco
AUGUST				
2	T6 + KL	Condé	Branville	War Flight
2	T6 + KL	Branville	Condé	War Flight
3	T6 + KL	Condé	Cherbourg	War Flight
3	T6 + KL	Cherbourg	Condé	War Flight
3	T6 + JL	Condé	Branville	War Flight
3	T6 + JL	Branville	Condé	War Flight
8	T6 + KL	Condé	Branville	War Flight
8	T6 + KL	Branville	Condé	Convoy in the Channel (nr. I. of W.)

Ground Casualties sustained during the main Stuka attacks against British mainland targets

Note: Comprehensive lists of Royal Navy or Army ground casualties sustained during the attacks covered in this book are not to hand and only partial listings are included where the names have been discovered, although that for HMS Peregrine (Ford) is thought to be comprehensive. Where known, the identities of civilian casualties have been added.

RAF Detling 13 August 1940

AC2 D. Argyle	Injured	AC2 W.J.Crote	Killed
Fg Off H.M. Aspen	Killed (53 Squadron)	LAC G.B. Currie	Injured (53 Squadron)
Cpl W.F. Bateman*	Killed (53 Squadron)	LAC A.F. Dancaster	Killed
AC2 G. Booth	Injured	Fg Off W.E. Davies	Injured
AC2 J.P. Bereton	Killed	Gp Capt E.P. Meggs Davies	Killed
AC2 A.F. Brooker	Killed	AC2 G.W. Dearlove	Injured
AC1 L.E. Brookes*	Killed	Cpl G. Deeley	Killed
AC1 A.F. Bussey	Injured	AC1 W.G. Elliott	Injured
FS W.F. Call	Injured (500 Squadron)	AC2 R.F.G. Elphick	Injured (500 Squadron)
Cpl A. Cassely	Killed	AC2 J.B. Farrell	Injured
AC2 J.E. Chambers	Injured	AC2 R. Foggin	Injured (53 Squadron)
Plt Off A.A. Christian	Injured (53 Squadron)	AC2 J.V.C. Gardiner	Injured (500 Squadron)
LAC W. Collerton*	Killed	LAC F. Goodbody	Injured
Sqn Ldr R.J.O. Compston	Injured (53 Squadron)	AC2 W.G. Gordon	Injured
DFC, DSC		Plt Off C.D. Gray	Injured
		AC2 F.H. Grieve	Injured
		FS W.H. Hipwell	Injured (500 Squadron)
		Sgt H.C.R. Hopwood	Killed (500 Squadron)
		Cpl B. Jackman	Injured
		Plt Off I.S. Jameson	Injured (53 Squadron)
		Sgt J. Jenkins	Injured (53 Squadron)
		AC2 J.A. Jones	Killed
		AC2 W.A. Latimer	Injured
		AC2 D.H. Lee	Injured (53 Squadron)
		LAC C.F. Lobley	Injured (500 Squadron)
		FS W.H.G. Loham	Killed
		AC2 E. Loughlin	Injured

Sqn Ldr Robert J.O. Compston DFC, DSC & two bars, was a World War One fighter ace accredited with twenty-five victories.

RAF Detling 13 August 1940 (continued)

Sqn Ldr J.H. Lowe	Killed
Cpl E.V. Lyons	Injured
AC2 W.A. Major	Injured
AC2 G.J. Martin	Injured
Stg F. Messent*	Killed (500 Squadron)
AC2 W.A. Moore	Injured
AC2 W. Neale	Killed (500 Squadron)
LAC R. O'Kelly	Killed
Sqn Ldr D.C. Oliver	Killed (53 Squadron)
LAC K. Park	Injured (53 Squadron)
LAC M.R. Powell	Injured (53 Squadron)
Cpl J.I. Price*	Killed
AC2 R. Quiemard	Injured
AC2 W.E. Regan	Injured
LAC A.H.Y. Roberts	Injured
AC1 L.E. Rookes	Killed
Sgt W.H.L. Richards*	Killed (53 Squadron)
Cpl C.F. Rubie	Injured
AC2 J.A. Scaife	Injured
AC2 J.W.S. Smith	Killed
AC2 J.R. Tait	Injured
AC2 A. Topham	Injured (53 Squadron)
Sgt K.W. Vowles	Injured (53 Squadron)
AC1 L.A. Watchous	Killed (500 Squadron)
FS G.J. Wilson	Injured (500 Squadron)

Six CWGC headstones in a single row at Maidstone Cemetery bear the individual names of these six men. Along the top of each of the six headstones is inscribed "Buried Near This Spot". According to the CWGC these memorials commemorate seven men who were killed in the air attack on Detling but who could not be individually identified. There is no indication as to the likely identity of the seventh man, neither is any information given as to where he might be buried.

Civilians

Walter F.A. Heron	Killed
Jesse G. Hunt	Killed
Frank Merrick	Killed

Air Attacks Lee-on-the-Sea and Gosport
16 August 1940

Cpl G. Atkinson	Killed
AC2 N.Q. Charlton	Killed
LAC A.J. Hoare	Killed (753 Squadron)
Sdn Ldr A.E. Knight	Injured (933 Balloon Squadron)
LAC T.J. Mortimer	Killed
AC2 B.S. Nicholas	Injured
Sgt R.B. Parham	Injured
Cpl A.J. Stewart	Killed
LAC G. Sturdy	Injured (781 Squadron)
Sgt O.J. Weeks	Missing* (785 Squadron)
AC2 R.T. Yates	Killed

Naval Personnel

Ldg Airman B.A. Cooke	Killed
Sub Lt (A) D. Drane	Killed

*(*No trace of thirty-four-year-old Sgt Owen James Weeks was found after the attack and he is commemorated by name on the Runnymede Memorial)*

Air Attack Tangmere 16 August 1940

AC2 R.E. Austin	Killed
AC2 A.W. Charlton	Killed
LAC E.J.F. Cork	Injured
AC2 S. Coutts	Killed
LAC A.E. Gainey	Killed
LAC R.O. Hewlett	Killed
Plt Off S. Janson	Injured
Cpl N.C. Kelly	Injured
LAC R.E.G. King	Injured (601 Squadron)
Cpl W.H. Lewis	Killed
LAC S. McGowan	Injured
AC2 J. Sheasby	Killed
AC2 R. Smith	Killed
LAC F.M. Strong	Injured
LAC D.A. Tolman	Injured
AC2 W.F.G. West	Killed
AC2 A.B. Young	Killed

Civilians

Henry Ayling	Killed
Alfred Ernest Quinnell	Killed
Alfred David Softley	Killed

Air Attack HMS Peregrine, Ford, 18 August 1940

RAF

AC1 W.H. Bentham	Injured (750 Squadron)
Cpl W. Hullett	Injured (750 Squadron)
AC2 J.G. Moverley	Killed
Cpl H.D. Starck	Killed
LAC L.W.T. Walker	Injured (750 Squadron)
LAC S. Worrall	Killed

This memorial to the casualties of the 18 August Stuka attack on Ford was erected in the adjacent churchyard of St Mary's, Clymping. In this photograph, the original grave markers can be seen and behind the memorial the coiled barbed-wire defences of Ford aerodrome.

Royal Navy – Fleet Air Arm

AM2 J.I. Ashton	Killed
AM A.H. Bavington	Killed
AM2 H.W.S. Cook	Killed
AM C.T. Connor	Killed
AM J.R. Coucill	Killed
Const A. J. Cunningham	Killed (RMP)
Lt Cdr The Hon M.J.R. De Courcy	Killed
Ldg AF I.L. Davies	Killed

Royal Navy – Fleet Air Arm (continued)

AM J. Heald	Killed
Lt Cdr W.J.M. Spens	Killed
Ldg SA F.A. Stanton	Killed
AM2 T.W. Trevithick	Killed
Lt Cdr M.H.C. Young	Killed

Army – Home Guard

Volunteer J.W. Diment (Civilian Driver)	Killed

Civilians

Ernest R. Ballantyne (Civilian Driver)	Killed
V.A.G. Berry (Civilian Driver)	Killed
Stanley J. Earnshaw (Civilian Driver)	Killed
Thomas H. Hill (Civilian Wireless Operator)	Killed
Catharina P. Murphy	Killed
Herbert J. Perring (Civilian Stoker)	Killed
John A. Pratt	Killed
Thomas Thomas	Killed

The Stuka in German Lore

The German propaganda machine was very quick to recognise that not only was the Stuka a powerful weapon on the battlefield but it was also a very potent propaganda tool. Uniquely German in concept and design, and somehow redolent of Nazi domination and superiority, the Stuka was much-loved by the Propaganda Kompanie (PK) and during the early part of the war it featured heavily in every medium through which the prowess of the aircraft and its fearless crews could be demonstrated to the German people and world at large. Heroic artwork featured Stukas diving to defeat the enemy and appeared in books, newspapers, posters, on magazine front covers and even postage stamps. In 1941 a film called 'Stukas' was released.However, by the time of its release the Stuka had long since been withdrawn from all operations against mainland Britain.

In common with most arms of the German military machine of the period, the Stuka force had its own battle-song, the *Stuka Lied* (Stuka Song). Rather improbably, the crews of the Junkers 87s depicted in the film are shown singing the song as they fly into battle, and although many of the Stuka crews from 1940 were familiar with the song it was not exactly belted out enthusiastically by the Stuka crews during rollicking drinking sessions around mess pianos! It was, of course, more to do with supposed morale-boosting propaganda and public consumption through the 1941 film and via the German broadcasting service. Nevertheless, to illustrate this rather odd piece of social and military history, the lyrics are reproduced here. Somewhat Wagnerian in content, and over-flowing with its overt triumphalist message, it is not difficult to see why, content aside, this was probably not exactly the song of choice for the off-duty Stuka men!

Song of the Stukas

Many black birds are filing
High above the land and sea,
And wherever they appear, there flees
The enemy before them.
They let themselves drop
From the sky steeply toward the ground.
They strike their bronze talons
Squarely into the foe's heart.

Refrain:

We are the black hussars of the air.
The Stukas, the Stukas, the Stukas!

Always ready whenever action calls us,
The Stukas, the Stukas, the Stukas!
We plunge from the sky and strike.
We do not fear Hell and we give no peace,
Until the enemy finally lies on the ground,
Until England, until England, until England is conquered-
The Stukas, the Stukas, the Stukas!

(Refrain)

If a thousand lightning bolts are flashing,
If danger threatens and surrounds them,
They hold together steadily like iron,
Comrades in life and in death!
If they spy prey,
Then woe be to it every time.
Nothing can evade their eyes.
The Stukas, like eagles of steel.

(Refrain)

Death they sow and destruction
Everywhere over the enemy's land.
Their tracks are wreckage and fragments,
And blazing firebrands through the sky.
There already goes in every land
Their name from mouth to mouth.
They strike the factories into rubble,
They sink the ships to the bottom.

(Refrain)

It had not taken long from the outbreak of war before the Stuka had become legendary; feared by its enemies and revered by the German people. The Nazi propaganda machine was intent upon ensuring that its reputation amongst friend and foe alike was both enhanced and broadened. That legend, though, was sometimes far removed from the truth but the Stuka's almost mythical role in World War Two, manipulated and manufactured by the German propaganda machine, has been one that has endured. Hopefully, through this book, the author has been able to put into some context its legendary participation in the Battle of Britain.

Der Adler magazine cover.

Selected Bibliography

The following books and publications were amongst those referred to by the author during the preparation of this work.

Air Historical Branch *The Battle of Britain – RAF Narrative* (A.H.B – circa 1949)

Ashworth, Chris *Action Stations – 9* (PSL, 1985)

Bateson, Richard P. *Stuka! Junkers 87* (Ducimus, 1972)

Beedle, Jimmy *The Fighting Cocks – 43 (Fighter) Squadron* (Pen & Sword, 2011)

Brütting, Georg *Das Waren die Deutschen Stuka-Asse* (Motor Buch Verlag, 1976)

Collier, Basil *The Defence of The United Kingdom* (HMSO, 1957)

Collier, Richard *Eagle Day* (Hodder & Stoughton, 1966)

Cornwell, Peter C. *Battle of France – Then & Now* (After the Battle, 2007)

Cornwell, Peter C. *Zerstörer* (JAC, 1995)

Creek, Eddie J. *Junkers 87 – Dive Bomber to Tank Buster* (Classic, 2012)

Crook, D.M. *Spitfire Pilot* (Grub Street, 2008)

Deichmann, Paul *Spearhead for Blitzkreig* (Greenhill, 1996)

Dempster, Derek *The Narrow Margin* (Hutchinson & Co, 1961)

Draper, Major Christopher, DFC *The Mad Major* (Air Review Ltd, 1962)

Eimannsberger, Ludwig von *Zerstörer Gruppe* (Schiffer, 1998)

Erfurth, Helmut *Junkers Ju 87* (Midland, 2004)

Foreman, John *RAF Fighter Command Victory Claims* (Red Kite, 2003)

Goss, Chris *Brothers in Arms* (Crécy, 1994)

Goss, Chris *Luftwaffe Bombers Battle of Britain* (Crécy, 2000)

Griehl, Manfred *Junkers Ju 87 Stuka* (Airlife, 2001)

Hewitt, Nick *Coastal Convoys* (Pen & Sword, 2008)

HMSO *British Vessels Lost at Sea 1939 – 45* (HMSO, 1947)

Johnstone, Air Vice-Marshal, CB, DFC, 'Sandy' *Enemy in the Sky* (William Kimber, 1976)

Jouineau, Andre & Leonard, Herbert *Ju 87 From 1936 – 1945* (Histoire et Collections, 2003)

Kent, Gp Capt J.A. *One of The Few* (William Kimber, 1971)

Knight, Dennis *Harvest of Messerschmitts* (Frederick Warne, 1981)

MacClure, Victor *Gladiators Over Norway* (W H Allen & Co. Ltd, 1942)

Mason, Francis K. *Battle over Britain* (McWhirter Twins, 1969)

McKee, Alexander *Coal-Scuttle Brigade* (Souvenir, 1957)

Parker, Nigel *Luftwaffe Crash Archive* (Red Kite, 2013)

Price, Alfred *The Hardest Day* (Macdonald & Jane's, 1979)

Ramsey, Winston *The Battle of Britain, Then & Now* (After the Battle, 1980)

Ramsey, Winston *The Blitz, Then & Now* (After the Battle, 1987)

Rudel, Hans Ulrich *Stuka Pilot* (Euphorian Books, 1952)

Robertson, Bruce & Scarborough, Gerald *Ju 87 Stuka* (PSL, 1977)

Saunders, Andy *Convoy Peewit* (Grub Street, 2010)

Shores, Christopher *Fledgling Eagles* (Grub Street, 1991)

Smith, J. Richard *The Junkers 87 A & B* (Profile Publications, c.1970)

Smith, Peter C. *Dive Bomber* (Casemate, 2008)

Smith, Peter C. *Junkers 87 Stuka* (Crécy, 2011)

Smith, Peter C. *Luftwaffe Ju 87 Dive Bomber Units, 1939 – 1941* (Classic, 2006)

Smith, Peter C. *Naval Warfare in The English Channel 1939 – 1945* (Pen & Sword, 2007)

Smith, Peter C. *Stuka at War* (Ian Allan, 1971)

Smith, Peter C. *Stuka Spearhead* (Greenhill, 1998)

Trivett, Hugh *Achtung, Spitfire!* (History Press, 2010)

Vasco, John J. *Bombsights over England* (JAC Publications, 1990)

Vasco, John J. & Cornwell, Peter C. *Zerstörer* (JAC, 1995)

Weal, John *Junkers 87 Stuka Geschwader 1937 – 1941* (Osprey, 1997)

Wood, Derek & Dempster, Derek *The Narrow Margin* (Hutchinson & Co, 1961)

Wood, Derek *Attack Warning Red* (Macdonald & Jane's, 1976)

Zimmerman, David *Britain's Shield* (Sutton, 2001)

Index